D0340788

## DATE DUE

## ALSO BY ERIK KIRSCHBAUM

*Burning Beethoven: The Eradication of German Culture*
*in the United States during World War I*
*Rocking the Wall: Bruce Springsteen: The Berlin Concert*
*That Changed the World*
*Swim and Bike and Run: Triathlon — The Sporting Trinity*

# SOCCER
# WITHOUT
# BORDERS

# SOCCER WITHOUT BORDERS

## JÜRGEN KLINSMANN, COACHING THE U.S. MEN'S NATIONAL SOCCER TEAM AND THE QUEST FOR THE WORLD CUP

### ERIK KIRSCHBAUM

PICADOR

NEW YORK

picadorusa.com • picadorbookroom.tumblr.com
twitter.com/picadorusa • facebook.com/picadorusa

Picador® is a U.S. registered trademark and is used by St. Martin's Press under license from Pan Books Limited.

For book club information, please visit facebook.com/picadorbookclub or e-mail marketing@picadorusa.com.

Designed by Steven Seighman

Frontispiece of Jürgen Klinsmann by John Todd/isiphotos.com

The Library of Congress Cataloging-in-Publication Data is available upon request.

ISBN 978-1-250-09831-3 (hardcover)
ISBN 978-1-250-09833-7 (e-book)

Our books may be purchased in bulk for promotional, educational, or business use. Please contact your local bookseller or the Macmillan Corporate and Premium Sales Department at 1-800-221-7945, extension 5442, or by e-mail at MacmillanSpecialMarkets@macmillan.com.

First Edition: May 2016

10  9  8  7  6  5  4  3  2  1

*For my children—Steven, Julie, Lukas, and Finn*

# CONTENTS

# ACKNOWLEDGMENTS

Writing this book has been on my mind for nearly ten years and I needed a lot of help to get it beyond the idea stage. I'd like to thank, first and foremost, Jürgen Klinsmann for all the time and energy he made available to help me write this story. I'd also like to thank Warren Mersereau for all his wisdom and support, as well as Berti Vogts and Roland Eitel for filling me in on some fascinating details. Thanks are owed as well to Lindsey Vonn, Phil McNichol, Fabian Johnson, DeMarcus Beasley, and Philipp Köster for their time and insights. I also owe my deepest appreciation to Stephen Barbara and Emma Schlee at Inkwell Management for helping get this idea off the drawing board, as well as Stephen Morrison and Peter "P.J." Horoszko at Picador for their cheerful support and skillful guidance in getting this story into print. P.J. was the young, bright associate editor at Picador whose enthusiasm, support, and skill helped make every page a little better. Sadly, he passed away as this book was going to press. Thanks, too, go to Michael Kammarman at U.S. Soccer for letting me pick his brain and to Rafal Gibek and Cynthia Merman for their splendid editing. As much as the longtime news agency journalist in me thrives on writing under impossibly tight deadlines, this was the most challenging ever, and I'd like to thank all the friends and relatives who altruistically read segments of the manuscript, offered critical suggestions, and helped keep me focused in countless ways on this journey outside of my comfort zone: Karolos Grohmann, Scott Reid, Iain Rogers, Mike Collett, Simon Evans, Tom Wagner, Joseph Nasr, David Crossland, Julie Kirschbaum, Martin Simon, Miriam Dieter, Markus Büttner, Olaf Zapke, Ingrid Kirschbaum, Karin Scandella, Don Grant, Lisa Luera, Tom Heneghan, Cora Lee Kluge, Michelle Martin, Steven Kirschbaum, Dean Grant, Paul Carrel, Rick Ostrow, Nick Fellows, Dean Grant, Thomas Krumenacker, Herbert Rossler, John Blau, Alex Mleczko, Rene Wagner, Deyan Sabourian, John Atkins, Jesse Spears, Georg Merziger, Henry R. Kaufman, Deirdre Preis, Elisa Oddone, Kevin Fylan, Markus Lepper, and Nick Fellows.

—*Erik Kirschbaum, Berlin, March 2016*

# AUTHOR'S NOTE

Along with millions of American baby boomers, I grew up in the dark about soccer. Unable to understand the appeal of the game with so little scoring, that felt so different, had almost no games to watch on television, and had such a foreign feel to it, I remained hopelessly unaware of and sadly uninterested in the nuances and excitement of soccer for decades. It was difficult to fathom the allure of a sport where there was so much activity, ostensibly, for so little tangible reward, like goal scoring. In the good company of millions of other equally unenlightened Americans, I kept my head buried in the sand, oblivious of the finer points of what was long known to the outside world simply as "the beautiful game." World Cup games weren't even shown on television in the United States until 1982, and only from the 1998 tournament in France were all the games broadcast live—as they had already long been shown in most countries around the world.

So it was quite a shock one day when, as a teenager in 1976 on the way to see my first pro soccer game live—a New York Cosmos play-off game—a friend told me that soccer was actually the world's most popular sport. *What?* No way! The rest of the world must have that all wrong was our ethnocentric consensus on the bus heading to Shea Stadium. Foreigners probably just didn't really understand American sports, like football, basketball, and baseball. Keep your soccer, and your silly metric system along with it, too! And, besides, the revelation that the world preferred soccer to sports like American football only made the game seem even more alien to me. How bizarre that so many people opted to play and follow a sport where you're not allowed to use your hands—the most dexterous part of your body! "Don't waste your time on soccer, kid. It's a sport for commie pansies," were the immortal words that summed up American attitudes on soccer in the 1970s from *New York Daily News* columnist Dick Young to a young sportswriter for the tabloid at the time named David Hirshey.

Even many years later, after moving to soccer-crazed West Germany for the first time in 1982, I hardly paid any attention to that country's most popular national sport—instead staying up well past midnight in the Central European time zone to watch fuzzy NFL and NBA broadcasts on the American Forces Network, a channel without commercials set up for American soldiers stationed in West Germany and other foreign outposts. To stay in shape I played pickup games of touch football with other American expatriates; we were the exotic ones in parks otherwise filled with pickup soccer games. And I even rather dim-wittedly insisted to German friends and colleagues at work that the National Football League, National Basketball Association, and Major League Baseball were all far more interesting than the national soccer league in West Germany, the Bundesliga, or the World Cup. They must have thought I was a moron with stubborn arguments that only exposed a regrettably closed mind.

The epiphany came later in my life, in 2004, well into my forties, and after having spent the better part of two decades living in Germany, Austria, and England. It suddenly dawned on me why soccer is so much more than just a sport in countries like Germany and

England, and why its popularity transcends cultures, borders, religions, and politics. In 2004, Germany marked the fiftieth anniversary of its first World Cup win in 1954, and a national radio station, *Deutschlandfunk,* rebroadcast the original live play-by-play radio coverage of the final game in which West Germany upset Hungary to win the tournament—in its entirety and at exactly the same time of day as the original broadcast on July 4, 1954. It was a magical experience to slip back a half century in time and feel the power of that magnificent moment in German soccer history and enlightening to understand the origins of the country's love affair with soccer. I finally grasped the profound impact that game has had on so much of its culture, psyche, identity, and indeed its entire postwar history. Almost every country across Europe has similarly unforgettable moments of collective elation or trauma because of a major triumph or defeat in a World Cup.

Also at about the same time in 2004, it was incredible to watch Germany's wrenching monthlong search for a new soccer coach after the team was unexpectedly eliminated from the European Championship tournament in Portugal in the first round without winning any of its three Group Stage games. At times the search for a new coach for the *Nationalmannschaft* seemed to be more important to most Germans than even a search for a new leader of government, and all other news got knocked off the top of front pages for nearly a month as the soccer federation struggled at first haplessly to find a coach brave enough to take on a difficult job just two years before Germany was going to host the 2006 World Cup. What started as an almost amusing problem quickly became a full-blown calamity. But ultimately, the crisis turned into a remarkable chance for change when the German Football Association's (DFB) specially created *Trainerfindungskommission* handed over the reins to Jürgen Klinsmann. It was fascinating to have a front-row seat to watch

Klinsmann, a former player with no coaching experience, boldly introduce his revolutionary reforms with far-reaching remedies at the venerable German Football Association. He worked his magic on the German *Nationalmannschaft* with ideas garnered from—of all places—the United States. That Klinsmann managed to overhaul and modernize the DFB and coach the team from his adopted home in California nearly six thousand miles away made the whole narrative all the more compelling. It was, as Klinsmann himself likes to say, one of those amazing stories that you can only get with soccer.

With its nearly universal appeal, soccer has the power to influence or even change history. Entire countries celebrate as one in the hopes of a victory, or collapse in collective heartbreak in defeat. It's a riveting experience to see the fate, well-being, and happiness of an entire nation hinge on their national team's performance at a big tournament like the World Cup or European Championships.

Many ingredients make the game special and, admittedly, it's an acquired taste. For Americans like me who grew up without watching soccer on television but with a wealth of other sports to watch and play, it can take time to appreciate the speed, savvy, artistry, endurance, genius, and incredible athleticism displayed by the world's top soccer players. Football, baseball, and basketball games that stretch on for hours seem somehow far less interesting, almost boring to me now with all the stops and starts—despite the high scoring. I've long since stopped staying up late in Europe to watch any American sports on television and can't even be bothered to watch whenever I'm in the United States. My world has been turned upside down to the point that I now find myself getting up early to watch European soccer games on television in the United States and checking out the results overseas on the Internet.

In soccer there are no TV time-outs, no injury time-outs, and—

as with life itself—no way to stop the clock. Its matches last the same ninety minutes, interrupted only by a short half-time break, as when it was created more than a century ago. There are few moments in sports as thrilling as the uninterrupted and unstoppable drama of the final two or three minutes of a close soccer game when one team is fighting desperately for a goal to win or tie the match—or doing everything to prevent that from happening. And it's impossible to match the singular joy that erupts in almost any big stadium anywhere in the world in an important match when a team scores. "Soccer is often mocked for its low scores, but precisely because goals are so scarce, the release of joy is greater than in other sports," Simon Kuper and Stefan Szymanski argue in their book *Soccernomics*.

Emotions about soccer can run so high that they once triggered a war between Honduras and El Salvador. The Soccer War, as it was called, lasted one hundred hours in 1969. Its roots went beyond soccer, but it was incredibly ignited after El Salvador beat Honduras two games to one in a Qualifying play-off for the 1970 World Cup. At the 1994 World Cup, Colombia was eliminated after the United States upset the South Americans 2–1, when Colombia's defender Andrés Escobar unintentionally scored the winning goal for the United States with an own goal. Escobar had tried to block a pass from America midfielder John Harkes but ended up deflecting the ball into Colombia's goal. Ten days later, he was murdered, shot six times by a gunman shouting, "*Gol.*"

Soccer is a game that people of all ages play on six continents. It unites the world like nothing else, especially at the quadrennial World Cup. Curiously, it is a game that the United States—for a complex variety of reasons—is still trying to master in the international arena, where soccer is played with so much passion. But it's a game in which the United States could one day be among the world's best—if Americans are able to fully appreciate soccer as *different* and accept that it's a game with international standards and schedules—and not a game in which the United States sets the rules and guidelines that everyone else will follow.

The United States has enormous untapped potential when it comes to soccer. It's also fortunate to have one of the world's top coaches with a wealth of experience in *both* Europe and the United States, Jürgen Klinsmann. He won the World Cup with West Germany in 1990 as a forward, scoring three goals in that seminal tournament, and is one of the World Cup's all-time leading goal scorers, with eleven goals from three tournaments. After retiring as a player, he moved to the United States in 1998, and he later coached the German *Nationalmannschaft* to third place at the 2006 World Cup, while staying based in California and commuting to Germany, forty-two long-distance trips across the Atlantic during the course of those two years. In 2011, he was hired to coach the U.S. Men's National Team, after an on-and-off courtship that lasted five years. He launched sweeping, at times controversial, reforms that helped the USMNT to a record-breaking year in 2013. The team had twelve straight wins, qualified for a sixth straight World Cup final, and defied all expectations by reaching the Round of 16—after emerging in second place behind Germany from the most difficult four-team group in the tournament, the so-called Group of Death. For that he was one of ten coaches around the world nominated for the 2014 *Fédération Internationale de Football Association* (FIFA) World Coach of the Year.

Klinsmann is a fearless, reform-minded coach and technical director with firm convictions who is well connected to the world's most important soccer network of Western Europe—the cradle of the game whose countries have dominated the World Cup. He knows what it takes to become one of the world's top soccer nations and is fascinated by the challenges of that long journey.

Soccer's rules, customs, tradition, and heritage are unlike those of any other American sport—even though there was a remarkable golden era in the 1920s before the 1929 stock market crash and the Great Depression when soccer, thanks to the high concentrations of newly arrived immigrants from Europe, was more popular than football in some parts of the United States. But rival leagues, the rising popularity of college football, along with the collapse of the stock market contributed to the early demise of professional soccer. Among soccer's many anomalies, which even today set it apart from other sports, are that the ball isn't out-of-bounds or a goal until all of it has crossed over the line; it's possible for a team that loses one game to still celebrate if it has a higher tally in the two-game aggregate score; and the best players usually play on multiple teams each season—for their clubs that pay their salaries and for their countries, mostly for honor. Teammates on top clubs from different nations often end up playing *against* each other in international games.

Complicating the picture further and adding even more games to long eleven-month seasons, the clubs play in several competitions concurrently: the league championship; their national cups, which are one-game knockout tournaments; and international club tournaments such as the Champions League—the world's most important club competition where Europe's best battle it out against each other in a tournament that runs parallel to the European leagues. It is thus possible for a player to claim four or more major titles in a single season, winning a so-called treble with his club along with a World Cup or confederation championship for his national team.

It's not a game that easily fits into the American prism with its penchant for TV time-outs, postseason play-offs, league parity, and U.S. domination. It's a game of patience and pleasure, both subtle and spectacular. It's a game that lasts ninety minutes where the players make the overwhelming majority of decisions on the field.

It's a game with about four hundred passes per team in which the average player has the ball for only about a total of fifty seconds, meaning the remaining eighty-nine minutes are spent dashing to get into the right position to try to score a goal or to try to stop one. Soccer games can be decided by a single split-second decision at any moment during the ebb and flow of those ninety minutes, where even a superior team can be defeated in an instant by an underdog opponent if they manage to score one "lucky punch" goal, like an outclassed boxer who scores a stunning knockout win against the odds. And it's an uncommonly unpredictable game where overwhelmed teams can, and do, upset the dominant teams with scrappiness, willpower, and that proverbial bolt out of the blue that knocks out the heavily favored team. That's how an unheralded U.S. team upset heavily favored England 1–0 at the 1950 World Cup in Brazil, the country's one and only World Cup win between 1930 and 1994.

Writing about soccer is also different from writing about any other sport. There might be fifty different sportswriters in the press box covering a soccer game who afterward might have fifty different interpretations of what happened. Soccer is a blank canvas with twenty-two veritable artists on the field, toiling, thinking, sprinting, tackling, and fighting their way to a masterpiece with plays and moves that can never be replicated. An equally important part of the soccer culture is the endless postgame debates about who played well or poorly, who won the game for their team or who lost it, which team deserved to win or not, or was it a goal or not. Soccer games are more open to interpretation than other mainstream sports because there are so few measurable "statistics" and "results"—aside from obvious goals, corner kicks, penalty cards, or miles run. There are also only three referees monitoring twenty-two players, leaving even more room for error and debate. Many Germans, for instance, still insist Geoff Hurst's overtime goal for England a half century ago in the 1966 World Cup in the final played in London's Wembley Stadium was *not* over the line and shouldn't have counted. It even gave the German language a new term, *"Wembley-Tor"* (Wembley goal), for undeserved or ill-gotten gains.

There are certain turning points to every game, as in other sports, that sportswriters focus on. But a soccer match is less an accumulation of "results" from each play, as in football, basketball, and baseball. Instead, it's a game of surprises, of changes in momentum, lightning counterattacks, brilliant saves, and underdogs suddenly scoring "against the run of play"—a scrumptious fast-break goal scored by a team that was being totally outplayed. And there are truly magical games where the two teams just seem to start playing over their heads, lighting up the crowd with creative attacks and nerve-tingling scoring chances or goals. Sometimes you can feel the power of an exuberant crowd cascading down the grandstands and onto the field, a surge of energy that seems to jolt the players to run faster and harder.

You can be sitting in an airport in Athens, on a bus in Berlin, a café in Cairo, a diner in Dublin, an eatery in Ecuador, a fan bar in Florence, a gym in Glasgow, a hotel in Helsinki, a market in Moscow, a nightclub in Nigeria, a pub in Pretoria, a restaurant in Rio, a taxi in Tokyo, a sauna in Sweden, or even at a zoo in Zambia—and the chances are good that you will be able to strike up a conversation with almost anyone there by talking about soccer, the latest UEFA (Union of European Football Associations) Champions League game, the last World Cup or the next World Cup Qualifiers.

Soccer is the game that unites the world more than the United Nations or anything else. "Big soccer tournaments provide some of the communal glue once supplied by trade unions, churches, and royal weddings," write Kuper and Szymanski in *Soccernomics*. "Big soccer matches have that sort of unifying role in most European countries . . . There may be nothing that brings a society together like a World Cup with your team in it. For once, almost everyone in the country is watching the same TV programs and talking about them at work the next day." Tellingly, it is soccer balls—not footballs or baseballs—that American soldiers bring along with them to try to connect with children near their bases in Iraq or Afghanistan or Latin America. Soccer, more than English, is the lingua franca of the twenty-first century. It is the game the world plays.

## WHY A BOOK ABOUT JÜRGEN KLINSMANN?

I was fortunate to get to know Klinsmann during the two years he was the coach of Germany's national team, leading up to the 2006 World Cup. At first I was just a pesky news agency journalist asking irritating questions at news conferences in Germany. Instead of clichés or clever attempts to skirt the issues, Klinsmann unfailingly offered disarmingly straightforward and thoughtful answers—unlike anything I'd ever experienced before. During those two years I also had several interviews with Klinsmann in his adopted hometown in Southern California, where he spent a few weeks each month in between commuting to Germany for games and training camps. I got to know and appreciate him as an interesting, uncomplicated, unpretentious, genuine, and eminently likable agent of change. As a journalist, I've always admired those who are unafraid to challenge conventional wisdom or the status quo, and Klinsmann was one of the most courageous movers and shakers I've ever encountered. The meetings continued even after he stopped coaching in Germany—sometimes in the United States and sometimes in Germany—and the conversations weren't always necessarily about soccer but were always enlightening, inspiring, and thoroughly enjoyable.

The Klinsmann interviews were some of the most memorable I've had in forty years as a journalist. He was not only candid about his job and goals, but also full of ideas and curiosity—and not only about sports. A few times he didn't want to do an interview but was happy just to meet to catch up. Sometimes we talked in German, other times in English. My German skills are almost on par with his English: with a trace of an accent and some mangled grammar. Sometimes he asked me as many questions about what I was up to or working on as I asked about him. Sometimes we talked about the pros and cons of living in the United States versus living in Germany. Sometimes he talked about the latest language he was learning, Spanish—in part to be able to better understand all the Spanish-language soccer games on TV in the United States and to communicate with Hispanic players in America, and in part because he simply enjoys learning languages. And sometimes about what he had just learned as a visiting coach observing the Los Angeles Lakers or the USC football team for a few weeks. He has an insatiable curiosity, and even though he wasn't coaching at the time, I couldn't help thinking his ideas about challenging the status quo and always looking for better ways to do things would be fascinating—and immensely enlightening—to read about in greater depth and detail in a book. But there was no Klinsmann book out there.

So about ten years ago I started asking him why there weren't any English-language biographies or books on his ideas, and whether he might be open to my writing a book about his life and overall coaching philosophies. It seemed like a great idea to me to try to capture some of his wisdom, his ideas on coaching and on soccer, and his vision for the game in the United States for a larger audience. The answer was always a polite "*Nein, danke.*"

He wasn't interested. He savored his largely anonymous lifestyle in California, enjoyed his independence, and was the antithesis of vain. He's usually deeply uncomfortable talking about himself, either quickly changing the subject or switching to the second-person "you" from the first-person "I." In German it's sometimes easier for people to refer to themselves abstractly as "man," which is either "one" or "you." It seemed that the idea of a book—with a tantalizing revelation or two that might be taken out of context for a news headline—was anathema to everything he valued. He had no scores to settle, no axes to grind, and has never been interested in looking back.

Finally, a few months after the 2014 World Cup, and in the middle of another riveting conversation that meandered into a discussion about some of the subtle differences between how Americans and Germans view patience and "long-term outlook," I threw up one last Hail Mary attempt to win him over: "Hey, Jürgen, I'm an American who's lived in Germany for half my life and you're a German who's lived in the United States for nearly half of your life. Why not let me try to write a book about where you're from and what you're trying to do in the United States?" He smiled and said, "Okay, I'll think about it." Maybe he appreciated the persistence? Maybe he appreciated that someone looking in from outside the United States might have an interesting perspective? Or maybe he just wanted to get me off his back? A few weeks later he said he wasn't interested in any kind of an autobiography but he wouldn't have a problem if I turned our interviews and conversations into a book.

I came to our early morning meetings at cafés with some of the best espresso in California, or met him in Europe when the U.S. Men's National Team was playing abroad, with loads of questions. But often we got through only two or three because he would talk at such length and with so much enthusiasm about soccer and the game's role in the United States. He patiently answered questions about his past but was clearly more interested in the future. I always wondered why in previous interviews he never seemed to enjoy questions about his experience as a player. Now I understood: "Klins-mann the player doesn't exist anymore," he said.

What has become abundantly clear is that Jürgen Klinsmann has only one goal—to do everything he can to make the U.S. Men's National Team the best it can possibly be and, he hopes, one day help the country that has become his home win the World Cup. It's based on a formula that he used so effectively in helping Germany as its coach from 2004 to 2006 to become a global power again after a spell in the wilderness, and some of the ideas he used to helped turn FC Bayern Munich into a stronger team in the Champions League. But he knows wishful thinking and desire alone aren't enough. There are uncomfortable truths to be told and challenges to resolve.

# INTRODUCTION

THE GLOBAL GAME of soccer has finally begun to catch on in the United States. The remarkably strong showing by the U.S. Men's National Team at the 2014 World Cup in Brazil, led by Klinsmann, created a sense of excitement across the country, stirring hopes that the United States might finally be on the verge of a great leap forward in soccer.

An especially encouraging development was the unbridled enthusiasm and the sheer numbers of American supporters in Brazil. The United States had more fans who flew to Brazil for the games than any other country except the hosts. There were 196,838 tickets to World Cup games in 2014 bought in the United States, according to FIFA—more than triple the number sold in the next-highest foreign country, neighboring Argentina, with 61,021, and nearly four times as many as the 58,778 tickets bought in soccer-mad Germany, which went to Brazil as a top favorite and won the monthlong tournament. Many of those U.S.-based fans had ties to and supported other teams in the World Cup, but most were cheering the U.S. team and many traveled to games with the American Outlaws, an enthusiastic fan group that was established by three supporters in Lincoln, Nebraska, in 2007 and by 2015 had grown rapidly to more than 30,000 members with 175 official chapters.

The United States managed to break out of the Group of Death, which was the most difficult of the eight groups in the World Cup, with stylish performances against three of the world's best teams: Ghana, Portugal, and Germany. What was arguably the most successful U.S. soccer team ever in the most competitive World Cup ever took second place of four teams in Group G, and advanced along with eventual World Cup winner Germany to the Round of 16. Both Portugal and Ghana were eliminated at the Group Stage.

Coach Jürgen Klinsmann's team played their hearts out as undaunted equals against some of the great powers of the game, earning respect and plaudits from soccer connoisseurs in the United States and around the world. The U.S. team, which many experts and TV pundits had forecast would end up in fourth place in the Group of Death against soccer's great powers and be sent home early, even had chances to win their group after beating Ghana and nearly defeating Portugal before Silvestre Varela headed in a cross, or long pass from the side, from Cristiano Ronaldo just before the final whistle that evened the score. It broke the hearts of American fans seconds before what would have been a major upset. The Americans then had mighty Germany nervously on the ropes in their showdown game that would decide the group winner, giving the team that went on to win the World Cup two weeks later one of its toughest games in the tournament before succumbing 1–0 to a second half goal.

After those strong performances against one of Africa's top teams, Ghana, and two of Europe's best, Portugal and Germany, the Americans were ousted in the Knockout Round in overtime by Belgium—another top-ranked team. The impressive run and surprisingly confident play that enabled the Americans to emerge from such a difficult four-team group alongside Germany to the Round of 16 caught the rest of the world by surprise and lifted the United States to fifteenth place in the FIFA rankings, right behind Italy and ahead of established soccer powers such as England, Croatia, the Czech Republic, Sweden, and Mexico. It also ignited hopes inside the United States that U.S. soccer could finally be catching up with the rest of the world—and possibly on the threshold of a breakthrough to greater glory. Even President Barack Obama got swept up in the enthusiasm of the 2014 World Cup, saying, "Our team gets better at each World Cup, so watch out in 2018."

There is no reason that the United States can't one day excel at the World Cup, the most important tournament in the world's most important game. It's been a riddle for millions outside the United States why the world's richest and most powerful country, with such a passion for sports, seemingly unlimited resources, knowledge, expertise, and an irrepressible drive to be number one, has nevertheless done so little in soccer on the international stage. It's one of the great sports mysteries of our times. Greater success for the United States in soccer could probably help the country better understand the rest of the world, while at the same time help the rest of the world better understand the United States.

It is a monumental task considering that seven countries—Brazil, Germany, Italy, Spain, France, England, and Argentina—have dominated the World Cup for years. They have won the last sixteen times, while the United States hasn't even made it to the Final Four since the inaugural World Cup in 1930, a thirteen-team tournament in Uruguay that most of Europe boycotted. Yet there are explanations—and some possible remedies—for anyone open-minded enough for the kind of honest examination and reforms that Klinsmann is pushing.

Americans want to be first. It's part of our DNA. Yet the country's failure so far to win the world's biggest sporting event—or even come close—is as much a mystery as it is an open wound. It's hard for Americans to fathom why so many much smaller countries with far more limited resources are consistently so much better.

Soccer is a game without borders. It's an international game on an international stage with an international set of rules and standards. Its developments are cascading forward, advanced through an international network of expertise closely associated with the best leagues in the world in Western Europe and the Champions League, a pan-European tournament for clubs where the world's best soccer is played with tactics and trends that national teams will likely be using in the next World Cup. A big part of the problem for the United States has been that, until recently, its focus was more on the domestic stage, and it tended to follow its own sets of rules and standards without tapping into that international network of the best and the brightest centered in Western Europe.

The United States' isolationist views on soccer reflect, to a certain degree, Americans' belief in their own exceptionalism and inward-looking attitudes in countless other areas. The United States is, of course, one of the few countries that still do not use the metric system. That isolationism is one of the key reasons the United States has lagged agonizingly behind the rest of the world in the global game for so long. And many smaller countries seem to delight in being able to tweak America's nose in soccer, savoring the superpower's prolonged agony in the only sport that matters for so many countries. Where else can Costa Rica, Jamaica, Chile, and Denmark all beat the United States in the same year? But soccer can level the playing field in surprising ways. In that same year—2015—the United States managed to beat the soccer superpowers the Netherlands, Germany, and Mexico. It's seen as poetic justice for many countries—where soccer is far more than just a game—that the United States has been a sleeping giant for so long.

But it doesn't have to stay that way. Soccer is, if nothing else, a game of momentum swings, and there's no reason why the United States can't become a global power—especially with Klinsmann at the helm. The sport is growing by leaps and bounds in the United States, and the U.S. Men's National Team—the focal point of the nation's attention in soccer—could certainly win the World Cup *one day,* as the U.S. Women's National Team has already done three times. The global situation in the women's game is almost the exact opposite of that of the men's. Women's soccer is more popular and has a longer tradition in the United States than in any other country. Forty percent of the registered youth players in the United States are female, according to FIFA, and girls make up 47 percent of all high school soccer players. At the college level, 53 percent of NCAA soccer players are women, and at the top college level, Division I, the women are even more dominant with 61 percent. Title IX, the 1972 landmark civil rights law that prohibited sex discrimination at colleges and opened the door for equal opportunities for women in sports, played a major role in strengthening women's soccer in the United States while lingering skepticism about the women's game in many other nations has held women's soccer back abroad. In England, women were even barred from playing soccer on fields or facilities that men used from 1921 to 1971, and women's soccer was banned in West Germany from 1955 to 1970.

In the men's game, there are many highly motivated smaller soccer nations that have taken enormous strides forward in recent years. They are tapping into the international network of best practices and soccer knowledge—and are eagerly sending more of their best players to test their mettle in the best domestic leagues in Europe, where frustratingly few American players are competing. They are also benefiting from the expertise of German, Italian, and Dutch coaches who have been spreading their knowledge in countries around the world. From Berti Vogts coaching Azerbaijan to Falko Götz coaching Vietnam, Germans have been out and about around the world helping develop the national teams of countries such as Cameroon, Jamaica, Thailand, Kuwait, Scotland, South Korea, Nigeria, Canada, Switzerland, Greece, Bangladesh, and Australia. There were German coaches leading four of the thirty-two national teams at the 2014 World Cup, more than from any other country: Klinsmann (USA), Joachim Löw (Germany), Ottmar Hitzfeld (Switzerland), and Volker Finke (Cameroon).

A strong showing at the World Cup can turn any player for any country into an instant hero back home—as demonstrated by James Rodríguez, who almost single-handedly helped Colombia reach the quarterfinals at the 2014 World Cup with six goals in five games. With legend status in the offing, it's no surprise that the global competition has been getting more intense—and the gap between the haves and have-nots in soccer has narrowed appreciably. Children and youngsters are playing soccer for six, eight, ten, twelve, or even fourteen hours a day over nearly twelve months a year in some countries. How will the United States fare in the years ahead if Americans aren't able to match that kind of effort?

The national teams of many smaller countries have raised their game enormously in the last decade, catching up to and sometimes even beating the established superpowers such as Germany, Spain, Italy, Brazil, and Argentina. Just ask the distraught fans of former European champions the Netherlands (1988) and Greece (2004) how it felt when their teams failed to qualify for the quadrennial European Championship tournament in 2016 in France while onetime minnows such as Iceland, Wales, and Albania all made it to the twenty-four-team finals of the tournament from a pack of fifty-three teams competing to qualify.

The way the game is advancing globally means that—truth be

told—the U.S. soccer team will have to keep improving just to maintain its level compared to other nations. The United States has been seen as one of the top regional powers alongside Mexico since the 1990s, ranked on average in nineteenth place since 1993 by FIFA, but often enough somewhere near the bottom of the world's top thirty. The United States has reached the thirty-two-team World Cup for the last seven tournaments, reaching the Round of 16 three times and quarterfinals once. But will the United States *really* be content to be a top-thirty nation in soccer? Even to become a top-ten team, which is one of Jürgen Klinsmann's primary aims, is a monumental challenge.

In part because the United States plays in what has been one of the weaker of the world's six continental federations, a region called CONCACAF (the Confederation of North, Central American, and Caribbean Association Football), American teams have made it to seven straight World Cup finals—a more consistent record than more established global soccer powers such as England or even Mexico, which failed to qualify in 1994 and 1990, respectively. But since 1930 the United States hasn't made it to the semifinals, a position Germany, with only a quarter as many inhabitants, has reached in eleven of the last fourteen World Cups. Why is that?

The United States has made it through the Group Stage to the final Round of 16 in three of the last four tournaments after qualifying for the World Cup only once, in 1950, during six decades in the wilderness between its appearance in 1934 to its next in 1990. Yet it will take a major leap forward to make it to a top-ten ranking—which last happened briefly in 2005—and to become a regular contender for the quarterfinals, semifinals, or finals.

To put the challenge in perspective, it is worth noting how strong the lock is that Western European nations have on the game at the World Cup. Not only have they won the last three World Cups and five of the last seven, but at the 2006 World Cup in Germany, teams from the core countries of Western Europe that are at the heart of the most vibrant network of soccer ideas and advancements won *every* match against teams from other regions except for one: Switzerland's loss in a penalty shootout to Ukraine in the Round of 16. Kuper and Szymanski argue in *Soccernomics* that it is the networking and intense exchange of ideas in Western Europe that make those nations so powerful.

"The region has only about 400 million inhabitants, or 6 percent of the world's population, yet only once in that entire tournament did a western European team lose to a team from another region," they write. "In 2006, even Brazil couldn't match Western Europe. Argentina continued its run of failing to beat a Western European team in open play at a World Cup since the final against West Germany in 1986 . . . Big countries outside the region, like Mexico, Japan, the U.S., and Poland, could not match little Western European countries like Portugal, Holland, or Sweden. If you understood the geographical rule of that World Cup, you could sit in the stands for almost every match before the quarterfinals confident of knowing the outcome." The top four teams were from Western Europe: Italy, France, Germany, and Portugal. The four core countries of the European Union—Germany, Italy, France, and the Netherlands—won a total of twelve World Cups and European Championships between 1968 and 2014. If Spain, which joined the trade bloc in 1986, is included and the dates are expanded from 1964 to 2014, the domination is even more complete: Those five countries have won seven of the last eleven World Cups and ten of the last thirteen European Championships.

At the 2010 World Cup, Western European countries were still dominant but not as invincible and lost six of their twenty-nine games against teams from other regions "in part . . . because other regions have begun to copy Western European methods," Kuper and Szymanski write. "Yet, even in 2010, first, second, and third place all went to Western European nations." Spain beat the Netherlands in the 2010 final and Germany beat Uruguay in the game for third place. "Western Europe excels at soccer for the same fundamental reason it had the scientific revolution in the sixteenth and seventeenth centuries and was for centuries the world's richest region . . . Geography has always helped them exchange ideas, inside their continent and beyond. In short, they are networked." At the 2014 World Cup, two of the top three teams were from Western Europe: Germany (first), and the Netherlands (third).

Europe, and especially Western Europe, is where the world's best soccer is played—the organization, tactics, discipline, and savvy of most European countries where soccer is by far the most important game are superior. The United States has played European teams seventeen times at the World Cup since 1990 and won only once, a 3–2 victory in 2002 with the help of Portugal scoring an own goal, while losing eleven times and playing five ties. In World Cup games against non-European teams, the United States has a better record, winning four of nine games, with four losses and one tie—1–1 against hosts South Korea in 2002.

The United States certainly has a wealth of assets when it comes to sports in general and soccer in particular. It has world-class training facilities; some of the best coaches, fitness experts, and scientific research; and more than enough money and infrastructure to be one of the world's top soccer nations. There is also an enormous and fast-growing pool of Americans playing soccer nowadays compared to the 1970s: Thirteen million Americans play some form of recreational team soccer, according to the Census Bureau, and even though the number of players registered on teams is lower than that, with

4.1 million, according to FIFA, surveys have found that soccer has become the third most popular team sport, behind basketball and baseball/softball.

The United States also has the world's largest economy and is one of the most populous nations, two key factors for long-term success at the World Cup, as convincingly argued by Kuper and Szymanski in *Soccernomics*: "Given the country's fabulous wealth and enormous population," it should have been performing better than it has, they write. The United States has nevertheless made enormous progress in the last fifty years. "We think the Americans, Chinese and Japanese will keep improving," they predict. "The U.S. has the most young soccer players of any country, and Major League Soccer is expanding fast . . . [They] are fast closing the experience gap. They have overtaken the Africans en route to the top."

There is indeed surging interest in the game of soccer in the United States, partly due to the increased television exposure as well as greater accessibility of the global game on the Internet. Major League Soccer (MLS), the domestic league, estimates there are seventy million soccer fans. Enormous crowds cheer from the stands whenever there is a game with top teams playing: 109,318 spectators filled Michigan Stadium in Ann Arbor in 2014 for an exhibition match between two of Europe's top clubs, Manchester United and Real Madrid, while more than 93,226 people were at the Rose Bowl in Pasadena, California, for a 2015 game between Spain's FC Barcelona and the Los Angeles Galaxy. There were 81,944 spectators watching a "friendly," or exhibition game, played between two foreign teams, Brazil and Argentina, at the MetLife Stadium in East Rutherford, New Jersey, in 2012. There were also 93,723 people watching the CONCACAF Cup play-off match on October 10, 2015, in Pasadena between the United States and Mexico—even though about two-thirds of the crowd, mostly Mexican Americans, was cheering for Mexico.

Watching some of the world's best soccer teams in Europe on television has also become a popular pastime for growing numbers of Americans. "After years of being greeted as the 'Next Big Thing' that wasn't, the sport (particularly England's Premier League, with its enhanced presence on American television), has become a conversation topic you can no longer ignore," wrote Alex Williams in an article "Soccer Growing in Popularity in New York Creative Circles" in *The New York Times* in 2014. "There was a time not long ago when Americans—even worldly New Yorkers—could float along in a happy bubble of ignorance, pretending for all practical purposes that the world's favorite sport, soccer, did not exist. That time appears to be fading quickly . . . This is particularly evident in New York creative circles, where the game's aesthetics, Europhilic allure and fashionable otherness have made soccer the new baseball—the go-to sport of the thinking class."

Despite all that, the United States hasn't even come close to winning the World Cup—a game that is watched on television by about one billion people, or about ten times as many as the one hundred million who watch the Super Bowl.

## WHY NOT?

Until now, some essential ingredients were missing. Part of the problem is that many of the most gifted American athletes still gravitate toward football, basketball, and baseball, which have long been the traditional focus of the media and also offer more lucrative contracts with greater financial security. Another significant part of the problem for the United States is that there is, on the one hand, a game of international standards and practices that most of the world follows, but on the other hand, there is the way the United States plays soccer.

In an interconnected world, it's hard to imagine how a nation that isolates itself—in certain crucial ways—from the way the rest of the world plays the game and cuts itself off from the global network of collective knowledge and wisdom can be strong enough to string together six or seven wins played over the four weeks of a World Cup to win that trophy. Winning the odd game in a tournament with a plucky destructive style might produce the occasional spectacular upset, as the United States did against England in 1950 and other overwhelmed teams have managed at times, but a team relying on such "lucky punch" wins with fast-break counterattack goals against the run of play is unlikely to achieve the six to seven victories in a row needed to win the World Cup.

The United States likes to do things its own way, and it's no different when it comes to soccer. Many in the United States tend to view the game through a domestic lens while the rest of the world sees soccer as an international competition. "Soccer (like religion) remains one of the few non-American narratives binding the world together," wrote Andrés Martinez in a 2014 article in *Time* magazine called "How Soccer Is Destroying American Exceptionalism." "The NBA and NFL have followings overseas, but sport still remains the weakest link in America's hegemonic control over global culture . . . For most of the 20th century, when so much of American culture was being adopted by others, Americans were adamant about not reciprocating by adopting the world's sport. Now things have changed . . . It's hard to exaggerate how much soccer's incursion into American life threatens to erode American exceptionalism."

While most of the world's best soccer players sharpen their skills and tactics by playing against each other on top clubs in the world's best four leagues in Europe, many of the best Americans stay home and play in the domestic league in North America. Major League

Soccer has certainly improved by leaps and bounds in the two decades since it was created, in the aftermath of the United States hosting the 1994 World Cup. Its increasingly attractive salaries for some of its best players are understandably an incentive for some of them to stay at home rather than play in top leagues in Europe to hone their skills. Reflecting the steady improvement of the MLS, the number of players on various national teams at the World Cup rose from six in 2010 to thirty-one in 2014—playing for eight countries, including England, Brazil, and Iran. Before that, there had been nineteen MLS players at the 1998 World Cup, eleven in 2002, and fifteen in 2006. By comparison, there were ninety-three players from Bundesliga teams playing for twenty-four national teams at the 2014 World Cup.

A major goal of MLS is to become one of the world's premier leagues by 2022, but it is still seen, from a global perspective, as a soccer backwater—a league for some of the world's greatest has-beens from overseas who are past their prime and are being put out to pasture. It is a league hurt by its cap on salaries. It is also undermined by its unique drive for parity, which fits the American mold but stands in marked contrast to leagues around the world that have dominant teams fans either love or love to hate. And it is hurt by its aversion to the promotion-relegation system that is used in more competitive leagues around the world. MLS has also been an attractive, low-pressure environment for some of the top Americans, evidently eager to avoid the hassles and intense competitive pressures in Europe. Despite its steady improvement, the truth is that MLS does not rank as one of the world's top-ten leagues and probably not even in the top fifteen. It is not hard for even an untrained observer to see the difference in skill, quality, and speed in an English Premier League game, a Bundesliga game, or top divisions in Spain, Italy, France, Portugal, the Netherlands, Switzerland, Brazil, Argentina,

Mexico, the Czech Republic, Denmark, Sweden, Poland, Scotland, or Ukraine compared to an MLS game. MLS games feel more like Germany's second or even third division.

At one MLS game on a warm Saturday evening in September 2015 in front of a sold-out crowd of 27,000 at California's StubHub Center between the Los Angeles Galaxy and the Montreal Impact, former England star Steven Gerrard of the Galaxy and former Ivory Coast star Didier Drogba of the Impact were suddenly going all out for a match-winning goal in the waning minutes of an at times entertaining 0–0 game, playing superbly to try to spark their teams to victory. But right at the most exciting moment of the game, several hundred American spectators stood up and made their way to the exits, presumably to get a head start on the traffic, even though they were missing the best action of the game. It was nevertheless a much more vibrant atmosphere than in 2006, when 20,145 watched at the same stadium, then called the Home Depot Center, as the Galaxy lost to the Houston Dynamo, 2–1. MLS is growing fast and had the seventh-highest average attendance for soccer leagues around the world in 2015—21,574. The most popular team, the Seattle Sounders, had an average attendance of 44,245 for its 2015 home games and 55,435 at its final against Real Salt Lake.

There is nevertheless an appreciable gap in the quality and intensity of the MLS from top leagues in the world. In *The Beckham Experiment,* Grant Wahl colorfully describes an awkward situation when the Los Angeles Galaxy was on an off-season tour of exhibition games in Asia, in part to raise appearance fees from those Asian teams that paid to host those friendlies, which helped to finance David Beckham's $6.5 million annual salary. Wahl writes that the Galaxy earned $1 million every time it played an exhibition game on the tour of Australia, New Zealand, South Korea, China, and Hong Kong. "The risk, however, was that once those Asian fans actually saw the Galaxy brand, they knew it wasn't a SuperClub. One MLS executive said his friend in Hong Kong took some high-rolling business executives to the Galaxy's 2–2 exhibition tie against Hong Kong Union. The Galaxy was 'an embarrassment,' he said. 'My friend goes, "They're thinking American soccer is crap. Because they view this as your best team, your Manchester United." And I tell him the Galaxy didn't make the play-offs last year. "But this is your team with Beckham, and they're crap." They thought it was a bunch of boys. That's not a good thing.' " The MLS's total salary costs that year, excluding Beckham, were $3.1 million, but five of the team's twenty players were earning $30,000 or less per year.

There is perhaps no better illustration of the gap between the quality of Europe's top leagues and MLS than players' salaries. MLS has a salary cap per team of $3.5 million. England's Premier League has no salary cap, and the average salary *per player* is about $3.5 million, as Robert Wilson notes in an analysis in *The Huffington Post*. He argues that the MLS's claim that it is closing the gap to Europe's top leagues is nonsense. "MLS has lost ground over the past 20 years, not gained it. MLS has established its own myth to the contrary, and that myth has been sold to the press and public extremely well. The European leagues since MLS's inception in 1996, have outgrown, outspent and created an increasingly better product. The gap with Europe widened from 1996 until now, and promises to widen further."

That cold reality of the disparity in quality is also reflected in what TV networks are willing to pay. American networks are shelling out twice as much to broadcast a *foreign* soccer league than their own top league. Indeed, NBC is paying $1 billion to broadcast England's Premier League games for six seasons through 2022. That amounts to $166 million per year for a league of foreigners playing in a foreign country five to eight time zones ahead of the United States, while MLS is getting $90 million per year from ESPN, FOX

Sports, and Univision. Can anyone imagine a U.S. network paying twice as much to broadcast games from a foreign basketball league—say, Spain—in the United States as it pays for the NBA?

That wide gulf in quality is one reason why large numbers of American soccer fans flock to the preseason exhibition matches of the top European clubs or tune in to Premier League games on television, yet don't go to see MLS games in person or watch them on TV. MLS is certainly an interesting and dynamic young league with a bright future, but it is not yet anywhere near the world's best. It is hurt by a complicated player allocation system, anemic TV ratings, and a pernicious practice of spending small fortunes on aging foreign has-beens with big names who have lost the speed and stamina to continue competing in the top leagues in England, Spain, Germany, or Italy. "It's not that the standard of play is bad (it's not, but it's nothing to fly across the country for either)," writes Ian Plenderleith in the monthly UK soccer magazine *When Saturday Comes*.

Another important factor that has so far held the United States back from winning the World Cup is that soccer clubs in most countries exist for one reason: to win games and put the best possible team on the field. Nothing else really matters. Soccer clubs around the world spend almost all their resources—and often more than they have—on acquiring players in the international transfer market and on player salaries. "Making profits deprives a club of money that it could spend on the team," write Kuper and Szymanski in *Soccernomics*. "The business of soccer is soccer. Rather, they are like museums: public-spirited organizations that aim to serve the community while remaining reasonably solvent. It sounds like a modest goal, but few of them achieve even that." Clubs abroad are thus often loss-making enterprises falling further in debt each year. They are in a sense more charitable trusts than sound businesses, which do not exist to make profits or pay shareholder dividends. Spain's top two clubs have more than \$1.2 billion in cumulative debt: Real Madrid owes creditors \$750 million and FC Barcelona has \$530 million in debt. Manchester United is third on the list of most in-debted clubs with \$510 million. Yet those three free-spending teams have won the Champions League in five of the last eight years.

Soccer clubs in North America, by contrast, are more businesses than public institutions, and thus they keep an eye on the bottom line. MLS clubs try to control costs and have no debt even though many still lose money. There is a vast gap in salaries in MLS between the haves and the have-nots as income inequality remains a major problem undermining the league's international reputation—in 2014 the top seven of the MLS's 572 players earned a third of the total wage costs of \$130 million. Keeping close tabs on the bottom line is certainly the American way of running a professional sports league, but does it produce great soccer?

The gap between the top European clubs and MLS can be illus-trated another way. Real Madrid had revenues of €660 million (\$700 million) in 2014–2015. That was more than the entire combined revenue of the four professional soccer leagues in the United States and Canada with a total of sixty-four teams—MLS, the National Women's Soccer League, the North American Soccer League (NASL), and USL Pro. "One European club, which is fan owned by the way, is worth more than all four leagues and their sixty-four teams combined in the USA and Canada. Two of the richest countries in the world," writes Wilson in *The Huffington Post,* referring to Real Madrid. He argues this is further evidence that the gap between MLS and the top European leagues has widened over the years. "In short, mediocrity and second tier status (when measured against our global benchmarks in the [English Premier League] and Bundesliga) has been institutionalized at the highest levels of the game in the USA and Canada. MLS is generating less revenue after 20 years than respectively, the English and German second divisions."

Soccer clubs around the world face a constant churning pressure to succeed on the field—or end up getting relegated, dropped unceremoniously to the next-lower league level. It is tantamount to the death penalty for clubs that fail to perform. In theory they can, and often do, bounce right back to top flight a year later by winning the lower league and getting promoted. It is a perpetual process that keeps players on every team at every level on their toes 24/7 right up to the final game. There is no "playing out the season" in most soccer leagues around the world because pretty much every team in every league is fighting for the championship, or to qualify for a spot in international tournaments the following season, or to avoid relegation. Soccer clubs in the MLS face no such existential competitive pressures.

Even though soccer's popularity has grown enormously in the last decade, it still has a way to go to catch up to the status of football, basketball, and baseball in America. The United States is a global superpower in so many areas, but it has cut a relatively minor figure globally in soccer.

That is changing. Jürgen Klinsmann, the German-born U.S. coach and technical director, is an agent of change, a mover and shaker par excellence. He knows what it takes to win the World Cup. He played an important role as player for his country at three of those tournaments—in 1990, 1994, and 1998—scoring eleven goals in seventeen games and becoming the first player ever to have at least three goals in three different World Cups. His eleven goals in total put him tied for sixth in the all-time World Cup scoring list, just one behind Pelé, the Brazilian superstar who played in four World Cups. Klinsmann was also a captain of Germany's 1996 team that won the European Championship. Later, after his seventeen-year career as a player, Klinsmann was the coach of Germany at the 2006 World Cup and of the United States in 2014—leading both teams to better than expected results.

As a player, Klinsmann had a knack for raising his game at the right time—when it mattered most in leading his country to two titles. He is remembered in Germany and around the world for playing his best soccer at the big tournaments—at all three World Cups and at the three European championships. "I just always enjoyed the tournaments and couldn't wait for them to start," he says. And, likewise, Klinsmann succeeded in getting more out of the two teams he coached at the World Cups.

A tireless reformer and catalyst for change, Klinsmann is forever searching for ways to do things better. He lived for six years abroad as a player in Italy, Monaco, and England, and has spent nearly two decades in California following his career as a player. After coaching Germany remotely from California, he is committed to making the United States strong enough to compete with—and even beat— the world's best teams, as they showed at the World Cup in Brazil when they defeated Ghana, played Portugal to a tie, and had Germany on the ropes. The United States has also had an impressive string of wins in friendlies against some of the world's best teams, beating Germany twice, as well as defeating Italy, the Netherlands, the Czech Republic, Bosnia and Herzegovina, Turkey, and a historic first-ever win against Mexico on Mexican soil, 1–0, on August 15, 2012.

A delightfully direct man who never hesitates to speak his mind or ruffle feathers in pursuit of his aims, Klinsmann is a maverick who wants to make the United States a soccer power after helping to revive Germany's National Team with revolutionary reforms that shook up the soccer establishment in his home country a decade ago. His changes upset the status quo—painful steps that nevertheless brought notable results and longer-term strength everywhere he has coached despite running into the resistance and wrath of many traditionalists along the way.

Overcoming that initial opposition as well as plenty of potshots from critics, naysayers, and those leery of change, Klinsmann managed to spearhead reforms that revitalized Germany's soccer program and put the country's national team on a trajectory to win the 2014 World Cup. Before that, Germany had reached the semifinals in both 2006 and 2010—with the help of many of the players Klinsmann picked and promoted as well as the new policies he put in place. He shook up the DFB, breaking up its archaic structures in the process, and tried to modernize the institution, creating more than a few enemies by the time he was finished in 2006. Germany has enjoyed the fruits of those far-reaching reforms ever since. Germany players and their coach since 2006, Joachim Löw, have regularly made it clear that Klinsmann deserves a share of the credit for Germany's success with the changes and reforms he introduced despite serious opposition when he was the German coach. Klinsmann also introduced extensive reforms at FC Bayern Munich that have increased the club's success, particularly in the Champions League.

Klinsmann turned his focus to U.S. soccer when he was named head coach in 2011. He has been following soccer's developments in the United States since he settled on the West Coast in 1998 with his family. With a voracious appetite to learn and the resolve to extract the best possible performance out of himself and his players, he has given a lot of thought to how he can unlock soccer's great potential in the United States over time.

He was often puzzled about what was holding America back in

the world's most favorite game, and he pondered what might be impeding the world's leading nation in so many areas from achieving greatness in soccer. A German native who has lived abroad for more than half his life, Klinsmann's meticulous research and eclectic insights have given him ideas about what needs to happen for the U.S. team to someday win the World Cup—despite the fact that not everyone likes the remedies he has introduced.

Klinsmann's soccer pedigree could hardly be more suitable for the task. Popular pretty much everywhere he played for both clubs and his country due to his contagious style of hard work, exuberance, and prolific goal scoring on the field, as well as his commitment to the sport off the field, Klinsmann is the epitome of drive and diligence. He rarely stops pushing himself, and he has even learned to speak four languages in addition to his native German as an adult—English, Italian, Spanish, and French—to be able to better understand his coaches, his teammates, and the mentality of the countries he has played or coached in.

Klinsmann helped rejuvenate Germany's soccer with pioneering reforms and a headstrong determination to restore the country's soccer glory after the proud and success-spoiled *Nationalmannschaft* had gone through a dismal and dispiriting trophyless period around the turn of the millennium. It was, above all, Klinsmann's courage—in the face of at times fierce opposition from the soccer establishment, the media, and especially Germany's professional soccer league, the Bundesliga—to push through the reforms that turned Germany into a world power again. He has faced similar resistance at times in the United States. In Germany, he introduced a new attacking style of play for the *Nationalmannschaft*. He also brought innovative ideas from the United States on fitness and organization that at first upset some of Germany's old guard. Klinsmann was a breath of fresh air, and even though it took some time for the changes to take hold, they helped make the team one of the world's most successful, and most admired, within the space of just two years with a highly entertaining and energized style of play.

In the United States, too, Klinsmann has faced criticism since taking the coaching job in 2011. He has one overriding aim—to make the U.S. Men's National Team successful over the long term, while making soccer more interesting and accessible for more Americans. He has, in the process, upset some in his first few years on the job. He has unintentionally made enemies of those who disagree with his views. But Klinsmann is used to criticism and was ready for the naysayers, remaining cheerfully undaunted and undeterred as he takes on the challenge at hand: He's on a mission to make the United States better and more respected in soccer circles, and a contender for the World Cup. He has some precise, painful, and yet refreshing ideas about what this will take.

Love him or loathe him, Klinsmann's ideas are changing the game in the United States and gradually taking hold. This book, based on dozens of interviews with Klinsmann and my twenty years' experience writing about soccer in Europe and the United States, attempts to answer some of the most pressing questions American soccer fans have been asking for years: Why hasn't the U.S. Men's National Team won the World Cup? What does it take to build dominant team? What separates the USMNT from Brazil, Argentina, Germany, Italy, and other soccer powers? And how will Klinsmann take the United States there?

PART I

———

# THE EARLY YEARS

# STARTING OUT

JÜRGEN KLINSMANN WAS an eight-year-old bundle of blond energy when he first put his foot into a soccer ball with a team. It was early in 1973, and like millions of West German boys, he had already been playing soccer with friends in pickup games—kicking balls around in parks, on the streets, or at school during recess. In a soccer nation like West Germany, it's what almost everyone did.

The national sport is everywhere. It's the game children play whenever they get the chance with their friends or family. Soccer is more than just a sport in Germany; it's a way of life. It is a part of the national identity, and it has been a source of intense national pride for more than six decades. Soccer is in many ways a bond that holds the nation—and its generations—together.

As much as eight-year-old Jürgen Klinsmann enjoyed kicking a ball around with friends in his small hometown of Gingen, he had never played soccer on a team—with uniforms, rules, and coaches. With encouragement from his father, he had given gymnastics a try at the club a year earlier. Siegfried Klinsmann, a forty-year-old master baker, had been a gymnast in his youth and was a part-time coach at the local club, the Turnerbund Gingen—TB Gingen. He thought gymnastics might challenge his son and expend some of his abundant energy. So he took Jürgen, the second oldest of his four boys, to the club when he was about seven years old to give gymnastics a try. But the tumbling, vault, and balance beam didn't especially impress Jürgen. There wasn't a lot of action, he recalled. A little while later, a few friends took Jürgen to handball practice, a popular indoor winter sport in pockets of Europe that's a sort of hybrid between soccer and basketball. But that didn't hold much appeal either.

Then in the winter of 1973, a few months after West Germany won the first of its three European Championships in 1972, he joined friends at a youth team soccer practice at TB Gingen. He took an immediate liking to the game in its organized form. He was captivated by the speed, the action, the energy, and especially the rush he got when he managed to score a goal.

"I just loved the feeling of running around, of letting all that energy out on the field, and the great feeling you have afterward," Klinsmann says, recalling his first formal practice sessions. "Soccer was just a wonderful outlet for all that energy that was bottled up inside. I was obsessed about running around and playing . . . I could go on playing soccer for hours at a time. I just really enjoyed it and had a lot of fun with it from the start. It gave me such a good feeling."

He signed up with that local amateur soccer club and started wearing TB Gingen's red-and-white jersey. The team was at the very bottom of Germany's soccer hierarchy, or pyramid—the entry level of organized soccer. There would be a direct line of promotion up that broad-based structure in the years that followed for Klinsmann. Thousands of other players his age joined a club in 1973, but only a few would make it all the way to the top of the pyramid: the Bundesliga and even onto the very pinnacle on the *Nationalmannschaft*. There still isn't such a clearly defined soccer structure in the United States, which Klinsmann has been working to change.

As a child, Klinsmann had no idea how far soccer would take him. He was simply having a great time playing the game, developing his skills with his friends and teammates. His focus at first was on making the starting team at TB Gingen, a club that had been established in 1870 as a gymnastics club. TB Gingen later added handball, track and field, and soccer sections. Long before anyone in Germany had heard of *Fussball,* the game of soccer that was imported to Germany from England in 1874, the *Turnverein,* the gymnastics clubs, were part of a popular nationwide nationalist movement in the nineteenth century—and that's why many of the top soccer clubs in the country still have references to *Turnen* (gymnastics) in their names.

Young Jürgen Klinsmann had a blast playing soccer on a team and felt the rapid improvement of his skills that naturally came along with so many hours of practice both with his club and at home. Unlike in the United States, where sports teams are an integral part of the school system, there are virtually no school sports teams in Germany, so children turn to sports clubs as their outlet for competition. Klinsmann's attachment to soccer can be traced back to his first club in Gingen.

There are many cultural differences small and large between towns in the United States and Germany. One of the most important distinctions is that time and progress are measured in other dimensions in towns like Gingen, a sleepy village of four thousand on the Fils River that was settled more than one thousand years ago. The pace can be glacial, and patience is part of life. When people in towns with a thousand-year history speak of a long-term horizon, they aren't talking about weeks or months. When Jürgen Klinsmann talks about a long-term perspective for soccer in the United States, he has his German roots in the back of his mind and is thinking in terms of many years, decades, and even generations.

TB Gingen's weekend games attracted scores of local townspeople—not only parents and friends but also local citizens eager to watch young children playing the country's most popular game. Klinsmann's father used to come out to the *Sportplatz,* the soccer field, to watch every game that he could make it to after finishing up for the day at his bakery.

Organized soccer is a serious matter throughout Germany. The German Football Association (FA), or *Deutscher Fussball Bund* (DFB), is the largest organization of its kind in the world, with 6.9 million members. Klinsmann was one of 112,858 West German children to sign up on a team for the first time in 1973 when he joined TB Gingen. The membership fee was affordable—a few dozen deutsche marks (about $20) per year. The coaches were invariably former players and mostly volunteers—another striking difference between Germany and the United States, where coaches are often paid and don't necessarily have playing experience themselves. Because soccer has always been such an inexpensive sport in Germany, it's been hugely popular with children from all walks of life, especially from families with limited resources. "We all came from families with moderate incomes and fought our way through," Klinsmann says. "Worldwide, soccer is a sport played by kids in the lower- and middle-class environments. In the United States it's different."

There were a total of 98,911 teams at 15,890 clubs in the DFB at the time. The number of players registered on teams with the DFB rose from 3,084,901 in 1972 to 3,197,759 in 1973, the year Klinsmann joined. The DFB doubled in size over the next four decades. To put some perspective on the DFB's size in 2015, it had 6,889,115 members—meaning there were more people playing on registered soccer teams in Germany than the entire population of Denmark, Finland, or Jordan.

Youth soccer ranked high on the sports calendar in countless small and large towns across West Germany, not only offering an outlet for young boys but also serving as an important community social function on weekends—not unlike Little League baseball games or high school football games across the United States that connect sports-minded children with their parents and communities. The number of new soccer players in Germany usually jumps significantly in the years after the country wins a major tournament, all of which are watched on television by virtually the entire nation—with market shares as high as 86 percent of the nation's viewers. The year 1973, one year after West Germany beat the Soviet Union 3–0 in the final to win its first European Championship in the tournament played in Belgium, was no exception. It inspired thousands of youngsters like Klinsmann to sign up with youth teams across the country.

There is no such thing as a "soccer mom" in Germany, and the concept usually needs a lot of explanation for Germans and others around the world. Soccer has widespread appeal across all demographics in Germany and is not by any means limited to stay-at-home mothers in affluent suburbs who shuttle their children around to after-school activities. Germany is also a country in which mothers, fathers, sisters, brothers, aunts, and uncles as well as *Oma* and *Opa* come out to watch the games and happily drive or accompany their children, siblings, or family members to and from practices and games. Soccer is ubiquitous in Germany, as it is in much of the world, played by all socioeconomic classes.

"You're a child of your environment, and my environment was a little club in my hometown that offered different sports—gymnastics, handball, and soccer," says Klinsmann, who is working to give soccer in the United States a similarly broad-based structure, feeding players through youth leagues to the top of the game. "My family had ties to gymnastics, so that was what you tried first. And then a friend takes you to a handball practice and you try that. And then the next friend takes you to soccer, and there you discover it's the thing you like the most. That's the way it was in West Germany back then. That's the beauty of the system of sports clubs there. You can just try things out to see what feels right. A lot depends on what your best friends are doing as well, and you end up going to the sport where your buddies are playing, and in Germany that's going to be soccer about ninety percent of the time."

Klinsmann was born in the village of Göppingen, near Gingen, on July 30, 1964. That year marked the peak of the baby boom in Germany, a record-breaking year for births: a total of 1,357,304 children were born in West Germany and East Germany. Never before or after were so many Germans born in a single year.

Klinsmann was fascinated by the competitive environment on the TB Gingen youth soccer team and encouraged by his ever-improving skills. Even at the age of eight, he had an abundance of drive and an insatiable appetite to improve. His aim was to be on the field as much as possible, then to become the best player on the field—while winning and scoring as many goals as he could—an ambition that propelled him on and upward over the next quarter century.

Klinsmann generally avoids dwelling on the past. But a smile nevertheless creeps across his face when reminiscing about his fascination with soccer as a youngster. "This little community was just driven by kicking a ball around. So you do that with your buddies in the street, and then you try it out at some point at your community club. That's basically where I started to play. That was pretty much the earliest age when you could play club soccer back then, starting at about eight. Before that there was nothing really organized. That's all changed now. Some kids start playing at clubs even at the age of five!"

Soccer had become an important part of West Germany's

national identity a decade before Klinsmann was born—in part a result of the euphoria that erupted when the country won the 1954 World Cup, beating Hungary in the final, and the afterglow of that historic triumph. The West Germany team's unexpected success was a trigger for the country's "economic miracle" and the nation's improbable rise from the ruins of World War II. The powerful influence that soccer holds over the German psyche can be traced back to that epic World Cup victory. Taking the Cup against such long odds contributed to a social, cultural, political, and economic chain reaction that economists said helped spark the legendary economic boom of the 1950s, lifting morale in West Germany after a decade of postwar deprivation and despair. It was the game of soccer, more than anything else, that wrenched the country out of its postwar lethargy. It brightened the national outlook and collectively helped millions of Germans feel they were a part of the world community again after decades of ostracism and isolation because of their destructive Nazi past. Understandably, soccer has been much more than just a game for Germans ever since.

Klinsmann's second birthday, in 1966, could have been a day of joy in West Germany but became a day of mourning instead. The country had been unable to repeat the success of the 1954 World Cup win in 1958 or 1962, and were knocked out in the semifinals by hosts Sweden, 3–1, in 1958, and by Yugoslavia, 1–0, in the quarterfinals in 1962. But in 1966 they were close to winning a second championship in twelve years, reaching the final against hosts England. But they were beaten when England's Geoff Hurst was awarded a controversial goal eleven minutes into the thirty-minute extra time period to make it 3–2. Hurst's shot hit the crossbar, bounced down on, but probably not completely over, the line before being cleared away from the goal by a West German defender. Was it truly a goal or not? It's one of the all-time great controversies of soccer and will likely never be conclusively resolved. England got a fourth goal one minute before the end of play as West Germany pressed forward desperately trying to tie the score again.

There are ordinarily three outcomes for a soccer match: win, loss, or tie. But there are no ties at big tournaments such as the World Cup, so if a game is still even after ninety minutes, the two teams continue on to play two fifteen-minute periods of extra time. If the game is still tied after the thirty minutes of extra time, the penalty shoot-out determines the winner. In what is invariably a high drama one-on-one showdown of kicker versus goalkeeper, the teams take turns taking shots from the penalty mark with the team that scores more goals from its five penalty shots declared the winner. If the score is still even after five rounds, the penalty shoot-out continues with one shot at a time until a winner is determined.

A week after joining the youth team at TB Gingen in 1973 and getting his first taste of the formal rules, Klinsmann came in as a substitute for the final ten minutes of a game against a club called FTSV Kuchen. He was sent onto the field following a quick briefing about a rule that no one had worried about in pickup games. *"Hei, was isch eigentlich Abseits?"* (Hey, what's this offside thing all about?) Klinsmann asked before going on, as Roland Eitel describes it in his biography, *Jürgen Klinsmann—Der Weg Nach Oben.* A week later in another game, against SV Altenstadt, Klinsmann scored his first goal in a 5–1 win. Playing on TB Gingen's *E-Jugend* team, or E-level youth team of eight- to ten-year-olds, Klinsmann soon made a name for himself with his goal-scoring prowess.

Germans are extraordinarily well organized about most things, and that is especially the case when it comes to soccer. Although it is not played at schools or universities but at clubs, there is, nevertheless, a pyramid system with a clear hierarchy in which players can rise steadily through the ranks, usually one level at a time.

When Klinsmann started, soccer for children began with the *E-Jugend,* where teams played seven against seven (instead of eleven on a side at the senior levels). After the E level, there were four higher levels—D, C, B, and A—separating him and his eight- to ten-year-old teammates from the club's senior adult team. From the *E-Jugend,* Klinsmann and many of his teammates were promoted to the *D-Jugend* (eleven to thirteen years old, with nine players a side), then to the *C-Jugend* (fourteen to fifteen), the *B-Jugend* (sixteen to seventeen years old, with eleven players a side), and finally the *A-Jugend* (seventeen to nineteen). Those still playing the game would graduate to the senior adult team—or jump off the pyramid and join the working world. Nowadays, the group levels start even earlier, with *F-Jugend* (seven to eight years old) and *G-Jugend* (under seven).

"In that organized form is where they start keeping track of the results, where you have a regular team and play in a regular league, and you have a jersey to wear," Klinsmann says. "That's where you take what you learn in your street game to an organized game."

In Germany, there has always been a subliminal message along with that kind of a tiered structure. The system provides perpetual incentive and encouragement for youngsters to aspire to the next level; it instills a desire to improve from an early age. There are subtle pressures and rewards embedded in the system, which is geared to keep players reaching for the next rung up on the ladder, as if that were the most natural thing in the world.

Klinsmann had boundless drive as an eight-year-old but no inkling that he could one day earn a living playing soccer—let alone become one of the country's most prolific goal scorers with eleven goals in three World Cups for his country. Like most of his friends and teammates in Gingen, he was unable to imagine going far enough with soccer to be able to make a career out of it. He simply loved playing and wholeheartedly embraced the competitive pressure from the start. "You have no idea how your life will develop at that point, absolutely no idea," he says. "You just play soccer because it's fun and it's what you and your friends do."

Even as he rose through the amateur ranks and each layer of West Germany's well-structured pyramid in the 1970s, Klinsmann maintained an infectious childlike enthusiasm on the field. In later years, it was a joy for fans to see Klinsmann maintaining such a youthful sparkle, and especially his unrestrained goal celebrations for his country—or for clubs in Germany, Italy, France, and England. This carefree innocence belied his age, years of experience, and professional status. The elation when he scored seemed no different from the way a ten-year-old Klinsmann would have celebrated his goals for TB Gingen. Even more than four decades later, anyone watching Klinsmann leap into 5 versus 2 keep-away drills at workouts on the field with his players on the U.S. Men's National Team marvels at the youthful enthusiasm of a coach well into his fifties.

In a nation so focused on soccer, it seemed beyond the realm of imagination for most youngsters that they could make it to the pros. The Bundesliga seemed light-years away. There were no club soccer games on live television in West Germany; instead there were popular highlight shows broadcast hours later on Saturday evenings. At that age, Klinsmann had a different long-term plan. He told everyone who would listen that he wanted to be a pilot when he grew up. Soccer was something he played for fun.

"In that peer environment of a soccer nation, every kid who comes through with a little bit of talent realizes there is just one goal—you go for the goal that you can see and feel right in front of you," Klinsmann says. He admires the bold self-confidence of twenty-first-century children in the United States, where dreams are big and youngsters watching the pros on television can easily picture themselves later on starring in an NBA final, a Super Bowl, or a

World Series. "When I was a kid, it was like, 'You're never going to reach a goal that's one hundred miles away right away.' That was all just so far away," he says, marveling at the capacity of young Americans to aim so high.

He had just turned nine years old in July 1973 and had been practicing hard—both with TB Gingen and at home with friends, kicking a soccer ball for hours on end against walls and garage doors. One day he was playing a game for Gingen against a rival club called Aichelberg. It was only a few months after he'd joined the club, yet Klinsmann scored sixteen goals, leading his team to a 20–0 win. The feat was all the more impressive considering the games at that level consisted of only two twenty-minute halves. He could feel that the countless thousands of hours of practice with his friends and with the club were paying off. His passing, ball-handling, and shooting skills were getting better all the time—a valuable lifelong lesson he would take with him about the rewards of hard work.

"There was just all this drive that came from playing soccer in the neighborhood," Klinsmann recalls. "The community club became just a little supplement with one game and one practice each week. The real practice was in a self-driven environment, every day. Most of the playing I was doing then was driven by neighborhood soccer. I was out there playing every day—three or four or five hours a day, after school or after doing my homework. I had no idea how good or bad I was. I was just driven by wanting to get better—and to score goals. I had no idea how it would develop. I just loved the feeling of scoring goals, whether it was on the field in an organized game or just two sticks or two piles of cloths. Whenever I scored, I'd run into the goal, get the ball, and take it right back to the midfield line as fast as I could. I'd put the ball down and tell the other team, 'Get going!'"

Klinsmann ended up with a total of 106 goals in eighteen games in that memorable first full season on the youth team, an average of six goals per game. That was quite an accomplishment for a novice in the region that was considered one of the many soccer hotbeds in West Germany. His rush of goal-scoring only whetted his appetite for more.

"Word began to spread that there was this extraordinary young goal-scoring phenomenon growing up in Gingen," Eitel writes about the prodigious star in his biography of Klinsmann. Eitel was a local sportswriter for the *Stuttgarter Zeitung*. He later became a friend of Klinsmann's and his media adviser in Germany. "The great talent Jürgen Klinsmann was discovered right there in Gingen. He soon started coming home, carrying a gym bag that was almost as big as he was, and announcing (in the local dialect): '*Mir hen g'wonne, I han a Tor g'schosse*' (We won and I scored). It didn't take long before he was coming home from almost every game with the same announcement."

# GERMAN ATTITUDE

Soccer's modern rules were first standardized in England in 1863. But it is a game that became closely entwined with German history. It could be argued that it has even been the country's raison d'être since 1954—the year when the team of rank outsiders from West Germany won the World Cup final against long odds. With four World Cup wins in total—1954, 1974, 1990, and 2014—along with three European Championships—in 1972, 1980, and 1996— some would argue that it has been the most successful soccer nation on earth over the last six decades; it has also made it to the semi-finals in ten of the last thirteen World Cups. The game might have been created in England, but it was perfected in Germany. Why? Why does Germany have so much success?

For a start, the number of Germans playing soccer is staggering. There is no other Football Association (FA) or even any other sports organization in the world with as many members as Germany's FA, the DFB. Founded in 1900, the DFB is the backbone of the game in Germany—Western Europe's largest country, with eighty-two million people.

An important reason that soccer is held in such high regard in

Germany is its 1954 World Cup and the impact it had on the nation. The quadrennial tournament was first held separately in 1930, in Uruguay. It had been part of the Olympics before that, from 1900, but wasn't in the plans for the 1932 Olympics in Los Angeles because the game—surprise, surprise!—was not considered popular enough in the United States. Germany took third at the 1934 World Cup but was eliminated in the first round in 1938. The two World Cups in 1942 and 1946 were canceled because of World War II.

In 1950, Germany was partitioned, occupied by the United States, Britain, France, and the Soviet Union. The country was banned from the World Cup, held in Brazil. Invited back to take part in the World Cup in 1954, the scrappy West Germany team was an unseeded underdog at the tournament played in Switzerland, but advanced all the way to the final in Berne. West Germany had already lost, 8–3, to the "Magnificent Magyars" from Hungary, the reigning Olympic champions, in its second match earlier in the tournament. Hungary's "Golden Team" had an impressive thirty-two-game winning streak during the preceding two years as they headed into the final against West Germany.

The game was played on a soggy Swiss field in Wankdorf Stadium on a rainy afternoon on July 4, 1954. There were only forty thousand television sets in West Germany at the time, but millions tuned in to hear the game on the radio, and the streets were all but deserted. Germans huddled together in bars or in homes of people who could afford radios and listened as the West Germany team fell behind 2–0 in the first eight minutes before fighting back valiantly to pull even at 2–2 and ultimately winning 3–2 thanks to a late goal from Helmut Rahn.

Germans were delirious when radio reporter Herbert Zimmermann bellowed the immortal words: *"Aus, Aus, Aus, Das Spiel ist aus! Deutschland ist Weltmeister!"* (It's over, over, over, the game is over.

Germany is the world champion!). Zimmermann's emotional reporting can still bring tears to the eyes of Germans old enough to
remember the game and gives younger Germans born after 1954
goose bumps as well.

That unexpected World Cup win gave the nation of fifty-two million a new lease on life and a chance to hold their heads high again.
It was only nine years after the end of World War II and helped mark
an end to an era of international isolation many Germans had felt
after the war.

This most unlikely triumph in the sixteen-team tournament became known in West Germany as the *"Wunder von Bern,"* the Miracle
of Berne. It gave a broken, bombed-out nation humiliated and dis-
graced by the war a new identity—*Fussball Weltmeister,* world soccer
champions. Especially for younger generations like Klinsmann's
father, who was twenty-one at the time, the World Cup win was a
turning point in their country's history. *"Wir sind wieder wer"* was
the sentiment West Germans expressed and felt in their hearts—
"We count for something again."

"My dad talked a lot about 1954 and how much winning the
World Cup meant," says Klinsmann, who as a coach in 2004 made
sure his younger Germany players knew all about the magic of 1954
by distributing CDs of the game's highlights. "The country was really
going through a difficult period back then after the war, and soccer
gave people hope and something to believe in again."

Some historians have pointed to that World Cup win as the moment the nation was reborn. It was a more significant event than five
years earlier, in 1949, when the country got a new constitution and
elected a first postwar parliament, or six years earlier, in 1948, with
the currency reform that replaced the deutsche mark with the reichs-
mark—or even the *Stunde Null,* zero hour, when the fighting in the
defeated nation was over at the end of the war in May 1945. Winning

the World Cup in 1954 was a moment of indescribable pride for West Germany, an unexpected victory that helped spark the *Wirtschaftswunder,* West Germany's legendary "economic miracle." It led to a period of rapid economic growth and prosperity that wrenched the country out of the postwar recession, putting it on a course of breathtaking expansion. It became one of the world's leading industrial nations by the end of the decade.

Fueled by the era of good feeling following the World Cup, West Germany's gross domestic product surged by 10.5 percent in real terms in 1954, the largest annual rise in GDP ever recorded in the country. Wages also shot up by 10 percent in 1955 on the wave of euphoria of that World Cup win, and the number of cars on the road increased by 19 percent. That surge in car ownership created an entirely new twentieth-century problem: the country's first traffic jams on the autobahns, the high-speed motorways crisscrossing the nation that had originally been built to facilitate troop and tank movements during the war.

The word "*Wirtschaftswunder*" was coined in 1955 to describe the powerful upturn that put West Germany on track to become the world's third-largest economy by 1960—behind only the United States and Japan. By 1960, West Germany's industrial output was two and a half times the 1950 level, and the unemployment rate had fallen from 10.3 percent in 1950 to a postwar record low of 1.2 percent. There were similar spurts of economic growth in the months immediately following the World Cup wins in 1990 and 2014 and the strong third-place performance at home in 2006. Economists attributed an increase in consumer spending to the "good feeling" and an irrational sense among consumers that they had more disposable income in the months after those triumphs in soccer. But those later upturns all paled in comparison to the eruption of growth after the 1954 World Cup win.

West Germans celebrated the win as a bright, shining moment in their young history. It was a badly needed tonic for the postwar depression and gave West Germans reason to hope and a newfound sense of self-esteem. It is hard to overstate the positive impact that the World Cup win had on the nation's morale.

Reflecting the outpouring of emotions for the triumphant soccer team, tens of thousands stood cheering at railroad stations along the route, and about five hundred thousand people jammed into the central station in Munich—a city of eight hundred thousand at the time—to welcome the players home. The epic World Cup win gave the country a new identity and turned the players into living legends. Even though they are all long since dead, many of the players on coach Sepp Herberger's team—including captain Fritz Walter—are revered.

Many Germans old enough to remember have vivid memories of that 1954 game. Some can even fondly rattle off the names of the eleven players on West Germany's starting lineup. In a country without many heroes, in part because of its belligerent twentieth-century past, many Germans are able to describe in detail how the irrepressible Helmut Rahn, who had set up West Germany's first two goals and scored the dramatic match-winning goal in the 84th minute—even though they only heard it on the radio and didn't get their first chance to see a grainy homemade black-and-white film of Rahn's deft right-left move to beat three Hungary defenders until years later. Rahn pounced on a loose ball outside the penalty box and got off a long-range left-footed shot that went into the lower left corner.

Soccer was thus something special, something more than just another sport for West Germany, a full decade before Klinsmann was born, with the first of its four World Cup wins. A decade later, in 1974, West Germany won its second World Cup, just three weeks before his tenth birthday. It won its third in 1990 with twenty-five-year-old Klinsmann as a key member of the team, scoring three goals in seven games. Germany won its fourth World Cup in 2014, with a team that he helped shape in important ways as its coach from 2004 to 2006.

# MOVING UP

KLINSMANN'S PRODIGIOUS GOAL SCORING as a youngster two decades after the 1954 World Cup did not go unnoticed for long—especially in a country filled with sportswriters and scouts focused on soccer.

In Germany, there are hundreds of daily newspapers and scores of sports newspapers and magazines. Like other newspapers and magazines across Europe, their pages are dominated by stories about soccer. Coverage of other "minor" sports such as Formula One, basketball, handball, tennis, track and field, skiing, biathlon, and cycling are dwarfed by soccer. With the close media scrutiny and the vast network of scouts, both amateur and professional, there is little chance of a bright, promising young talent like Klinsmann being missed. That network has been further expanded in the last decade with more than fifty *Leistungszentren,* DFB-approved academies, spread across the country to identify, cultivate, and coach talented young players as well as train coaches.

By the age of ten, Klinsmann's ambitions were already becoming apparent. He was becoming the proverbial big fish in the small pond of Gingen and was hungry for a new challenge. His neighbor Werner Gass, who was several years older, coached a youth team while also playing on the senior team at a larger local club just seven miles down the road from Gingen called SC Geislingen.

The town of Geislingen, with a population of about twenty-six thousand, was more than six times larger than Gingen. Its soccer club was known far and wide as one of the best for youth development in the region. Gass was coach of the *D-Jugend* team, the Under-12 team, at SC Geislingen and an eighteen-year-old player himself on the club's senior team, which played in Germany's fourth division. Gass later moved further up the pyramid and played for VfB Stuttgart. Determined as he was, Klinsmann was eager to take his game to the next level at the bigger club. He was confident and bold enough, even at that age, to make a move—displaying the same flair, courage, and proactive strategy that would serve him well throughout his career as a player and as a coach.

"One day I just decided, 'I gotta go, I gotta go to the next level,'" Klinsmann recalls. "I wanted to go to the club in Geislingen. I knew where Werner lived. It was just a hundred yards away from the bakery. So one day I just went over there, knocked on his door, and said, 'I want to come and play for you.' And he said, 'Ah, sure.'"

Klinsmann had enjoyed his one and a half years at his hometown club. But he was training every day in the neighborhood with his friends, and his improved skills were putting him so far ahead of his contemporaries that there was hardly any challenge left in Gingen, where the club had only one practice and one game per week. "I had one teammate who basically kicked the long ball to me and then I had to do the rest while the other teammates were just standing around," says Klinsmann. "Everyone was saying, 'This kid can't play here anymore, it's too much.' So after a game one day, I just came to the conclusion: 'I gotta get out of here.'"

It was an early illustration of his resolve to keep getting better and reaching for the next level, a drive that would accompany Klinsmann throughout his career. Even though there were hardships and risks associated with the move out of his comfort zone, his early ambition was a harbinger of what would follow in the years ahead. In Geislingen, the *D-Jugend* team practiced more often and had more experienced as well as more knowledgeable coaches. Klinsmann could tell the difference right away. There were three practices a week and one game on Saturdays.

Klinsmann was only ten and had to figure out how to get to and from the workouts in Geislingen. "For the first two years, Werner basically picked me up for training and brought me back home—or I had to ride my bike the seven miles each way," says Klinsmann. "It was all good. But then Werner turned pro at VfB Stuttgart when he was twenty so he had to give up coaching the team in Geislingen. After that I had to ride my bike all the time."

Even as his abilities improved and his goal-scoring skills began drawing more attention, Klinsmann says he still harbored no illusions of becoming a pro. Climbing through the ranks, he was happy reaching the next level and patiently seeing how far the increasingly competitive game would take him. "My goal as a little kid was to play on my sixth-division team in the adult league. And then when you do that, you move your goal to the next higher level. I wanted to play for their first team, which was in the fourth division. So it was always just looking from one level to the next, one at a time."

When Klinsmann joined SC Geislingen in 1974 and started wearing the club's black-and-white colors, his father presented him with a *Rekordbuch* in which he could keep track of his statistics, results, and goals. Siegfried Klinsmann penned an inscription at the front of the book that stuck with Klinsmann over the years: "*Olympisch sein heisst: Ehrlich im Kampf, bescheiden im Sieg, neidlos in jede Niederlage und sauber in Deiner Gesinnung. Das hofft dein Vater und Turnkamerad, Siegfried Klinsmann*" (To be Olympic means being honest in the contest, humble in victory, not envious in defeat, and clear in your convictions).

"I still have that record book at home," Klinsmann says with more than a little pride, adding that the inscription meant a lot to him later during his career, even though he didn't fully understand all the words at the time. "My dad gave it to me because he thought, 'If the only thing he talks about is scoring goals all day long, maybe he should keep track of his goals scored.' So I kept that with me for my whole youth career. Every goal I scored all the way until my last youth-level game is in there. It just made me feel good when I came home and could add another goal into the book. And I would think to myself, 'Hey, it was a good day today, it was productive.'"

Klinsmann was close to his father, admiring his stoic dedication and tireless work ethic. He was a modest man who got up between midnight and 3:00 A.M. six days a week, working through the night to bake fresh bread, rolls, cakes, and pastries in time for Bäckerei Klinsmann to open at 6:30. "I know what it's like to work twelve hours a day or even more," says Klinsmann, adding that his father sometimes toiled fourteen or even up to sixteen hours a day. He says he never understood how his father managed to stave off sleep as well as he did. He acquired a lifelong appreciation for hard work from his father and mother. "I owe my parents a lot."

The Klinsmanns were part of West Germany's broader middle class in the 1960s, '70s, and '80s—part of neither the country's small wealthy elite nor its small indigent population. West Germany had become one of the more prosperous countries in the world by the 1970s, and this economic success was widely distributed across the middle class. With comprehensive national health insurance for everyone and good public schools across the country, West Germany's "social market economy" had a magnificently egalitarian feel about it. Its generous social welfare network prevented anyone, even those without jobs, from slipping through the safety net into serious financial trouble, while its relatively high tax rates served as a deterrent to accumulating wealth, or at least against making any ostentatious displays of affluence. Most Germans nevertheless worked hard to make ends meet, and Klinsmann's upbringing at the family's bakery shaped him in important ways.

"He was an athlete himself, an enthusiastic gymnast and cyclist, and I got my sports genes from him," says Klinsmann of his father, who died in 2005 at the age of seventy-one—to Klinsmann's great sorrow just a year before he coached Germany at the World Cup at home. "As a baker, it was always a challenge for him to come out to the games on Saturday afternoons. That's the toughest day of the week for a bakery in Germany, Saturdays. He worked through the night and was always fighting off the tiredness. My games weren't until two o'clock or three o'clock in the afternoon. It was sometimes hard for him to keep his eyes open because he was so tired. I don't know how he fought off sleep. He would drive out to the field with a big bag of pretzels, twenty or twenty-five pretzels for the whole team . . . and the guys on my team couldn't wait until they got their pretzels after the game. He'd always watch the games from behind the goal, just standing there. He kept doing that all the way to the point where I started playing professional soccer. He was probably very, very tired, but his standing there watching me meant a lot."

Klinsmann says his father never had to push him to play soccer and never tried to meddle in his career but was instead always ready to support his growing interest in the national pastime. "He came to every game he could make—without saying a word no matter if I played well or not. He would never comment on the game because he would say, 'I didn't grow up with soccer; I'm a gymnast. Just have fun.' The one thing he would always ask me is, 'Did you have fun today? Did you have a good time?' I was lucky to have guidance and support like that all throughout my childhood."

Even as a youngster, Klinsmann was known as a fierce competitor who loathed losing—something he still despises whether he's playing or coaching a national team at the World Cup or playing table tennis with his players. It still bothers him as a coach to see a player squandering talent or not living up to his potential. He developed an intense fighting spirit on the field at a young age, a drive to win that often helped raise the level of his entire team, especially later for Germany in big international tournaments.

"It makes me furious whenever I see someone not giving one hundred percent," Klinsmann says. Even though every player can have an off day, his motto was, "*Kämpfen bis zum Umfallen*" (Fight 'til you fall), even if they were having a bad day. In *Klinsmann, Stürmer, Trainer, Weltmeister,* German sportswriter Michael Horeni writes that Klinsmann's work ethic made him enormously popular with fans wherever he played: "His career was marked from the start by his enormous willpower, discipline, and ambition. It's no coincidence that he is one of the few pro soccer players that the crowds never accused of not putting out and giving everything he had on the field."

As passionate as he was about his effort on the field as well as the play of his teammates, Klinsmann rarely got visibly angry over a loss or disappointing result as a youth player. Instead, he would simply stew quietly inside, letting the frustration slowly dissipate. Sometimes it might take a few hours, sometimes a few days, and sometimes even a few weeks—especially later on as a pro after a talent-laden Germany team was upset and knocked out of the 1994 World Cup, in the quarterfinals by Bulgaria.

Klinsmann says his father—and teammates—understood the intensity of his frustrations at an early age and gave him plenty of space when he needed to decompress. "My father saw that I was sometimes angry because we lost and maybe because I didn't score any goals. Then he would just leave me alone because he knew the best thing was to 'just give him some time.' Those cooldown periods could last between a couple of hours and a day, even when I was still playing in Gingen. So my teammates just left me alone. Sometimes I would have to apologize to them afterward because I was so angry. But then they learned to understand it. That I always needed some time to cool down is something that stuck with me."

With all that practice and determination, Klinsmann's career was on a steep upward path. A regional soccer newspaper in 1977 wrote a prescient feature article about thirteen-year-old Jürgen Klinsmann under the headline "*Auf den Spuren Gerd Müllers*" ("In Gerd Müller's Footsteps"). Müller was a star forward with an uncanny knack for scoring opportunistic goals for Bayern Munich and West Germany in the 1970s. The article described Geislingen's young center forward as "lithe and lissome, not especially big but a player who is as swift as an arrow and has dynamite in his legs." The report in the *D- und C-Jugendzeit* youth newspaper noted that Klinsmann had scored an incredible 250 goals for Geislingen in less than four seasons, and the writer concluded with a prediction that he surely must have been proud of years later: "He's got a great future in front of him."

Jürgen Klinsmann played with SC Geislingen from 1974 to 1978. He even continued playing at the club after his family packed up and moved from Gingen to the Botang section of Stuttgart, a city of six hundred thousand some thirty miles west of Geislingen. The family acquired a three-story house with its own small bakery on the ground floor. But Jürgen felt a sense of attachment to Geislingen and wanted to stay on the successful team that had upset some of the bigger and better clubs in the region, from Stuttgart to Ulm. Klinsmann also had many friends and teammates in Geislingen, several of whom he stayed in close contact with over the decades. "It's your decision—you're the one that has to be happy with it at the end of the day," his father told him. He wanted to instill a sense of responsibility and independence in his sons from an early age— to be accountable for their own decisions.

He was only thirteen, and despite the tantalizing offers to switch to bigger and more prestigious clubs such as the Stuttgarter Kickers or VfB Stuttgart, Klinsmann opted to continue playing with the club in Geislingen. He couldn't be lured away by the bright lights of the state capital or the fancy names of its soccer clubs. He was happy to stay with his provincial small-town club. He commuted several hours a day after school for about half a year from Stuttgart to Geislingen high up in the Swabian Alb, in the rolling hills east of Stuttgart, for the workouts several times each week. He managed to catch rides after school with a commuter from Geislingen who worked in Stuttgart, and he often took the train home later after workouts or slept over at friends' houses in Geislingen.

"I kept playing for Geislingen because I didn't want to leave my friends—and because we were better than the Stuttgart teams," Klinsmann says with a laugh and a flash of the competitive streak that is still intact some forty years later. "That's actually how we looked at it. We won the state championship in Geislingen in the Under-12 and the Under-14 and were better than the two big clubs in Stuttgart, the youth teams from the Kickers and VfB Stuttgart. So when they heard my parents were moving to Stuttgart, both clubs wanted me. I said, 'No, that's okay, I'll take the train to Geislingen.'"

# STUTTGARTER KICKERS

THE COMMUTE BETWEEN Stuttgart and Geislingen was finally beginning to take its toll on fourteen-year-old Klinsmann in 1978, after about six months. At around the same time as he was growing weary of all that travel, the young forward was being recruited more intensely by one of the two big professional clubs in Stuttgart, the capital city of his state of Baden-Württemberg: the Stuttgarter Kickers. This was the first time he had been so seriously courted by another club, and it was another tacit affirmation that hard work pays off. The Kickers were doing everything they could to make Klinsmann, who had been beating them for years with his Geislingen teammates, feel welcome.

As the U.S. Men's National Team coach, Klinsmann is now on the other side of recruiting and is known far and wide for his courting skills—especially of dual-national players he has invited to play for the United States. Klinsmann has not forgotten the lessons he learned as a bright young prospect being wooed by the Stuttgarter Kickers. "He called me up and invited me to a U.S. training camp," says Fabian Johnson, a dual-national right back who grew up in Germany. He fondly recalls Klinsmann and the U.S. coaching staff making him feel welcome from the start. "There's a really good vibe here. That's why I decided to play for the United States."

Klinsmann's grades at school dipped during that half year of commuting. He sometimes fell asleep on the train home to Stuttgart after a long day of school and practice. "My dad said, 'You gotta make a decision here because school comes first.' That was at about the same time the Kickers approached me again and asked if I wanted to just come around and train with them, to see if I liked it. I told Geislingen I wanted to train with the Kickers and that my dad was angry with me because of my grades, and they understood. They said no problem."

It was the right time for a move, even though he wrestled with the decision for a while. He was impressed by the Kickers' persistence and found their offer tempting. He soon sensed it would be a fresh challenge and welcome change of pace with the Kickers, and after working out with the team for a short while decided to switch completely to the Stuttgarter Kickers' youth team in the summer of 1978. The Kickers were the second club in town behind Bundesliga team VfB Stuttgart. He would stay with the Kickers for six important years—longer than at any other club—from the age of fourteen in 1978 until the age of twenty in 1984, learning a lot about soccer and about life. He was shifted for a while to midfield and helped *"die Blauen"* (the Blues), as the Kickers are called, to win the *B-Jugend* regional championship in the Württemberg region in his first season.

"Geislingen was my comfort zone," Klinsmann says, looking back at the move nearly four decades later. In retrospect, he views it as a good decision—an early lesson on the virtues of guarding against complacency. "I stayed with Geislingen because I felt that because we were better than Stuttgart, why should I go there? Just because they're a bigger name while we're a better team? But Stuttgart made me feel really welcome in those first workouts, and I realized it was the right thing to do. At some point, I said to myself, 'You know what? You gotta move on, you gotta get out of your comfort zone and take the next step.' It was the right time to move, it was a good move. It was a good wake-up call for me too, because the Kickers' workouts were more intense than what I had been used to in Geislingen. And I went with that Kickers team right away to winning the youth state championship."

The Stuttgarter Kickers then narrowly lost the West German national *B-Jugend* championship to FC Augsburg, an unfortunate defeat that still annoys Klinsmann all these years later. Despite his growing success on the bigger stage in Stuttgart, Klinsmann was still unsure how far he could go with soccer. There were so many thousands of talented young players working their way up through the ranks across the country. He was happy to take on one challenge at a time, and most of all to savor his steadily improving play. He was confident of his skills but still didn't have the audacity to see himself making it into the Bundesliga, let alone one day playing for the West Germany National Team.

"My goal was just whatever I could see right in front of me. It wasn't a goal of playing on a team that you could only see on television," he says. "Even when we watched the West Germany team that won the 1974 World Cup, I'd go outside and celebrate goals by Gerd Müller, but I'd never have said as a ten-year-old, 'You gotta play the same position that Gerd Müller plays one day,' because that was just not reachable at that point. You couldn't feel you'd end up at that level that you saw on television in those days. I only had a sense for wherever I lived and was playing at the time. I never had a sense that I could jump up more than one tier at a time. Every little next step in my career only came into focus when I got to the step before it. That's what's so good about the tier system, the way it helps you evaluate yourself and gives you an honest answer about where you are. I never felt any kind of pressure to make it all the way to the top. I always thought that if it doesn't work out with soccer, then I'd just keep working as a baker.

"When I was fourteen and moved to the Kickers' youth team, I saw that the second division of the Bundesliga, where the senior team was playing, was another huge level higher from what I was used to. I said to myself, 'That's where I want to play one day.' Then one day you're playing there in the second Bundesliga and then you look up again and see there is the first Bundesliga ahead of you, and you say to yourself, 'That's where I want to play one day.'"

Klinsmann never lost his sense of humility even when he advanced closer to breaking into the second division as a pro—getting nearer to the top of the soccer pyramid. He says he still banished any thought of playing for his country. He began to entertain thoughts about a call-up to the National Team—the ultimate achievement for most soccer players—only when he had firmly established himself in the Bundesliga later on with VfB Stuttgart, and was regularly scoring goals as a first-team player in the country's top league.

He remained hungry for more goals and promotion to the next higher levels, warding off any signs of self-satisfaction that could derail the momentum of his career. As the U.S. Men's National Team coach, Klinsmann sometimes wonders and worries about some American soccer players who seem content once they reach a certain level. "You see it with all the top players in the world that there's a specific mind-set, a certain hunger," he says. "There's something special that keeps driving players like [Lionel] Messi, Cristiano Ronaldo, or Bastian Schweinsteiger or Miroslav Klose or Wayne Rooney through their youth years and to the senior teams. The United States hasn't consistently been able to develop players with that kind of mind-set yet. Maybe it's because it was never asked of them and maybe it's because they grew content once they had reached a certain level and just settled with it."

It was hard to become complacent in West Germany because the competition was everywhere. There were always teammates and other players who were unapologetically after your spot on the field. As at other stages in his life, Klinsmann made the most of his chance to play on the bigger stage with the Stuttgarter Kickers' youth team.

His prowess and determination on the field did not go unnoticed with the Kickers' senior team—as well as at the West German DFB headquarters in Frankfurt. A letter arrived in the mail one day out of the blue from the *Deutscher Fussball Bund*. "We've nominated you to play with the youth national team for a game in Portugal," the letter said. Klinsmann was bewildered. He had to read the invitation several times before it sank in.

"I just couldn't comprehend that," says Klinsmann. "I was just a small-town kid, and reading this letter from the DFB that said, 'We'd like you to play for the youth national team.' I didn't know what that all meant, I just didn't get it. It was all a bit too much for a fifteen-year-old kid."

His debut for West Germany's youth team was not especially memorable for fans even though it left a lasting impact on Klinsmann. His coach was Berti Vogts, a former West Germany international player who would later coach the Germany team that won the 1996 European Championship, and would incidentally be the man who got Klinsmann into coaching. West Germany's *B-Jugend* team was beaten by the Netherlands, 2–0, and by Spain, 2–0, in the next game before it beat Switzerland, 3–0, in the final game. Klinsmann played in only those three games with the Under-16 team without scoring a goal, but he found the international experience invigorating nonetheless.

"It was a huge eye-opener for me," Klinsmann says of the games played in Faro, Portugal. "It was a different country and a different language. You couldn't understand what the people were saying. It was an incredible experience. I had never been to Portugal before, and it was all just so fascinating. I saw the beach and I freaked out," he adds of his first glimpse of an ocean. "It was just so fascinating . . . I would just go to the beach and stare out at the ocean."

Vogts fondly tells a story of how Klinsmann showed an independent streak at an early age. It's a quality that's important for helping players make instant decisions with confidence on the field, but it is also a challenge for coaches intent on maintaining team discipline. According to Vogts, fifteen-year-old Klinsmann would slip away from the West Germany team hotel after lunch—instead of taking part in the team's strongly recommended *Mittagsruhe,* post-lunch nap. As a chaperone as well as a coach responsible for the welfare of the youngsters on his team, Vogts would secretly follow Klinsmann as he quietly walked away from the hotel—just to make sure he wasn't running away or getting into trouble and soon enough realized it was all harmless.

Klinsmann, too, recalls the episode. "The ocean was just two hundred yards from the hotel, and Vogts freaked out because he thought, 'What is he doing?' But after a couple of days of that he realized I was just going to admire the ocean. After that, he told his staff, 'Don't worry, it's okay, he's fine.'"

The Stuttgarter Kickers played in an unofficial European Championship youth tournament in the Netherlands that summer. The atmosphere of the tournament was electrifying. The Kickers made it to the semifinals before being beaten by Vejle BK of Denmark, but Klinsmann had the first of his many strong performances on the international stage, scoring seven goals in six games. "The Kickers had long since recognized what a jewel they had with Klinsmann," writes Roland Eitel in *Jürgen Klinsmann.* Impressed with his performance, the club offered him a preliminary contract for their professional team that played in the Bundesliga's second division even though he was only sixteen and the pact wouldn't take effect until he turned eighteen two years later.

# SCHOOL OR SOCCER?

It was a pivotal moment for Klinsmann when he was offered a pro contract at the age of sixteen. He was torn between a yearning to go as far as he could with soccer and a desire to go to an academic high school, which are called *Gymnasium* in Germany, and to college after that. He was a curious and inquisitive teenager, hungry to learn. Before far-reaching reforms at German clubs were introduced in 1998 and expanded further in 2000, when soccer academies for talented young players that combined schooling with top-level soccer training were established, the overwhelming majority of players had to make the same choice as Klinsmann: playing soccer or staying in school to go to college.

Klinsmann enjoyed learning and school. He had wanted to become a pilot up until that point. He didn't start entertaining thoughts about playing soccer professionally until he was offered the contract with the Kickers. Yet there were so many thousands of players in West Germany that the odds of succeeding were incredibly poor.

"I was always fascinated by flying," Klinsmann says. "When anyone asked me when I was a little kid growing up what I wanted to be, the answer was always a pilot. I was always thinking, 'I'm going to be flying airplanes one day.' Soccer was something I did for fun, and I always had a lot of fun playing it."

The contract offer from the Stuttgarter Kickers changed those plans and forced him to shelve his flying ambitions—but not forever. He did get his license to fly helicopters a quarter century later and enjoys flying around Southern California. The offer also made the curious young man, who had been so eager to learn, decide to alter his plans about education, abandoning at least for now his hopes of going to college even as some of his friends from Geislingen went to universities.

In Germany, the *Gymnasium* are rigorous college-preparatory schools with an emphasis on academics. Only about half the children of each school year gain admission. The students are taught more than in American high schools and are expected to work more independently—the final two years of *Gymnasium* have more in common with the first two years of college in the United States. Those who pass the difficult final exams and graduate are rewarded with free admission to college.

It may seem rather cruel, and especially unfair to late bloomers, that the children are separated into different academic or vocational career paths at such a young age—about fifteen. Some get the fast-track academic treatment to the *Gymnasium* and colleges, while the other half start vocational training at trade schools or apprenticeships at companies, jobs they are likely to stay at for the rest of their working lives. When Klinsmann was fifteen, hardly any professional soccer players had gone to a *Gymnasium*. Now, with the soccer academies that promote and encourage academic schooling, more than half of the professional players have received their *Abitur*, their high school diploma.

It was a major crossroads for Klinsmann. "My grades weren't good enough to go straight to high school," he says. He considered taking an indirect path to college by going to a *Wirtschaftsgymnasium,* an academic high school with a focus on business-related subjects. But that would have meant a full-time schooling commitment all the way to the thirteenth grade—or the age of nineteen. "At the same time, the Kickers came to me and offered me a preprofessional contract. I wasn't even sixteen yet, still just fifteen. I asked my dad, 'What should I do? I want to go to the next level in school even though I know my grades aren't the best, and I think I should stay in school.' He said he understood what I wanted, but then said if I wanted to continue with school, I couldn't sign the contract with the Kickers."

Siegfried Klinsmann wanted his son to have at least one completed training degree to fall back on to be able to earn a living in case his professional soccer career didn't pan out. It was typical pragmatic German advice. At that time, there were indeed hundreds, if not thousands, of young soccer players in Germany each year whose dreams of playing soccer professionally were dashed, and many found themselves caught in a trap without anything to fall back upon. Others made sure they got a degree of some sort: Some of Klinsmann's predecessors coaching the National Team also left school at about fifteen to learn a trade: Franz Beckenbauer, West Germany's coach from 1984 to 1990, became an insurance salesman; Berti Vogts, Germany's coach from 1990 to 1998, was a trained toolmaker; Rudi Völler, the German national team's coach from 2000 to 2004, was an office clerk; and Klinsmann's former assistant coach and successor since 2006, Joachim Löw, was trained as an import-export merchant.

If Klinsmann had chosen the academic route and schooling full-time, he wouldn't have finished his *Abitur* before his time-consuming professional soccer career started at the age of eighteen. He could well have ended up having to drop out of high school a year or two before getting his diploma. His father was worried that in a worst-case scenario, Jürgen could end up empty-handed, without any kind of diploma and without a soccer career. It was a tough decision for Klinsmann to leave school at fifteen, and it sometimes seems to be one of the very few regrets he has, despite having since acquired a wealth of knowledge and learned four foreign languages. Leaving school at fifteen was not uncommon for soccer players in Germany, an age where millions leave school for apprenticeships in trades from butchers to carpenters, cosmeticians, mechanics, and clerks.

"My dad said, 'Okay, if you work with me as an apprentice and get your baker's diploma, then you'll always have at least one finished degree if something happens with your soccer stuff,'" Klinsmann says. "He always called it 'soccer stuff.' I said, 'Okay, yeah, that makes sense.' I already knew the practical side of becoming a baker because that's what I grew up with, making all the things you see in a bakery. So that was no problem."


Several years later, while playing at Inter Milan in Italy, Klinsmann made another stab at completing high school—in Italian—and spent long hours with two private tutors trying to get a school-leaving certificate. But he ultimately had to abandon that in his final season in Italy, when Inter Milan was struggling on the field.

"Going to college was something that I could have imagined doing, but at some point I just realized that I could get a kind of university education by living in different countries," he says. "I might not have as many theoretical lessons in the classroom, . . . but I had a lot of practical lessons in dealing with people in a lot of different places. That was my education."

For his apprenticeship at the family bakery in Stuttgart, Klinsmann worked for several hours before dawn making and baking the tasty pretzels, rolls, pastries, and loaves of bread that Germans are so fond of buying hot out of the oven every morning from their local bakery just around the corner. His favorite was Swabian pretzels—dough twisted in two symmetrical loops. The Swabian pretzel differs from its rival, the Bavarian pretzel—it has thinner "arms" and a fatter "belly" that is partially sliced open. He also spent one day a week attending theory lessons on baking and operating a bakery at a nearby vocational school, the Berufschule Hoppenlau. He went to soccer workouts during the mornings with the Kickers' first team while playing games on the weekends for their Under-18 youth team. He earned his baker's diploma in 1982.

"Everything worked out in the end, and it turned out to be a huge advantage because just a couple of months later the coach of the Kickers asked me to practice with the first team—that was unheard of at the time," Klinsmann says, fully aware that this was a stroke of good fortune. He was already in a place he increasingly liked to put himself—over his head and beyond his comfort zone.

"I got my baker's diploma, too. It was a time of transition. You could train every day with the pros as a sixteen-year-old, but you know that you're not fully developed physically and that you're not quite there yet. But you also know that if you keep working at it every day, you'll get stronger and your confidence will grow. So I finally made my debut on the first team at seventeen. It was a great feeling."

Klinsmann was getting up at 3:00 A.M. to do his apprenticeship in the bakery and working until about 7:30, then eating breakfast and going to practice at 10:00. Even on Saturdays, the busiest day at the bakery, he was up at 3:00 and working until 7:30 before taking a nap ahead of his games in the afternoon. "I still worked on the day I had a game," he says. "I guess it's just a work ethic you get from your environment. My parents were just that way, and it's just automatically the way you are. You see it, you do it yourself, and you just think it's normal. It's a generation that's used to working hard and enjoying working hard. I'd never be able to sit on the beach all day long either. It would be impossible for me."

That same year, in 1981 at the age of seventeen, he started his professional career with the Stuttgarter Kickers. It was a huge moment in Klinsmann's life even though the salaries in the Bundesliga at the time were modest. He started out earning just 1,500 West German marks (about $600) per month, according to Eitel. That amounted to about 18,000 marks a year—only just above half the average annual income in West Germany but not bad for a seventeen-year-old in a country that puts an emphasis on wage equality.

Klinsmann, from the Swabia region where people are famous for their thrift, maintained a humble lifestyle even after turning pro and managed to save a good portion of his small income. He focused on improving on the field. He made his debut on March 27, 1982, as the youngest senior team player in Kickers history. He got into six games that season. He played his way into the starting team for the Kickers in his first full season, 1982/83, and by the end of the 1983/84 season he was one of the second division's top scorers, with nineteen goals for the club that plays in the tree-covered and hilly district west of the center of the city famous for being the home of Mercedes-Benz and Porsche.

The Stuttgarter Kickers got caught up in an intense but exciting relegation battle in 1983/84, his third season as a professional, when he was nineteen. This is another experience that he believes made him a better player and is a life lesson that he would like to see American players face. Relegation battles in Germany and in leagues across Europe and around the world provide some of the most exciting action and do-or-die games anywhere in sports. They are invariably tense, nerve-racking fights for survival that can often be more exciting than the competition for the championship at the top of the standings. It is a Darwinian fight for survival that brings out the fight in the players, who can feel the constant pressure on their shoulders. The bottom four teams from the Bundesliga's twenty-team second division that the Kickers were playing in got relegated at the end of that season to Oberliga, the third tier and out of the pro leagues.

The consequences of being dropped are harsh, almost existential: A lot of staff workers at the clubs relegated lose their jobs; the demoted club's budget is slashed; and the better players are often snatched up by other teams in the second division, usually for transfer fees at fire-sale prices. In essence, relegation can feel like the end of the world for clubs going down—even though their purgatory might be ephemeral. It often lasts only a season or two until the demoted club can win promotion again. Winning promotion is another exciting, heartwarming story of triumph over adversity for clubs and their towns that plays out in soccer nations around the world.

But sometimes relegated teams sink over the course of a few seasons from the top tier all the way down to the amateur levels in the fifth or sixth tier, falling from one division to the next one season at a time. One renowned German club, Alemannia Aachen, for instance, was in the Bundesliga until 2007 but fell from top flight to the second division that season, then to the top amateur league in the third division in 2011, before falling another tier to the fourth division, the Regionalliga West, in 2014.

Of course, there are plenty of tales of teams going the other way. The story of a small-town club called Turn- und Sportgemeinschaft 1899 Hoffenheim, or TSG 1899 Hoffenheim, is one of the most remarkable in German soccer history. Based in the small southwestern town of Hoffenheim with a population of just 3,270, the club traces its roots to the gymnastics movement of the late nineteenth century. It was an obscure fifth-division team wallowing in the amateur leagues as late as 2000. Then it climbed four rungs in eight seasons to win promotion to the top tier, the Bundesliga, in 2008. And in the club's magical first season in the top league, Hoffenheim even soared all the way to the top of the standings through the first half of the season, winning the Bundesliga's unofficial *Herbstmeister,* Autumn Champion, title before slipping to seventh by the end of the season.

For Klinsmann, winning the relegation battle with his team in Stuttgart was unforgettable. The Kickers surged away from the drop zone in the second half of that 1983/84 season and ended up in a respectable ninth place, finishing safely above the drop zone with FC St. Pauli (17th place), VfR Bürstadt (18th), Kickers Offenbach (19th), and SSV Ulm 1846 (20th) going down to the third division, while 1. FC Nürnberg, Hannover 96, and 1. FC Saarbrücken won promotion to top flight, the Bundesliga.

As a reward for his players, who fought their way out of the drop zone at the bottom of the standings, the Kickers' president, Axel Dünnwald-Metzler, made good on a midseason promise to take his players on an all-expenses-paid trip to Florida. He had made the vow when his team was stuck in the penultimate spot in the standings—if the team finished tenth or better, he would take them on a summer vacation.

Klinsmann cherishes the memories of that first relegation battle as a pro. "It's another whole emotional part of soccer that people in America unfortunately don't get to experience," he says of the roller coaster he went through that season fighting to avoid the drop. Klinsmann is an advocate of the competitive intensity that the promotion-relegation system creates because it keeps players and clubs at all levels on their toes right up to the end of the season. He admits he still wakes up before dawn in California each year in the springtime to watch on television those special fight-to-the-finish games of teams in the Bundesliga or Premier League going all out to stay in the top tier. "It means you always have to perform," he says.

# MAIDEN VOYAGE TO AMERICA

THE PRIZE FOR WINNING that relegation battle left a lasting impression on Klinsmann. He was only nineteen years old when he made the ten-day excursion that changed his life. He smiles at the irony of his first journey to the United States, which has been his home since he retired as a player in 1998—a reward to visit the only soccer country in the world *without* a promotion-relegation system for winning a relegation battle in West Germany. "So that's how I got introduced to the United States for the first time—because of the relegation battle with the Kickers," he says with a laugh.

Postwar West Germany was by and large full of admiration and appreciation for the United States—a country that helped its erstwhile battlefield enemy get back on its feet after World War II with Marshall Plan aid starting in 1948 and 100 million CARE packages of food that ordinary Americans sent to ordinary West Germans and Europeans threatened by starvation. Many postwar West German structures and institutions had a thoroughly American feel to them because they were modeled on those in the United States—everything from the federal system of states to the central bank and the constitution.

As a bulwark of the West and a frontline nation lined up against the Warsaw Pact countries during the Cold War, West Germany was the temporary home to 250,000 American soldiers who were stationed there as a deterrent against any military threat from the Eastern Bloc. Several of the dual-national players on the U.S. Men's National Team that Klinsmann has recruited are the children of American servicemen who lived in the country.

West Germans were already well acquainted with the American way of life from American television shows and movies, usually dubbed into German. But in an era before transatlantic travel had become affordable for the masses, relatively few West Germans visited the United States. Klinsmann's first trip was an eye-opener for the young soccer pro.

"It was like, 'Whoa!' " he says. "The trip to Florida opened up a different world, which I had never thought about before or could even have imagined. We had a great time in Florida. We were so fascinated by America. I had no idea what the United States was really about. I had no idea what Florida or Miami was all about. It was crazy. They took us on a channel boat ride in Fort Lauderdale, and we couldn't believe what we were seeing. This was just another example of the places soccer can take you. It opens doors to things that you couldn't ever imagine seeing. It was all just so unbelievable."

He also got the chance to meet one of his childhood idols— former West Germany forward Gerd Müller. But the encounter wasn't at all what he was expecting. Müller had played for three seasons for the Fort Lauderdale Strikers in the North American Soccer League and was now retired, running a restaurant in Fort Lauderdale. He was a legendary figure in Germany and one of the world's greatest goal scorers ever, with an incredible sixty-eight goals for West Germany in sixty-two appearances—an astonishing rate of more than one goal per game.

Nicknamed *"Der Bomber"* for his famous "finishing" skills in putting the ball into the goal under pressure, Müller was the European Footballer of the Year in 1970 after scoring ten goals for West Germany at that year's World Cup. He also scored four goals at the 1974 World Cup, including the game winner in the final against the Netherlands. Müller, who also had 365 goals in 427 Bundesliga games for his club Bayern Munich, was one of the champion players who moved to the United States to join the nascent NASL along with West Germany teammate Franz Beckenbauer, Manchester United's George Best of Northern Ireland, and Pelé from Brazil.

"We played a friendly against the Fort Lauderdale Strikers because Gerd Müller had played there," says Klinsmann. "He ran a steakhouse in Fort Lauderdale at the time. He was the striker I looked up to in my childhood. When he scored goals at the 1974 World Cup, I'd go running around and screaming at our little pickup soccer field and pretending to be Gerd Müller. And now you see him in Florida in a steakhouse entertaining German tourists? And you look at him and you think, 'What are you doing? You're Gerd Müller.' It's just kind of stunning because you have this picture of someone very, very special and then you see him in Fort Lauderdale, and it doesn't really belong there. Gerd Müller? Steakhouse in Fort Lauderdale?"

It was a haunting experience for Klinsmann seeing a player he had once, like millions of Germans, so admired for his heroic performances on the field now living off his past, living off his name as a storyteller for German tourists in a steak house—while still in the prime of his life at the age of thirty-nine. It was an encounter he would never forget and is another reason Klinsmann has no interest in dwelling on his own life as a player. He never wants to become a prisoner of his past.

"You have to think about today and tomorrow—and not what you've done already," he says. "Whenever I bump into a group of people who start out by saying, 'Hey, remember ten years ago when . . .' or, 'Remember fifteen years ago when . . .' I just try to get away as fast as I can. It's all about today and tomorrow. That's the wonderful thing about soccer: It's always moving forward, there's always the next game ahead."

Klinsmann and a Stuttgart teammate had such a fabulous time in Florida that they returned to the United States on their own, almost immediately after returning home to West Germany. They visited New York, Chicago, and California. He says he fell head over heels in love with the United States on those first two trips as a teenager because of all the energy and friendliness of the people as well as the optimism he ran into everywhere. It was all somehow so completely different from what he was used to at home.

"I just found the openness and the energy of America so fascinating," he says. "It's such a huge country and so overwhelming for a little kid from Germany. I got to see the extremes in the country, the bad ones but also the unbelievably beautiful ones too. What I've always liked about America is that you have this feeling that everything is possible."

Klinsmann discovered a lot about himself on those trips—foremost that despite having studied English in school for many years, he had forgotten most of it. The frustration of not being able to express himself in the United States stirred something deep inside him to devote more effort to learning English properly, and languages in general.

"Our English was horrible," he says. "I felt a little embarrassed that I forgot all the English that I supposedly had learned. But that was good because it gave me so much drive to learn the language. After that, I studied my English books and everything I could get my hands on."

Shortly after finishing his apprenticeship at the age of eighteen, in 1982, Klinsmann moved out of his parents' house above the bakery and into his own apartment, returning to the quiet rural town in Geislingen. Obtaining his baker's certificate was an important milestone, a sort of rite of passage. The level and quality of training during those three years in Germany was extraordinarily high. Mechanics, hair dressers, carpenters, bus drivers, and bank clerks—they all go through the rigorous training with little or no pay. After that, they can study to get their *Meisterbrief,* their master's certificate, which is often proudly hung on the wall. It's an important and difficult-to-get prerequisite to open any business. Klinsmann's father was duly proud of his own *Meisterbrief,* and Jürgen was just as proud of his baker's *Diplom.* "I learned how to bake, and my degree is hanging in the bakery," he says.

# PART II

# GERMANY, ITALY, MONACO, AND ENGLAND

# BREAKING INTO THE BUNDESLIGA

KLINSMANN MADE ANOTHER major step up the soccer pyramid in 1984, when he switched teams, moving to crosstown rivals VfB Stuttgart after six years at the Stuttgarter Kickers. He had finally made it into the Bundesliga, the country's first division. It was one of the world's best four leagues in the 1980s, although the quality and salary gap between the Bundesliga and the more superior leagues in Italy, England, and Spain was still considerable.

The Bundesliga was created as a national professional league only in 1963. That was eighty-nine years after the first soccer club in Germany was established in 1874 by a group of English laborers living in Dresden—called simply the Dresden English Football Club. The Bundesliga, literally "federal league," was created in the midst of a crisis in 1963 after years of debate and resistance from the powerful regional leagues that were loath to see their stature diminished by a single centralized pro league.

Before 1963, soccer was played at semiprofessional and amateur levels with a number of regional leagues. A play-off system was used to determine the national champion. The DFB also long opposed the formation of a single central professional league, fearing the influx of money and commercialism would somehow spoil the purity of the game. The lack of a top professional league had clearly been stunting the development of soccer in West Germany compared to other countries, and it was increasingly handicapping the West Germany National Team as well—which had failed to even come close to repeating its 1954 World Cup win in the next two Cups in 1958 and 1962. International soccer had evolved since 1954, but in West Germany it seemed to be standing still.

It took a crisis to break through the impasse. The problem came to a head following the humiliation of the 1962 World Cup played in Chile, when West Germany was eliminated in the quarterfinals. The *Nationalmannschaft* got knocked out by Yugoslavia, 2–1, in a game played in Rancagua. That just wouldn't do for West Germany, where expectations had risen enormously following the glory of 1954. Yet pragmatic as they are, some Germans saw the defeat as an opportunity to push through badly needed reforms—such as the creation of the Bundesliga. The DFB and the National Team's coach, Sepp Herberger, had previously opposed a professional German league. But after the disappointing 1962 World Cup, they realized it was a question of the nation's honor and saw that a professional league was needed to keep the country competitive at an international level. Four years later, in 1966, after the Bundesliga had become established, West Germany had a better run at the World Cup, reaching the final in London. But there the team lost the controversial 4–2 decision to hosts England in extra time—the same day Klinsmann was celebrating his second birthday.

Within two decades, by 1984, the Bundesliga would become one of the world's top four pro leagues. By 2015, its status had risen further and it was considered to be the world's third best, not far behind only England's Premier League and Spain's Primera División. Major League Soccer, the North American pro league, is generally not ranked in the world's top fifteen. The Bundesliga teams had an average attendance of 43,500 in the 2014/15 season, more than any other soccer league in the world, with the Premier League in second place at 36,695. The only professional league anywhere in the world that has more spectators than the Bundesliga is the NFL, with an average of 68,776 in 2014/15.

The switch to the Bundesliga was a giant leap for Klinsmann. It was also, on a more personal level, an awkward move because he had earlier vowed never to play for the better-funded crosstown rivals, a club that was despised in his section of West Stuttgart. After all, he had spent the last six years playing for the Kickers and shared a deep emotional attachment to the *Blauen* with the club's fans, making it difficult to transfer from the Blues, the team he loved, to the *Roten,* the Reds, which he had long loathed. These intense "derbies" are part of the soccer lore in Germany and other soccer nations, where teams in the same town or region are seen as mortal enemies, and anyone walking on the streets in a rival's section of town wearing even a scarf or jersey or the other team's colors runs the risk of verbal taunts or abuse—and not always good-natured.

The president of Kickers, the benevolent industrialist Axel Dünnwald-Metzler, who had taken the team to Florida a year earlier, had to persuade Klinsmann to accept the move to VfB Stuttgart. The top-tier club had just won the Bundesliga championship and was willing to pay a handsome 700,000 deutsche marks (about $300,000) transfer fee for the talented young forward. Soccer clubs in Europe do not trade players like teams in other pro sports in North America do, but instead sell or buy them, not unlike a commodity, in an open transfer market that transcends national borders and leagues. The transfer window is open for about twelve weeks each summer before the season begins and for another four weeks, approximately, at midseason in the winter. The transfer fees are in general not kept by the owners or paid out to shareholders but are instead used to help pay for the costs of training younger players or buying new players in the increasingly efficient transfer market. The market is an important vehicle for clubs with ambitions to reinforce their teams and for smaller clubs to spot and nurture talented youth players. The transfer market is at the same time a chance for talented players to move further up the pyramid—to improve their skills and play against the world's best players. That is how the top clubs in Europe enhance their rosters for the Champions League—by acquiring, usually for enormous transfer fees, the *crème de la crème* from lesser teams and lesser leagues around the world. And it is how ambitious players leapfrog their way up to the top leagues in Europe and then, once there, jump to the top teams in those top leagues.

Dünnwald-Metzler had to absolve Klinsmann of his earlier promise that he "would never" transfer to VfB. For Dünnwald-Metzler it was not necessarily the transfer fee—although that was certainly an important consideration—that was so essential. It was obvious that Klinsmann was more than ready for the jump to top flight, to the Bundesliga, where VfB played. He realized that Klinsmann was too good to stay stranded in the second division of the Bundesliga, where the Kickers played.

Dünnwald-Metzler was eager to see the energetic player, who was quickly establishing himself as one of the country's brightest young forwards, at least stay in Stuttgart, where he already had a following excited by his goal scoring, fighting spirit, and work ethic. Klinsmann had a lot of respect for Dünnwald-Metzler after playing for the Kickers for six years. "He was always interested in your development as a person, not just as a player," Klinsmann recalls.

It was in any event a proud moment for Klinsmann when he joined VfB Stuttgart in 1984 at the age of twenty. It had been a long and exciting journey up from the *D-Jugend* at TB Gingen. He was one of 379 professional players that season in the Bundesliga. There were more than three million players in the pyramid and fewer than four hundred at the top in the Bundesliga. A straight line could be drawn from that novice level in the *D-Jugend* in Gingen all the way to the top—only one in ten thousand who started out made it. One of Klinsmann's long-term goals is to further develop what has been a largely disconnected soccer structure in the United States into a clearly structured tier system based on the European model.

Already a thinking man's player as a teenager and always looking for better ways to do things, Klinsmann was determined to make the most of his chance to play in the Bundesliga. In the months before jumping to top flight, he was anything but complacent. He wanted to make an instant impact in the Bundesliga in case it was the only chance he got, and he reasoned he might give himself a small but important advantage by arriving on the first day of the preseason training camp in peak physical condition. He worked out with extra intensity during that summer vacation on his own before he had even arrived at VfB Stuttgart preseason training camp. "I wanted to have an advantage at the first practice by being in the best possible shape before the season even started," he told Roland Eitel.

In one telling illustration of his determination to squeeze the most out of his abilities and take advantage of every opportunity to succeed, Klinsmann also worked with a sprint coach on his own before his first Bundesliga season. His goal was to try to improve his speed, even gain a crucial half step. The extra sprint coaching turned out not only to be successful for Klinsmann but also opened his eyes to the potential of specialized training—an area he has tried to tap even more as a coach decades later with Germany, FC Bayern Munich, and the U.S. Men's National Team.

Speed is an essential part of a forward's game, the ability to outsprint a defender to get off a shot on goal or win the sprint to a loose ball to get the first touch. Klinsmann had thought he was already fairly quick—along with an ever-improving instinct to be at the right place at the right time in front of the goal. But before starting out in the Bundesliga with VfB Stuttgart, he got an unsolicited and not necessarily welcome tip from his older brother. Horst Klinsmann was a decathlete at a local sports club, and after watching Jürgen playing he noticed that Jürgen's speed, especially toward the end of games, seemed to wane.

"When my older brother saw me playing and saw me getting tired after the hour, he just told me one day, 'You know, Jürgen, you have no upper-body strength and you're losing a lot of speed late in the game because you're tired and getting more uncoordinated when you run. You really need to build up your running because you've got basic speed but you don't get it all out on the field,'" Klinsmann recalls. "And I thought, 'What's he talking about?' But he was right. Every game after about an hour, the other team started to bang me around and I would lose some coordination. So I started seeing this track and field coach twice a week for extra workouts."

His brother's track coach, a man named Horst Allmann, first timed Klinsmann as a 12.0-second sprinter for one hundred meters. They then worked on improving his technique and strength—but clandestinely, because his soccer coaches wouldn't approve. Klinsmann took the pointers from Allmann and worked on his sprints on his own as a supplement to workouts with VfB Stuttgart. And a year later Klinsmann was able to run the same one hundred meters a full second faster—in 11.0 seconds.

"We measured the times because I wanted to have proof, I wanted to see if it made a difference," Klinsmann says. "I started working with the sprint coach to get stronger and faster. But my [soccer] coaches wouldn't let me do it, so I had to do it without them knowing about it. It helped me get a lot faster, actually. My upper arms were stronger and I wasn't being pushed around as much late in the game anymore. I was obviously more explosive, and because I was far more efficient energywise, I lasted ninety minutes. In soccer, it's the last twenty minutes of a game when big things happen. So I started to run people into the ground. After seventy minutes I could see they were getting tired, and I'd say, 'Now, I'm going to finish you off.' "

It was an extremely valuable lesson that had lasting reverberations for Klinsmann. It was not just about getting faster but also about turning to specialist help from a personal trainer long before anyone in West Germany had heard of the concept, and about how to improve a small but important part of his game. His philosophy is that those incremental improvements can have a major effect at some point down the road, the difference between scoring an extra goal or two a year and possibly winning or losing a couple of games each year. It was also an affirmation of his hunch that any player of any ability can reap the rewards from improvements in his or her game and fitness, both small and large, with hard work and focused training.

"It was a great lesson that you have to be persistent," he says. "You have to kind of grind things out, keep working on them, and don't give up just because things are not working your way at the moment. We have a culture in the United States where many people tend to want things to pay off right away. Unfortunately there is a culture in some countries where people want things to pay off right away. Sometimes it takes time. And if you put in all the extra work, it *will* pay off in the long run."

That some of his former teammates were not always able to get everything out of their talent is frustrating, he says. He is also baffled by a creeping complacency that sometimes stunts the growth of young players in the United States and elsewhere once they reach a certain level of proficiency. What happened to the drive that got them there? Where's the hunger to keep reaching for the next level? What the game needs are the players who constantly push even after they have achieved success. What happened to killer instinct in what he sometimes refers to as the "Facebook-Twitter-Instagram" generation?

"That's sometimes difficult for me to understand," he says. "Often when you tell the players what they might be lacking or need to work at, they say they understand. You hope they'll do something about it, but many don't. If you say, 'You need to be more flexible,' or 'You need to have more stability,' or 'You need more speed,' or 'You need more one-on-one training,' or whatever comes out of the analysis, it's not really clicking. A lot of players don't develop that inner drive to say, 'Okay, I understand that's what I need to work on, so I'll be out there every day after training or before training working on it.'" Klinsmann points out that even in the "Facebook-Twitter-Instagram" generation, there are top players around the world who have the necessary drive. "That's why Cristiano Ronaldo is who he is or why Lionel Messi is who he is. They're going out to hit free kicks for half an hour after training, or they're going to be working on this or that after practice. They never stop working."

Identifying his own weakness, waning speed late in a game, and finding a way on his own to improve it—with a year's worth of hard work—was an enlightening discovery. The lesson learned not only made him a few steps faster but also taught him to always be on the alert for ways to do things better, on and off the field. Cultivating that inner drive to improve even after reaching a certain level of success is one area where many of the players in the United States have scope to improve.

# FIVE GOALS

KLINSMANN THRIVED IN THE Bundesliga from the start, even though he had just turned twenty and was suddenly lining up against the best players in West Germany. He fed off the electrifying atmosphere in the Bundesliga stadiums, where up to eighty-eight thousand people watched the games on Saturday afternoons. He loved the frenzy that built up in town all week, a crescendo of excitement in the days immediately leading up to the game. The stadiums were often sold out and the crowds on edge and standing for the full ninety minutes, erupting into deafening cheers whenever a goal was scored.

Klinsmann heard those cheers often during his rookie season for VfB, scoring fifteen goals and playing thirty-two of his team's thirty-four games—more than any other outfield player. Klinsmann was able to maintain that solid scoring average of about one goal in every second game throughout his career.

Klinsmann grew not only as a player but also as a person at VfB Stuttgart, playing in the same Neckar Stadium where his father had taken him as a youngster to see Hertha Berlin play. In those days in the late 1980s, many of the Bundesliga clubs traveled in a team bus—the distances between most West German cities were short enough that journeys rarely exceeded more than a few hours. While many of his teammates played cards or listened to music, Klinsmann often used the idle time to read and answer fan mail. He decided at an early age he was not going to bring the letters home with him. It was a process of separating his professional life from his private life. He's stuck with that philosophy ever since.

The reputation of the game so many loved had been tarnished by scandals earlier in the decade. Klinsmann's impressive debut season, as well as his energetic play on the field and his exuberant, uninhibited celebrations after scoring goals, proved to be a welcome tonic for many fans who were yearning for fresh faces and a new start.

Klinsmann's second Bundesliga season in 1985/86 didn't start as well as his first. VfB Stuttgart fired its coach, Otto Barić, in March. The players had been struggling to get along with Barić, who had been extremely critical of most of the team, and as soon as the Croatian was gone, Klinsmann erupted for five goals in the very next game to help Stuttgart win at Düsseldorf by a score of 7–0. He was only the eleventh Bundesliga player to score five goals in a single match. "Stuttgart fired Barić a week before that game," says Klinsmann, who admits they just didn't get along. "When the assistant manager took over, it got me all free and self-confident. And I showed that in the next game."

Barić's replacement, Willi Entenmann, managed to turn things around, and VfB made it to the final of the German Cup, a prestigious knockout tournament created in 1935 and open to teams in the pro and amateur divisions that run parallel to the Bundesliga season. The Bundesliga season ends without any play-offs. The team with the most points—three points for a win and one for a tie—during the season is crowned the champion. In many countries, the league championship is held in slightly higher esteem than the cup tournaments that usually run parallel to the league play because it is a reflection of how the title-winning team played all season long, not just in a single knockout tournament. The German Cup, by contrast, is a straightforward six-round tournament that, in 1985, started off with sixty-four teams from the first, second, and third divisions.

All teams in all German tiers can qualify for the single-game-elimination German Cup, which includes extra time and penalty shoot-outs that are often needed to break deadlocks. Occasionally, teams from the lower divisions of the amateur leagues triumph against long odds in the winner-take-all matches and make it all the way to the final. But in May 1986, it was two Bundesliga teams, Bayern Munich versus VfB Stuttgart, that made it to the final. The favorites from Munich won 5–2 in front of seventy thousand spectators in West Berlin's Olympic Stadium. Klinsmann had played an important role in getting his team to the final and was devastated by the loss, weeping openly afterward. The moving pictures of Klinsmann losing control of his emotions after playing his heart out on the field offered Germans a welcome glimpse of his passion, showing the country that there were indeed players who cared as much as they did. It was a small but significant moment that helped revive the popularity of and public's support for the game near the end of what had been a difficult decade for soccer in West Germany, accompanied by a prevailing sense in the public that there was too much commerce creeping into the game, and that many of the players were overpaid and underperforming.

# THE GOAL THAT GOT
# HIM NOTICED

Klinsmann's career at Stuttgart blossomed further in his third season in the Bundesliga. He was becoming known not only for his aerial skills, heading in goals, but also for his clever finishing, a predator able to make the most of his chances in front of the goal. Klinsmann also had superb technique, able to turn defenders inside out before getting off powerful shots. He was catching attention nationwide for his elegant runs into open space and quick-thinking readjustments, latching onto passes, and converting even the smallest of chances into goals. He scored nineteen goals in the 1987/88 campaign and won double honors as the league's leading goal scorer and West Germany's *Fussballer des Jahres* (Player of the Year)—winning the vote by the country's 785 soccer writers with a record 70 percent backing.

It was a phenomenal breakout season for the twenty-three-year-old. Perhaps the most memorable goal was a stunning overhead bicycle kick that led the way for Stuttgart to defeat Bayern Munich at home 3–0. The opening goal in that November 1987 game also got him noticed at home by West Germany's coach, Franz Beckenbauer, as well as by some of Europe's top teams. The acrobatic strike against Bayern was later voted West Germany's prestigious *Tor des Jahres*

(Goal of the Year) honor by more than three hundred thousand viewers who cast their ballots in the popular soccer highlights TV program *Sportschau.*

The sequence began with Stuttgart playmaker Ásgeir Sigurvinsson lofting a long pinpoint pass from the center of the field across the box to teammate Günther Schäfer on the right wing. Schäfer volleyed the ball back into the center of the field in the box. His cross appeared at first to be too high and too far away from the goal to be of any danger. Yet suddenly Klinsmann whirled around in the center, and with his back to the goal launched himself into a perfectly timed back flip, brilliantly smashing his foot into the ball—with his right leg extending to its apogee some six feet into the sky—and pounding it like a pinball flipper into the goal while flipped upside down. Two Bayern Munich defenders and goalkeeper Jean-Marie Pfaff watched in awe, dumbstruck as they struggled to register what had happened in the blink of an eye.

The *Fallrückzieher,* literally "falling backward kick," as the bicycle kick goal is called in German, is one of the most spectacular ways to score in soccer. It can look brilliant when it works but ridiculous when it doesn't. Klinsmann's bicycle kick against Bayern was about as good as they come. There was something extraordinarily artistic about the timing, the seemingly unreachable altitude of the ball when he hit it—as if he defied gravity—the velocity of his shot, and the circumstances in a top-of-the-table game. Highlight films of the goal went around the world and helped to etch Klinsmann's name further into the minds of soccer fans everywhere.

"It was just instinct," Klinsmann says. "For me it was no big deal. We won the game 3–0, and looking back it was one of the most beautiful moments I had at Stuttgart—beating Bayern Munich 3–0 at home and scoring on a bicycle kick." It was, in any event, a big deal for West German soccer fans, who couldn't stop talking about the goal. It also put Klinsmann on Beckenbauer's radar—just as single spectacular goals that draw notice to already strong performances have helped launch the international careers of other players, such as David Beckham's goal from midfield in 1996 that led to his first call-up for England.

"A bicycle kick is something special for a striker, no doubt about it—it's something you love to do," Klinsmann says. "You dream about scoring one as a player, but then when you get one in a really big game at home in front of seventy thousand people and against Bayern Munich, then it's even better. I started practicing bicycle kicks as an eight-year-old just like other kids do. I knew I could do it blindly because I'd been doing them for so long, and then you do one against Bayern and you freak out, but at the end of the day you only just did what you've always been doing in practice."

The bicycle kick eventually led to his first call-up from Beckenbauer to the National Team for two matches in South America at the end of 1987, an enormously important step in his career that meant he was considered among the best two or three dozen players in West Germany and a candidate for the squad for the 1988 European Championship tournament that would be selected in less than a year's time. "It was the goal that opened the door for me internationally. A month later Franz Beckenbauer called me up, and shortly after that I had my first international cap [appearance]—so that's why it was the most special goal for me. Your whole world changes after a goal like that," Klinsmann says. "It takes you from being a domestic player in West Germany to being an international."

Klinsmann's bicycle kick goal was not the only extraordinary thing that happened on that chilly Saturday afternoon in Stuttgart's Neckar Stadium. Late in the game, with Stuttgart leading 2–0, Bayern defender Norbert Nachtweih brought Klinsmann down with a hard and needlessly clumsy tackle—he was going for the ball but cut down Klinsmann instead. The referee, Dieter Pauly, was right on the spot and whistled the foul against Nachtweih.

Pauly reached into his hip pocket and was about to pull out a yellow card to book Nachtweih with a second caution in the game, which would have meant he would be sent off for getting booked with two yellow cards and his team would have to play the rest of the game with only ten men. But Klinsmann saw what was happening and rushed over, intervening on the Bayern player's behalf by urging Pauly *not* to book him with another yellow card even though Nachtweih's exit would have helped Stuttgart secure the win. It was an exceptionally rare show of sportsmanship. Klinsmann told the referee the foul wasn't that bad and not worth giving Nachtweih a yellow card for it.

The referee could hardly believe what he was hearing, and after an instant of mild shock and befuddlement, he stuffed the yellow card back in his pocket. It all happened quickly and not everyone in the stadium grasped what had transpired, so Pauly went out of his way to tell sportswriters about it after the game. "It's such a wonderful story that the public ought to know about it," Pauly told them. Bayern Munich's commercial manager, Uli Hoeness, was so amazed by Klinsmann's gesture that he went out of his way to thank him in the Stuttgart dressing room, telling him that kind of sportsmanlike conduct was good for the game.

Klinsmann tries to downplay the incident a quarter of a century later. "I knew the guy already had one yellow card, and when I saw the referee reaching for his pocket I just instinctively said, 'Hey, it wasn't that bad—it was a foul but not that bad,'" he says. "It wasn't anything that I thought about. It was just instinct. We were already ahead 2–0 and it was late in the game and I just thought to myself, 'No, not now, don't send someone off now.' For me it was no big deal."

But the gesture of sportsmanship drew considerable attention in West Germany, where soccer fans wanted to believe in the good of the game after some pernicious influences in the 1980s. Soccer was still by far the dominant sport there but had fallen into disrepute thanks to questionable judgments by players on and off the field. After recovering from a match-fixing scandal that affected some Bundesliga players on clubs such as Arminia Bielefeld in the early 1970s, attendance fell steadily from an average of 26,000 per game at the end of the 1970s to 17,600 by 1984/85. League games were often graceless, rough-and-tumble battles, and Bayern Munich dominated the league with suffocating regularity, winning the title six times in ten years. Widening the gulf between fans in the stadiums and the pros on the field, the league's top salaries rose eightfold during the 1980s, from around €500,000 as measured in today's currency to €4 million per year—although certainly not every player earned anywhere near that much. Those salaries were at first not easy for ordinary West Germans to fathom. Many believed the relation between wages earned by ordinary workers and managers, or soccer stars, should not become so disparate—especially if the players didn't seem to be giving everything for their team.

Compounding troubles of the 1980s was the 1982 World Cup, when the West Germany team was involved in two infamous games in Spain. First, they played to a scandalous 1–0 win against Austria in their final group game—a match later remembered as the "Disgrace at Gijón." The 1–0 result was an acceptable outcome and was achieved after just ten minutes, enabling both teams to advance. But both teams stopped making any effort to score after that, to the dismay of soccer fans around the world, especially in West Germany and Austria. The West German–Austrian *Nichtangrifsfpakt* (nonaggression pact), as it came to be known, was a collaborative farce that robbed Algeria of its rightful spot in the Round of 16 and stained the reputation of the World Cup as well as the teams involved. After West Germany scored a goal in the tenth minute that produced a result suitable for both teams to advance, they seemed to stop playing, harmlessly kicking the ball back and forth to each other for the remaining eighty minutes without any semblance of a move toward the opponents' goal. It was considered such a sporting travesty that FIFA changed the rules afterward so that all final group match games were played simultaneously to prevent any such shenanigans from happening again. The German television commentator Eberhard Stanjek was so distraught at the lack of effort that he almost started crying: "What is happening here is disgraceful and has nothing to do with soccer." When German fans went to the team's hotel after the game to voice their displeasure, some of the players made matters worse by throwing water bombs at them from their upper-story windows.

West Germany's players were unapologetic about the results-oriented soccer against Austria. They had not violated any rules aside from the spirit of fair play. They were pleased to advance later to the semifinal match against France, where goalkeeper Toni Schumacher was involved in the next scandal: He knocked French striker Patrick Battiston unconscious while both were going for a ball at the edge of the penalty box. It was an attack that left Battiston flattened on the ground, with a serious back injury. Schumacher also punched out two of Battiston's teeth, and he later fell into a coma. Adding insult to injury was Schumacher's reaction. He stared down at the Frenchman, lying flat on the ground, with bored disdain. He fanned the flames yet more after the game by callously offering to pay to have the Frenchman's teeth repaired. Diplomatic relations between France and West Germany cooled precipitously after that game, which West Germany won on penalties. It remained a contentious issue in France for decades. Further blackening their image with the public was an incident involving a West Germany player who had scornfully poured water on journalists following media reports from West Germany's pretournament training camp that some of the players had been drinking heavily.

By the end of the 1980s, the country, with its proud soccer legacy, was hungry for untainted new talent. West German soccer fans wanted to love the game again. And players like Klinsmann, who celebrated his goals with unbridled joy and took defeats as hard as they did, seemed to epitomize what many fans had been craving.

# DEBUT AGAINST BRAZIL

KLINSMANN'S HARD WORK was paying off once again. He had already got a first tantalizing taste of international soccer with VfB Stuttgart in the 1987/88 season, playing in the UEFA Cup (now called the UEFA Europa League) that runs parallel to the domestic league season. Klinsmann relished the chance to travel abroad for the tournament's midweek games in between weekend Bundesliga games and test his skills against some of the top clubs in Europe. Playing in the UEFA Cup made him even hungrier to play more on the international stage.

The UEFA Cup was a tournament for clubs that didn't quite qualify for the European Cup tournament, as the Champions League, made up of the very best teams from each league, was called then. It is the most important club tournament in the world. The UEFA Cup, made up of clubs near the top of Europe's leagues, was a chance for players to gain international experience and recognition. Klinsmann once again made the most of the opportunity to play on the international stage for VfB Stuttgart in the season leading up to the European Championships (Euro 88), where the best eight national teams in Europe would play, after the 1987/88 season ended in the summer of 1988. West Germany would host the Euro in 1988.

In the UEFA Cup, VfB Stuttgart beat the Czechoslovakian team Spartak Trnava in the first round but was eliminated in the second round by the Soviet team Torpedo Moscow. Klinsmann nevertheless was excited to visit other cities in Europe and has fond memories of Moscow, where he got to see the Red Square. He was determined to make the most of his opportunities to explore other cities and vowed to do so during future away matches—a practice he followed throughout his playing career and into his coaching career as well.

Klinsmann was nominated for West Germany's Olympic team in the fall of 1987, also known as the Under-23 youth team because the Olympics allows countries to include a maximum of only three players above the age of twenty-three. He was enthusiastic about the chance to play in the 1988 Olympics a year later. Thanks to his strong performances for the U-23 team and for VfB Stuttgart, Klinsmann also got called up by Beckenbauer to the senior team.

In his first international appearance for West Germany's senior team, on December 12, 1987, Klinsmann played the full ninety minutes in a game against Brazil, a 1–1 tie, in Brasília. It was the first of Klinsmann's 108 international appearances—also called "caps"—for his country over the next decade—a record of durability that puts him in sixth place overall on Germany's all-time list of most capped players. He also played in the 1–0 loss to Argentina in Buenos Aires four days later, getting rave reviews in a game he played against Diego Maradona, who was considered the world's most complete player at the time. "It was impressive the way that Jürgen asserted himself out there," Beckenbauer said of his performance in the two games, adding that he thought Klinsmann had showed he was an equal of the other two regular forwards, Rudi Völler and Klaus Allofs. It was an important endorsement coming six months before the European Championship was to be held at home.

After the two exhibition games in South America, Klinsmann got another taste of the United States and its enormous size. He flew to San Francisco and then Hawaii while the rest of the team went home to West Germany for the Christmas holidays. He promised to meet two close friends—Stefan Barth from his youth days in Geislingen and teammate Rainer Zietsch from Stuttgart. "My two best buddies and I had planned a vacation before I got called up," he says. "They always wanted to go to Hawaii. So not knowing geography at the time, I told them I was already in South America and could meet them in Hawaii. It was like, 'You guys are already there so I'll come join you.' So the DFB booked a flight from Buenos Aires to Miami, to San Francisco, and then to Hawaii. I had no idea of what I was getting myself into. It was one long flight after another. But that's how I got to Hawaii for the first time. We had an awesome time." They are all still close friends—Barth is the managing director of a children's charity foundation called Agapedia (Greek for "love for children") that Klinsmann set up in 1995, and Zietsch is head of the FC Nürnberg youth soccer academy.

Klinsmann thoroughly enjoyed his early trips to the United States and made some friends in California. "I like to get off the beaten path and break away from the daily routine," he told Eitel in *Jürgen Klinsmann,* adding he enjoyed being able to improve his English and learn more about the United States. "I think that's the only way a soccer player can find some peace of mind. Most of my friends (in the United States) know that I'm a soccer player, but they couldn't really imagine what that is."

He was also especially curious about life outside soccer in West Germany, and with Eitel's help organizing a meeting, he spent several hours visiting young inmates at a youth prison near the town of Heilbronn. He wanted to learn more about their lives. "I had done a lot of thinking about why and what the causes were," he said, referring to the issues that got the young men sent to jail.

Klinsmann finally got the first of his forty-seven goals for his country in a 1–0 win in an exhibition game against Switzerland on April 27, 1988. It was his fourth appearance for West Germany, shortly before the start of the Euro 88 at home. Klinsmann's improving form helped make him a regular on Beckenbauer's team at the Euro. It would be the first of six major international tournaments for his country—the European championships of 1988, 1992, and 1996 as well as the World Cups in 1990, 1994, and 1998.

At the Euro 88, Klinsmann helped West Germany make it to the semifinals with the first of six strong performances. He raised his game for his country with bursts of brilliance at the right moments in all six of those tournaments held over a ten-year period. Klinsmann says he just had a drive to make the most of every tournament, even small ones, and that he never wanted to go home with a sense that he or his team could have played better.

"Just give me a tournament—I always enjoyed them," he says when asked why he always seemed to be able to do so well in them. German teams have long enjoyed a reputation around the world for producing "tournament teams," or teams that might not always play well in between tournaments but manage to rise to the occasion when it matters most—especially as the World Cup or European Championship moves from the Group Stage to the Knockout Stage. In that sense, Klinsmann was a "tournament player" who also seemed to play his best soccer when the stakes were high. "I couldn't wait for the start of a tournament. I kind of understood that these were moments that were never going to come back again. With your club, you've got a regular eleven-month season and you want to win the championship. You want to do well with your club in the national championship, but the season is stretched out and you'll have good games and bad games along the way. In a compact situation like with a World Cup or European Championship, it's easy to tell yourself, 'You better step it up now,' because you can't say it'll last for a long period of time."

Klinsmann says although he wasn't always satisfied with the outcome of those six tournaments—his German teams won only two of them—at least he always had a clear conscience of having given everything he had. Some of the world's best players virtually disappear on the field at big tournaments, ill-timed drops in performance that cast shadows on their careers. But not Klinsmann, who seemed to save his absolute best for the World Cup and European Championships. "I just lived for those moments of the big tournaments," he says. "I loved the pressure and the high expectations and staying cool in front of the goal. It's really just down to you making sure that once the tournament begins, you're at peace with yourself and that you can say to yourself, 'No matter how this ends, I did everything I could.' Maybe qualitywise it wasn't good enough, but at least from an attitude approach, you want to know you went to the extremes, you did everything you could and gave everything you had. That's why I think it's really important that players recognize the tournaments are truly special once-in-a-lifetime moments that aren't going to come back again."

In 1988, Klinsmann gave everything he had for West Germany, scoring the first goal in its 2–0 win over Denmark; he also played well in a 2–0 win against Spain. West Germany also played a 1–1 tie against Italy. But the former was ultimately eliminated in the semifinals by archrival Holland in 2–1 in Hamburg after West Germany had scored first. Despite the bitter loss at home to the Netherlands, Klinsmann got plaudits from the media as the revelation of the tournament. He was nevertheless shattered about the semifinal defeat. He later said he was surprised and disappointed when three of his teammates started playing cards on the bus as it pulled away from the stadium—as if nothing had happened.

The next day when a journalist told him he was one of the "winners" of the tournament, Klinsmann was baffled. "How can you talk about winners? I don't feel like a winner when we just lost. Soccer's a team game," Roland Eitel quotes him saying.

"People have an enormous amount of respect for Klinsmann's Swabian integrity," Eitel wrote after the 1988 tournament, describing the mood in West Germany and the impact Klinsmann had made in just six months playing for his country. "When he scores a goal, like the opening score in the 2–0 win against Denmark, the entire nation erupts with him in celebration like it hasn't done for years. And the people feel his pain when he fights off tears after losing to the Netherlands 2–1. There is nothing new about these kinds of authentic and contagious emotions from Klinsmann, but it was the first time that Germans got to see all that live in their living rooms."

Summer 1988 was a busy time for Klinsmann. After the Euro, he helped West Germany's Under-23 team win four of its six games and take the bronze medal at the Summer Olympics in Seoul, South Korea, along with several others, including Thomas Hässler, who would help the West Germany team win the country's third World Cup two years later in Italy. Klinsmann, who had only just recently turned twenty-four, scored four goals in six matches in the Olympic tournament, including a hat trick against Zambia and one in their 4–0 win against Italy in the match for third place after West Germany was beaten by Brazil in a penalty shoot-out in the semifinal.

Klinsmann calls the chance to play in the Olympics one of the highlights of his career and said it was special to be part of the Olympic Village. He went to see other events in between games and was in the Olympic stadium when middle-distance runner Dieter Baumann, a friend from a small town near his, won the silver medal in the five-thousand-meter race. "I was screaming and cheering for him. It was a special experience," he says.

Klinsmann continued to grow and improve as a player and a person after the Euro and Olympics. He got plenty more experience abroad in his fourth—and what turned out to be his final—season with VfB Stuttgart as the team advanced to the finals of the 1988/89 UEFA Cup. He relished the chance to travel across Europe with his club, getting to see and learn more about countries on both sides of the continent divided by the Iron Curtain and Cold War, such as Hungary and Croatia as well as Holland and Spain. One of the more intriguing road trips was to a city behind the Iron Curtain, in Communist East Germany. VfB Stuttgart was playing a series of home-and-away semifinal games against Dynamo Dresden. It was in April 1989, with tremendous change and upheaval sweeping across East Germany and just seven months before the Berlin Wall fell. Klinsmann's team was up against the East German powerhouse Dresden in a country where the Stasi security police had an army of spies and informants keeping close track of foreigners, especially celebrity soccer players.

"I had been to East Germany almost every year with my parents— we traveled there to see my father's folks," says Klinsmann of trips to his father's hometown in Hohenwutzen, northeast of Berlin, near the Polish border. "But coming to East Germany as a player for a very important game was a kind of shock because these were Germans, these were our own people but in another country. And you know that your every move is being watched. You don't know where they are, the cameras, but you know they're everywhere. It was weird, a weird feeling. My dad's side of the family still lived there, my cousins, my uncles, my grandpa and grandma. So now you're playing in the East and you know they're not far away but they are somehow still very far away. And then we were playing against a very good team in Dresden, so it was, 'Okay, now you really have to zoom in and get down to business.' "

Stuttgart won the first leg at home 1–0 and played to a 1–1 tie in Dresden on April 19, thus winning the home-and-away series by an aggregate score of 2–1 to advance to a two-game final against Napoli, a team from Italy's league Serie A that was led by the great Diego Maradona, who in 2000 was voted FIFA's Player of the Century. Napoli beat Stuttgart by an aggregate score of 5–4. It was a bitter defeat for Klinsmann, an experience he vowed to avenge the next time he made it to a final.

# MOVE TO ITALY

As disheartening as the defeat at the hands of the Netherlands in the Euro 88 at home had been for Klinsmann and his West Germany team, Klinsmann's strong performance wasn't forgotten. Also, about an hour before the semifinal game, Dutch captain Ruud Gullit had gone out of his way to talk to Klinsmann during warm-ups. The midfielder for the Netherlands was one of the biggest stars in the game at that point and had been named the 1987 World Player of the Year. Gullit was playing for one of the world's top clubs at the time, AC Milan, and had met Klinsmann earlier in the year at a charity event. They were talking for about ten minutes about the challenges of the game at the club level in Italy when Gullit suddenly blurted out, "Hey, what about you? When are you going to come to Italy too?" The idea of playing in Italy one day stuck with Klinsmann.

Klinsmann was having a great time playing for VfB Stuttgart and especially playing internationally for West Germany. But a part of him was eager for new challenges and—once again—to break out of his comfort zone. He also got some sage and remarkably candid advice from his VfB Stuttgart coach, Arie Haan. The Dutchman, rather astonishingly, quietly encouraged Klinsmann to move on, saying he thought Klinsmann could raise his game to the next level in a more challenging league.

"He came up to me and said, 'You gotta move on,'" Klinsmann recalls, smiling at the memory of the coach willing to put the player's career ahead of his own vested interests. "Even though the club really wanted to keep me, he said that. I looked at him and said, 'What do you mean?' And he just said, 'You gotta move on, it's time for you to go.' This coach was actually putting his job on the line by advising one of his key players to leave because, for the player's development, it was time to go to the next level. That was the best advice I ever got from a coach."

Klinsmann was floored by Haan's altruism, especially as Haan could be putting his own job with Stuttgart in jeopardy by urging his top goal scorer to move on to a more challenging league. It was an important lesson about integrity and honesty for Klinsmann, a lesson he wouldn't forget. It was also something he took with him into his coaching career with Germany and the United States—giving his players his honest assessment and straightforward advice on how and where they might be able to play in order to take their game to the next level.

At the end of the 1988/89 season, Klinsmann was certainly ready for a change. He had already scored 79 goals in 156 appearances for Stuttgart—an average of one goal in every second game. He had also advanced from a top second-division player to a starter in the Bundesliga, becoming the league's leading scorer in 1988, and then getting called up to the West Germany national team at the pinnacle of the pyramid. He had gotten a taste of the international game, for both his club and country, and was eager for more.

The conversation with Gullit piqued his interest about playing in Italy's Serie A, which was considered the best league in the world at the time and a step up both professionally and financially for anyone in the Bundesliga. Italian clubs had won three of the previous six European Cups. Goals were scarce in a league that placed an emphasis on airtight defenses—not the most enticing prospect for a goal-hungry forward like Klinsmann. But the quality of play in the league was excellent, and he believed his skills could be sharpened by the greater competition.

"It was just time to see something new," says Klinsmann, adding he was simply ready to start a new chapter of his life with new challenges. "Italy was the only place to go. It was the best league in the world. I was already part of the National Team at the time. Not only did they pay three times as much as the Bundesliga, but at the time in the early 1990s it was the mecca of soccer. The only thing that drove me then was that I wanted to be where the best players were, period. And the best were playing in Italy. I got to see that in the UEFA Cup final, playing against Maradona."

But it was more than just honing his skills against some of the best players in the world that prompted Klinsmann to move abroad. After four seasons in the Bundesliga, he was starting to fear that a certain complacency could set in at some point, worried about the many backslappers and sycophants, and fearful that he might fall into the trap of becoming satisfied with what he had already accomplished without pushing to find out how good he could be or explore how much he could get out of his abilities.

"When you first become a professional soccer player, you end up getting what is relatively quite a bit of money and a lot of things are made easy for you—and that can make you complacent and sluggish," Klinsmann told Michael Horeni in *Klinsmann*. "That's why the transfer to Italy was so important. It got me out of my daily routine and gave me all sorts of new challenges: learning a new language, coming to terms with a different mentality. The new experience was more important to me than scoring goals."

Several of West Germany's best players were also in Italy at the time—captain Lothar Matthäus, Andreas Brehme, and Rudi Völler. So were Holland's best players: Ruud Gullit, Marco van Basten, and Frank Rijkaard. Another attraction was that Italy would be the host country for the next World Cup in the summer of 1990, at the end of the following club season. He'd had a promising start with the West Germany National Team in 1987, 1988, and the first half of 1989 with three goals and eleven caps. With one year to go before the 1990 World Cup, Klinsmann was looking forward to the opportunity to play on an even bigger stage. The challenge of competing against the world's best in Italy could only make him better, he reasoned. And it certainly wouldn't hurt to get acquainted with the country, its culture, and its soccer stadiums.

Klinsmann had negotiated his own contract with VfB Stuttgart four years earlier, and he was not a free agent but instead bound to the club for another year. But he had an exit clause written into the contract that would allow him to transfer anywhere if he could find a club willing to pay a fixed transfer fee of 4 million marks (about $1.6 million), probably well below his market value for West Germany's Footballer of the Year but nearly six times the 700,000-mark transfer fee that VfB Stuttgart had paid to the Stuttgarter Kickers. The advantage for Klinsmann of such a clause was that he could decide if and to which club he would transfer—and not have to wait to be auctioned off to the highest bidder, as was often the case. VfB Stuttgart club executives—unaware of Haan's private advice to Klinsmann—did not want their star forward to leave and were eager to sign him to an extended contract.

Club executives from Internazionale Milan, however, pursued Klinsmann with gusto after the 1988/89 season. They met at the Stuttgart airport. The club had been following Klinsmann for the last two years and offered a lucrative three-year contract. But for

Klinsmann, more important than the money was the chance to play in one of the world's best leagues and learn about a new culture. A lot of Stuttgart fans as well as fans across the country were hoping Klinsmann would stay in West Germany, even though most understood his desire to join the more competitive Italian league. He had played an important role in revitalizing the game in West Germany, helping to win back broader public support for the game with his charisma and enthusiasm after scoring important goals and his tireless work ethic on the field.

"The generation of international players before Klinsmann's had caused considerable damage to soccer's image in the early 1980s," writes Horeni. "Soccer still had its fan base but no longer had the broad-based support by the society at large." He notes that West German industry and advertisers had a bit of an aversion to the Bundesliga during that era because of the tarnished image, and a prevailing sense that many players were little more than passionless mercenaries. There had been a disconcerting disconnect between the enthusiasm that German fans carried in their hearts from their own soccer playing in their youth near the bottom of the pyramid and the detached, self-indulgent, and at times almost apathetic approach some of the highly paid professionals showed on the field.

The president of VfB Stuttgart, Gerhard Mayer-Vorfelder, was acutely aware of all that and was thus understandably eager to keep Klinsmann. Mayer-Vorfelder, who years later, in 2004, would be the president of the DFB who hired Klinsmann as Germany's coach, offered to try to tap new sponsors to raise his salary, but he was unaware of coach Arie Haan's unorthodox advice to Klinsmann. Mayer-Vorfelder realized quickly enough that it was not a bigger paycheck motivating Klinsmann but rather the quest for a new challenge and a desire to learn a new language. VfB capitulated and accepted the fixed transfer fee from Inter Milan. Klinsmann moved to Milan in the summer of 1989. He negotiated his own three-year contract with Milan—after getting useful tips on strategy from Bayern Munich's commercial manager, Uli Hoeness. "I knew what my value was," he says.

Klinsmann was determined to learn as much as he could about Italy and its culture. He had quietly been preparing for the move to Italy by taking Italian lessons from a tutor in Geislingen for about six months prior to the move. "I was always fascinated by trying to understand people in a different culture," says Klinsmann. "And that can only happen if I speak their language. Language is the key to understanding a country. I studied it before I went because I wanted to be prepared. But then here comes the shock: The moment you get to that country you're hardly able to say anything because you're so overwhelmed by the speed of the language. So that was a bit intimidating. It took me three months to start talking. What was fascinating about taking classes every day and learning the language was that suddenly there's a moment where it all comes together. For a while you're a student thinking, 'I'm never going to get that,' and then there's the moment when it clicks, the moment when you get it. It feels really good. I was literally obsessed with learning Italian."

To Klinsmann's chagrin, his coach at Inter Milan, Giovanni Trapattoni, put him in an apartment with two other West Germans on the team, Lothar Matthäus and Andreas Brehme, for a preseason training camp. Klinsmann protested Trapattoni's well-intentioned plan to put the West Germany teammates all together, saying he wanted to learn Italian and more about the local culture—and not be trapped in German-speaking isolation.

He lost that argument but plunged into learning Italian nonetheless. He would study the language for hours on end after practice—to the point that Trapattoni once stormed into his room and shouted at him to stop. "I was studying Italian every day, after practice and after lunch," says Klinsmann, who still speaks the mellifluous language fluently. "He came in and said, 'You're not studying Italian anymore, you need to sleep.' I said, 'Coach, I want to understand you. I gotta study the language.' I just had this kind of feeling that if I'm not speaking their language, they'll never let me into their culture. They'll never tell me the stuff that I'm not supposed to know."

Trapattoni expected Klinsmann to put all his effort into soccer, not learning Italian. Years later, when Trapattoni was rather famously struggling to learn German and delightfully mangling the language to the point that he became a cult figure for his poor German (coining such slogans as "*ich habe fertig,*" or I am finish) while coaching Bayern Munich, he admitted that, in hindsight, he envied Klinsmann's far-sightedness to work so hard to learn Italian at the start of his career in Italy.

Klinsmann took learning Italian so seriously that he even went back to school to try to get his degree. Even though he did not get his diploma in Germany or Italy, he had an insatiable appetite for learning—whether it was languages, cultures, or business. He enjoyed negotiating his own contracts with the clubs he played on. There didn't seem to be any limits to his curiosity.

"I went to a type of college that I could never have gotten a degree from—it's a school where you go to Italy, learn Italian, and learn Italian culture," he says. "Then you go to France and Monaco, and learn French and French culture, and then you go to England and you experience things in England you had no idea about. In a certain way you're thankful because the game of soccer took you there; your talent took you to experience all these different cultures and people. You realize that you've gotten a completely different education now than anyone else could have gotten. And it never stops because I'm always eager to learn more. I don't have a degree to hang on the wall. But I went to a different kind of school and got a different education."

Klinsmann soon enough had his own apartment, and he packed up and moved himself from Stuttgart to Milan. He tried to lead a comparatively modest lifestyle in Italy, not letting the bigger paychecks change his naturally thrifty outlook on life. He got by each month on just a small fraction of his income. He saved as much of it as possible and invested part of it in rental property back home in Germany with the idea of having a nest egg to fall back on after his playing career—which he knew could end abruptly. "Soccer gave me the once-in-a-lifetime chance to achieve something that not a lot of people have a chance for at my age: independence," he said after moving to Italy. "No one can tell me, 'You have to do this or you have to do that.' I'm free, I'm my own boss."

Savoring his freedom as well as soaking up the language and culture, Klinsmann quickly became popular in Italy, in part thanks to his distinctively hardworking style on the field and his candid interviews *in Italiano* after the games as well as his rapidly improving Italian skills. Klinsmann thrived on the frenzy of the fans. The chant *"Jürgen Klinsmann, facci un gol"* (score a goal) sometimes rained down onto the field. He also acquired the nickname *"La Pantegana bionda"* (The Blond Rat), supposedly a reference to his distinctive nose, from an Italian sports TV show when one of the moderators spoke admiringly of Klinsmann's performance with the sentence *"Che bella settimana per la bionda pantegana"* (What a beautiful week that was for the blond rat).

His language proficiency and genuine interest in Italian culture made life all the more enjoyable. He got to know people in Italy away from soccer who became close friends. But he struggled a bit at times to come to terms with the Italian mentality. While being on time is normal for Germans, punctuality isn't a virtue of any special merit in Italy. Klinsmann showed up on time for practice and was surprised to find himself the only one there. Many of his teammates didn't start arriving until a quarter of an hour later; their thinking was: Practice starts when everyone gets there. Punctuality and precision are traits that perhaps explain Germany's success in many areas. Trains run on time, workers are paid on time, soccer players come to practice on time. Klinsmann was also baffled to read fabricated interviews that he had purportedly given to journalists—"interviews" that were in fact figments of the journalists' imagination. It's an odd practice of Italian journalism, as Klinsmann discovered.

"In Italy I had to learn to take the people the way they were and not the way I wanted them to be, otherwise you run up against the wall and can end up going crazy," says Klinsmann, adding that it was a valuable lesson in tolerance that would serve him well at later stops in other countries. "They're never on time and things like that. It's like if you make an appointment with someone and he shows up two hours or two days later, he still shows up. You have to build a level of tolerance to the people but also toward yourself, or you'll go nuts. That's why certain players left and went home early from Italy. They said, 'I can't give you that.' But I learned how to cope with that mentality. I said to myself, 'You can change yourself but you won't change them.' I changed in Italy and became more tolerant toward people but also more tolerant toward myself." At the same time, Klinsmann quickly came to appreciate the positive aspects of life in Italy—especially the Italians' cheerfulness and undying optimism. "It's just in their nature," he says. "It's their nature to be positive no matter what the problem is."

Klinsmann figured out how the game was played in Italy and soon became one of the most popular foreigners playing in the Serie A. He thrived in the hothouse atmosphere of the big stadiums, some of which held crowds as large as eighty thousand. In his first season, he scored thirteen goals for Inter Milan, helping the team take third place in the league—scoring that often was quite an accomplishment considering many games ended with a score of 1–0 and the defensive-minded Italian game with its heritage of *catenaccio* defensive style. The *catenaccio*—literally "door-bolt" style of play—was brought to Italy in the 1960s by the Argentine coach Helenio Herrera. He led Inter Milan to three league championships and two European Cup titles with the tight defensive style in which players stay deep in their own half.

In Klinsmann's second season, 1990/91, he scored fourteen league goals and also helped Inter Milan win the UEFA Cup, beating Roma 2–1 on aggregate. In his third and final season, Inter struggled under a new coach, Corrado Orrico, and ended up eighth in Serie A. With key players on his team injured, Klinsmann scored just seven goals in that season, and even though his three-year contract had been extended, he was ready for a new challenge in a new country.

"Things were falling apart in my third year at Inter," he says. "The team fell apart. Matthäus got injured, and I didn't see a ball up front and didn't score a lot of goals. Then the move to Monaco came. It was a very rewarding experience in Italy, and that's one of the things I took from those years. Could I live in Italy again today? Oh, easily, yes. I get them, I understand them with all the good and bad there is there."

# WINNING THE WORLD CUP

THE 1990 WORLD CUP finals in Italy turned out to be a major turning point for Klinsmann's career—another important tournament where he was able to raise his game when it counted the most to help his team, further burnishing his reputation as a clutch player. The World Cup is the ultimate test for the game's best players—some of soccer's greatest club players wither under the bright lights, disappearing under the pressure.

Adding to an atmosphere of expectation for the Germans, the Cup was played against the backdrop of sweeping political and social changes in Germany after the Berlin Wall, the most potent symbol of the Cold War, had been torn down on November 9, 1989, amid the peaceful revolution in Communist East Germany. The tournament was being played just three months before East and West Germany reunited in October 1990.

The powerful West Germany team was among the favorites to win the World Cup and got off to a flying start with Klinsmann scoring their second goal in a 4–1 win against Yugoslavia at his home stadium in Milan to the cheers of German followers and thousands of Inter Milan fans. He scored the second goal again in West Germany's 5–1 win against the United Arab Emirates, before they were held to a 1–1 draw against Colombia both also in Milan. West Germany faced the strong team from the Netherlands in the Round of 16 game—again in Milan. The Dutch had struggled in the Group Stage but dominated the start of the elimination round game against the Germans.

But there was a dramatic turn of events about twenty minutes into the tense game. In a fit of anger, Holland defender Frank Rijkaard spit onto the back of the head of West Germany's striker Rudi Völler, which led to scuffles and verbal abuse going both ways. Both Rijkaard and, bizarrely, Völler were sent off with red cards. Just when things were looking bleak for West Germany, Klinsmann stepped into the void as the team's lone striker and put on what some called his greatest performance ever, running everywhere, outplaying the Dutch defense, and inspiring his teammates.

Klinsmann's indefatigable efforts finally paid off, and he put West Germany ahead 1–0 in the 52nd minute with his third goal of the tournament. Andreas Brehme doubled the lead in the 84th minute to 2–0 before Ronald Koeman scored a penalty kick for the Netherlands in the 88th minute for a final 2–1 score. "I've never ever seen a striker fight for the rest of the team with such utter self-sacrifice," said Karl-Heinz Rummenigge, a former West Germany captain and executive at Bayern Munich, of Klinsmann's phenomenal performance against the Netherlands on his home field in Milan. The *Süddeutsche Zeitung* praised Klinsmann for saving the day: "Never before in the last decade has a striker had such a brilliant, near-perfect performance." After that, West Germany struggled to a 1–0 win in the quarterfinals against Czechoslovakia before advancing to the semifinal, where it got past England 4–3 on penalties after the game and overtime ended in a tie.

The final in Rome against Argentina is remembered for Brehme scoring a penalty to break a 0–0 deadlock with six minutes left. But

Klinsmann was involved in one of the most dramatic moments of the game that helped turn the tide not long before that, when he was tackled in a reckless challenge from Argentina's defender Pedro Monzón in the 68th minute as he was sprinting down the right side. The attack sent Klinsmann spinning through the air and left him with a six-inch gash on his shin. Monzón got a red card from the Mexican referee and became the first player ever to be sent off the field in a World Cup final.

Rudi Völler was tackled in the penalty box by Roberto Sensini with six minutes left, and Brehme scored the penalty to win the World Cup for West Germany—the country's third title in thirty-six years. This win pulled the country even with Brazil and Italy (each with three championships) as the most successful soccer nations in the world.

"It was an aggressive game and it's too bad that Argentina didn't open up," Klinsmann says. "They just sat back, trying to kill the rhythm of the game instead of playing their own game. It's unfortunate that it was decided by a penalty, but we were clearly the better team. They never had a chance. The game wasn't very exciting, but we deserved to win."

# STRONG IN SWEDEN

TWO YEARS LATER, at the European Championship in Sweden, Klinsmann again managed to raise his game at the right time. He had lost his starting position for Germany in the run-up to the tournament. United Germany's new coach, Berti Vogts, welcoming the former East German players whose team had been disbanded with reunification in 1990, had been critical of Klinsmann's play in the fall of 1991 and benched him for a while because he was not playing up to Vogts's expectations for his club in Italy or for the National Team. It was harsh, but it was an important wake-up call for Klinsmann, twenty-seven at the time. "He really let me have a piece of his mind," Klinsmann told Horeni in *Klinsmann*. "Yet it helped me realize once again what a wonderful life soccer was making possible for me—even if every day wasn't going as well as I'd have liked."

Klinsmann got a chance to play early in the European Championship and once again made the most of it. "I was having a bad run before the tournament and was on the bench for the first game," Klinsmann says. "But then I got lucky and got to play because Rudi Völler broke his arm." Klinsmann came off the bench to play alongside Karl-Heinz Riedle. He had another strong tournament, and he got better each game. He scored a goal against the Netherlands in a 3–1 defeat at the Group Stage, and helped Germany beat Sweden 3–2 to advance to the final. But there Germany was upset by Denmark, 2–0.

It was the third straight tournament in which Klinsmann had shined as one of Germany's best players, raising his game once again when the pressure was the greatest. "Once the tournament was over, I could say I gave everything I had," he says. "I didn't stop for a second, and moments like that are, I think, really, really important for players to recognize: Hey, this moment isn't going to ever come back. It's a question every player has to ask themselves at the end of a tournament: 'Did I give absolutely everything I had every minute I was out there?'"

# MILAN TO MONACO

AFTER THREE YEARS in Italy, Klinsmann was ready to move on. He was twenty-eight and felt he needed a change of scenery after the difficult third season in Milan. He had talks about a possible transfer to Real Madrid or Paris Saint-Germain, but a few weeks after the Euro ended, Klinsmann ended up agreeing to a transfer to AS Monaco, a team that played in France's top division, Ligue 1. It was not one of Europe's top four leagues, but it was also not far behind Italy, Spain, England, and Germany. And he had a chance to learn a new language, French, get to know a new culture, and enjoy a break from the 24/7 pressure of playing in soccer-mad Milan.

Klinsmann also welcomed the chance to play for Monaco's innovative and dynamic coach, Arsène Wenger, who was forty-four and in the process of making a name for himself in France and beyond with his attractive attacking style of play. Klinsmann scored nineteen goals in thirty-eight matches to become the third leading scorer in the French first division—a nice change of pace after the stifling defensive style in Milan, where he got only seven in his final season there on a team increasingly racked by internal disputes.

"It was a great opportunity," he says of Monaco. "I met different people, learned French, and was exposed to a different way of thinking." At that stage in his career, Klinsmann started giving more thought to what he would do after his playing days were over. There are not many strikers older than thirty playing soccer at the highest levels, because one of their most important weapons—speed—often starts to fade at about that age. Klinsmann had even briefly considered retiring a year earlier while taking a five-week vacation to South Africa and Namibia. But he realized that he wasn't yet ready to live without soccer and quickly abandoned the idea of retiring at the prime of his career. The new environment in Monaco, where soccer was not the only game in town, was a tonic for Klinsmann; Monaco also hosts Formula One and major tennis, golf, and cycling events. It helped give him a breather from the intense pressure of playing before crowds of seventy thousand by instead playing in front of as few as two thousand.

It was also liberating to play for a coach like Wenger, an advocate of a more attacking style of play that Klinsmann preferred to the grinding, defensive style of play that he had grown accustomed to in Italy. After three years of *catenaccio,* Klinsmann flourished in Wenger's flowing, open style of play. Klinsmann scored three goals in his first five games and ended up with nineteen in his first season, leading Monaco to second place. For his energetic play on the field, which also inspired his teammates to raise their games, Klinsmann was given the nickname *"La Locomotive"* by France's *L'équipe* sports newspaper.

"I enjoyed working with Arsène. He's open-minded," says Klinsmann, who gleaned a number of ideas for later use from the Frenchman. For instance, Wenger was the first coach Klinsmann had who had a special nutritionist working for the team. "I was lucky to learn from so many different coaches over the years. I had Arsène and many good teachers. He's not only a good soccer coach. He's got a wealth of knowledge off the field too, so for a player it's like going to one of the best universities in the world. It was always the long-term picture with Arsène. He knew he needed results in the short term, but he was always looking at how a player would develop in two or four or six years from now."

Klinsmann led Monaco to the 1994 Champions League semifinals; he was their top scorer in the tournament, with four goals. Thanks to this and his five goals at the 1994 World Cup that summer, he was voted Fussballer des Jahres, Player of the Year, in Germany for the second time after 1988.

# WORLD CUP IN THE USA

KLINSMANN WAS ALSO PLAYING a more important role in Germany coach Berti Vogts's plans for the 1994 World Cup in the United States. He was one of the senior players on the team—with ten years of pro experience and five years of international experience, along with some forty caps for Germany. Klinsmann welcomed the added responsibility and believed Germany had a strong enough team to become the first country to win back-to-back World Cups since Brazil accomplished the feat in 1958 and 1962 (Italy also won twice in a row in 1934 and 1938). But it would take a total team effort where there could be no room for selfishness.

Vogts, struggling to break out from the shadow of his predecessor, Franz Beckenbauer, was already under pressure in the success-spoiled domestic media after Germany lost in the 1992 European Championship final to Denmark. There were tensions beneath the surface on the 1994 World Cup team. Distractions, turmoil, and self-inflicted wounds knocked the team off course. First, midfielder Stefan Effenberg was thrown off the team after he made a rude gesture to Germany fans for booing him, flipping them the bird as he came off the field in Germany's final group game—a 3–2 win over South Korea in Dallas. Effenberg might have been able to have the dismissal reversed if he had apologized, but he refused and was sent home.

Germany scraped past Belgium 3–2 in the Round of 16 but was eliminated by underdog Bulgaria in the quarterfinals 2–1, squandering a 1–0 lead by giving up two late goals. Throughout the tournament there were problems on the team; some of the players complained about their accommodations even though they were staying in hotels as luxurious as the Waldorf Astoria, while others got embroiled in a public debate raging back home in Germany about how much time they could spend with their wives or playing golf.

Klinsmann was stunned that the team, one of the top favorites to win the 1994 World Cup, had been beaten, knocked out of the tournament so needlessly and carelessly. He was upset that the team seemed to beat itself, and that some individuals were unable to put their own interests aside for the good of the team. The chemistry was not right, and that cost Germany dearly in the tournament that Brazil went on to win.

Once again, he had a great tournament, scoring five goals in five games, but was shattered by the defeat—the earliest exit for a German team since 1978. He stayed silent after the game and opted not to say anything about it for weeks. Klinsmann thought long and hard about all that went wrong, zeroing in on the importance of team chemistry. In a tournament with twenty-three players, everyone must be aware of his role—whether on the field or as a reserve—and pulling in the same direction. What might have been one of the best Germany World Cup teams ever got eliminated in the quarterfinals by Bulgaria, by allowing destructive distractions off the field by a few players to sink the whole team. He would remember the lessons from that debacle when, as coach, he picked Germany's team for the 2006 World Cup and the U.S. Men's National Team for the 2014 World Cup in Brazil. The lesson learned was that it is almost impossible to exaggerate the importance of getting the team chemistry right and selecting the right players who will accept their roles even if it means sitting on the bench as a reserve player.

It took Klinsmann two months to process the 1994 World Cup debacle before he finally broke his silence and aired his views about it in a German newspaper interview.

"The fact of the matter is that some players weren't able to put the interests of the team ahead of their own interests," Klinsmann told the *Süddeutsche Zeitung.* "It's not acceptable that we allowed secondary issues to distract us from the task at hand and the reason we were in the United States—to defend our World Cup title. We weren't there to prattle on about women issues or leisure-time activities. I felt like I'd been cheated. Everyone should be able to do whatever they want away from the game. It doesn't matter to me who has what issues away from the game. But those who are out there on the field with us simply have to give everything they've got for the team. That wasn't what happened, and that's why we failed."

Vogts agrees that the 1994 Germany team was probably stronger than the squad that won the World Cup in 1990, but he says the harmony was disrupted by a small number of selfish players. Klinsmann says he learned from the fiasco, lessons that he took with him into his coaching career for Germany and now the United States. When he picks his teams for the World Cup, Klinsmann is not only looking to select the best possible team but also thinking ahead to the tournament and ensuring that the twenty-three players have the right chemistry, cohesion, and drive to be able to spend more than a month together. It's important, he says, that the reserve players understand their roles and won't try to thrust themselves into the spotlight if they are sitting on the bench.

"I definitely learned from Berti's experience in 1994 and how important it is that everyone on the team is there for the bigger

picture—winning the tournament," says Klinsmann. "A lot happened, unfortunately, off the field. We were the best team in that
World Cup, by far. If we had made it to the final against Brazil, we'd
have been the only team that could have put them under pressure.
But we blew it because we were too confident, too arrogant, and too
complacent. And then obviously on the field there was the Stefan
Effenberg situation. We, the players, and Berti begged [DFB presi-
dent] Egidius Braun to let Effenberg stay after that, saying, 'Come
on now, just be cool about this, just give him a fine or whatever.'
But on the other side, the guy didn't want to apologize. So there were
two worlds clashing there. I said, 'This is crazy. This is one of the
best midfielders in this World Cup and this is the situation?' We all
make mistakes, but for me it's important you say that you made a
mistake. It didn't happen there. People made mistakes and they said
they didn't do anything wrong. Some people went golfing at eight
o'clock in the morning, playing nine holes in ninety-five-degree
heat before training. They came back with red faces, and I thought,
'What the heck are you doing? We're playing in a World Cup here.'
No problem if we have a day off, but don't go play golf right before
our team workout."

# CHANGE OF PACE IN LONDON

JÜRGEN KLINSMANN TURNED thirty in the summer of 1994, an age when many strikers who might have lost a bit of their speed are approaching or passing their sell-by date. But he was still full of life and hadn't lost even a half step. He was on the verge of having possibly his best and most exciting year in soccer.

He had once again raised his game for a major tournament—his fourth straight exceptional performance at a World Cup or European Championship since 1988. Despite Germany's bitterly disappointing quarterfinals' ouster in 1994, Klinsmann had perhaps his best World Cup, with five goals in five games. That had made him one of the world's most sought-after players and, despite his age, the target of some of the top clubs in Europe looking to bolster their lineups for the upcoming club season. He had already announced months before the World Cup, toward the end of his second season at AS Monaco in the spring of 1994, that he wanted a new challenge and to move to a new club.

It was all very nice playing on the shores of the Mediterranean in Monaco, which had plenty of agreeable distractions and drew low-key home crowds averaging 10,000 in a stadium with a capacity of 18,500. Monaco, a tiny principality that is the world's second-smallest country with 37,800 citizens, is also the world's most densely populated country with luxury high-rises built upon a small slice of land of just five hundred acres on the coast between Italy and France. Monaco was one of the top teams in France's Ligue 1 and played in the Champions League. But after two years of that, Klinsmann was feeling an urge to play again in a major soccer nation with all the accompanying pressures from passionate crowds and demanding fans. AC Milan, FC Bayern Munich, Barcelona, Aston Villa, Atlético Madrid, and FC Genoa were among the suitors. Yet shortly after the World Cup, it was Tottenham Hotspur that unexpectedly won the sweepstakes.

Tottenham owner, Alan Sugar, boldly showed up one day on a yacht in Monaco to personally persuade Klinsmann to come and play in England, convincing him he would fit perfectly on the offensive-minded club that had always been a haven for extraordinary and eccentric players who nevertheless had the skills to make a difference on the field. "If you stick your head out the window, mate, you'll see my blue boat bobbing about in the harbor," Sugar told Klinsmann one day in late July 1994. It was a major coup for Sugar to sign a player of Klinsmann's caliber, especially considering that the Spurs were in rather desperate straits. They had finished fifteenth in the standings in the previous season, just three points above relegation. And because of charges that financial rules were breached by the club's previous owners in the 1980s, Tottenham had been handed a twelve-point penalty before the season began and was banned from the FA Cup. The club appealed, and those penalties were later revoked.

"Things were changing, and by 1994 it was all starting to shift away from Italy. You saw that it wasn't the same in Italy as it had been during the golden years before that," Klinsmann says, explaining how he ended up in England. "I had offers from Spain and to go back to Italy, but I just really wanted to go to a vibrant new place like London. I was always a fan of English soccer. Tottenham for me meant London—a very traditional club, a good name, but certainly not Manchester United or Liverpool. I thought, 'This is a good club,' and I had always admired the coach, Ossie Ardiles. He was an amazing technical player and World Cup winner."

Hardly any foreign players went to England in the early 1990s. In the Premier League's first season, 1992/93, there were only thirteen foreigners in the whole league. That was the year before Klinsmann became one of the first big foreign signings, a harbinger of change that helped make the Premier League arguably the best in the world. The number of foreigners playing in England surged after 1995 and the so-called Bosman ruling at the European Court of Justice. The ruling was named after the Belgian player Jean-Marc Bosman, whose transfer from his Belgium club to a French team had been foiled. It put an end to the practice of domestic soccer leagues in the European Union imposing quotas on the numbers of foreign players. The court ruling opened the door for players to switch clubs on free transfers when their contracts expired. Nearly 70 percent of the players in the Premier League in the 2014/15 season were foreigners.

Moving to London to play for Tottenham would be one of the most exciting and fulfilling experiences in Klinsmann's career. In a certain way, he was following in the footsteps of his father, who as a journeyman baker had worked in different bakeries around Germany and Switzerland in the 1950s before settling down, enriched by new experiences along the way.

Klinsmann spent one and a half seasons total at the Premier League club beginning in 1994 and counting in 1998 season. It was an exhilarating time for him and—duly appreciated by the fans and his teammates alike—he played some of the best soccer of his career.

His move to England was also pioneering just before the Bosman ruling, indirectly helping to open the country to top foreign players. It would also send his own career into orbit, and even helped modernize an outdated image of frumpy, humorless Germans that had lingered in Britain since the World War II era. Klinsmann had no intention of becoming possibly the best ambassador to Great Britain that Germany ever had. Instead he went to London with an open mind and thrived on the high-energy, attacking game that was played by the clubs in the Premier League. In his youth he had been a fan of Liverpool—along with Borussia Mönchengladbach, which had great teams in the 1970s. "As a little boy I was a crazy Liverpool fan," he says. "It was Liverpool and Mönchengladbach. As a kid, you admired players like Kevin Keegan and Kenny Dalglish."

Like many Germans, Klinsmann admired the soccer traditions and culture in England, the pulsating atmosphere in the stadiums, the crowds so close to the field, the sportsmanship, and the polite, almost theaterlike applause that regularly erupts whenever a player makes a good effort.

"I didn't have a really deep understanding of football in England," Klinsmann says, "so it was another cultural adventure that I couldn't have foreseen. I had literally no expectations, positively or negatively. I just thought to myself, 'Premier League? Tottenham? Let's give it a shot.' And then comes the 'diver story.' I had no clue."

Klinsmann was surprised and a bit dismayed that some of the newspapers in England were at first trying to portray him as a "diver," a player who deliberately falls to exaggerate or feign physical contact from a defender to fool the unsuspecting referee into awarding an unwarranted penalty kick. But he tried to take it all in stride.

Dives are frowned upon, even despised, considered cheating in England and the United States. But, broadly speaking, the practice of going down artfully when fouled in the penalty box is seen as somewhat less objectionable, if not exactly condoned, in continental Europe and South America—provided the stumble is generally in line with contact clumsily caused injudiciously by an overly zealous defender.

Klinsmann found the accusation that he was a diver unfair, off the mark, and probably even a bit insulting when he first heard about it, but he understood it was an attempt by some English newspapers to provoke him, to try to get him upset about it in order to keep the story running for several days of headlines. He never had a reputation in Germany for being a *Schwalbenkönig*, the unflattering term for a diver named after the swallow, because of the way the bird glides to the ground. Germans, who have a bit more tolerance for clever dives than the English or Americans, have an even more colorful and disdainful term—"*sterbende Schwan*" (dying swan)—to describe players who exaggerate their fall to the ground theatrically with arms outstretched in search of an unwarranted penalty call. Klinsmann had long enjoyed a sterling reputation in Germany, in part due to his extraordinary act of sportsmanship in 1987 when he had urged a referee not to give Norbert Nachtweih a second yellow card. Miffed though he was, Klinsmann knew he had to try to understand and defuse whatever was behind the accusations—and not get worked up about it.

"You just have to accept them [English journalists] right away the way they are," he says. "You shouldn't get offended because there are some media people trying to provoke you. It's just the way they do it there. They're not being mean. They just want to sell their newspapers. Going through a situation like that not only helped in terms of success on the field but I think it helped me as a human being."

Klinsmann reasoned that humor might be the best way to deal with the diver tag. Some newspapers were trying to dub him *"Der Dive Bomber,"* corrupting Gerd Müller's nickname *"Der Bomber,"* and casting aspersions on his character before he had even arrived at Tottenham.

"I was never a diver and never dived, but when I first came to Spurs I heard about this story, and it was a big lesson for me about how to handle the English media," he says. "Suddenly, I'm in England and there's this diver provocation and some talk about the fact that you're a German, and I just said, 'I'm okay with that, I can laugh at myself, I can crack a joke, I can convince them that we Germans are all right and that we're good at what we do.' And within two weeks this whole thing just turned around into completely different story. But I think the key was I just took them the way they are and adjusted myself to them, going with the teammates to eat fish and chips, and just be one of them—and obviously play your game. That's why you're there. To win them over with your game, you use the language of your sport to convince them of your qualities."

Klinsmann did his homework before going to London. He got some useful tips from a German friend in Monaco who had lived in Britain. He went to London prepared to deal with the taunts from the media—with a strategy to defend without appearing to be defensive. At his first press conference, he started off with a lighthearted joke, disarming the skeptical reporters assembled in front of him: "I just want to ask you fellas: Are there any diving schools in London?"

After the laughter subsided, Klinsmann extended an invitation to meet with reporters again in a few weeks' time to discuss replays of any moments in his career where they thought he was guilty of diving. "I'll bring the beer and you bring the videos. We'll take a look at the videos, and you show me where I tried to trick anyone." No one took him up on the offer, and that part of his answer did not make it into many newspaper accounts of the press conference. He had nevertheless touched a nerve with self-deprecating humor, turning their doubts upside down by acknowledging and poking fun at the allegations. His honor was at stake and he wanted to clear the air.

He even had a diving mask and snorkel as a prop tucked into his backpack—ready to pull out and strap on for emphasis if the moment had been needed. It wasn't. Klinsmann had won them over with his one-liner. He then managed to win over any remaining doubters in England with his play on the field. He scored his first goal, an exquisite header and match winner, that gave Tottenham a 4–2 lead on the way to their 4–3 victory over Sheffield Wednesday in his first game. Some of the Sheffield Wednesday fans had been trying to taunt him as a diver, holding up signs reading "5.8" and "5.9" as if they were Olympic diving judges.

After scoring that first goal for Tottenham, a jubilant Klinsmann made fun of the diving tag once again by celebrating with five teammates—taking a playful forward dive in front of the crowd. It was an idea suggested by a fellow Tottenham forward. "Teddy Sheringham said to me, 'When you score your first goal, we're all going to dive.' Then it actually became popular with the kids in the park, so for a while every celebration was a dive and everyone was laughing about it. There couldn't have been a better way to start the season." The next game, his first at Tottenham's home field, White Hart Lane in north London, Klinsmann scored twice in a 2–1 win against Everton, including a spectacular bicycle kick goal.

Sheringham had told Klinsmann that his six-year-old son and many other children in town had become enthusiastic fans of the self-mocking dive. "Everyone was ready" after his first home goal against Everton, Klinsmann says. He led the way, sprinting to the sideline and pointing his teammates toward the area for their collective dive with their arms spread out in front of them as if they were all diving into a lake. "The goalie came running from eighty yards away and we all ran together into the corner and we all went down, the whole team," Klinsmann says with a broad smile. "I don't think I experienced an atmosphere in the stadium like that ever before. Everyone was singing after that, and I could feel goose bumps running down my back."

Energized by the pace and energy in England after two seasons in front of smaller and subdued crowds in Monaco, Klinsmann got off to a flying start, with ten goals in his first seven games in all competitions. He had a brilliant season for Tottenham and scored twenty-nine goals in all competitions, including twenty league goals, five in the prestigious FA Cup tournament and four in the League Cup, another domestic tournament in England. Feeding off the energy of the crowds while giving them plenty to cheer about on the field, he was enjoying some of the best moments of his career on the team, with its flowing, fast-paced attack stacked with five forwards.

Klinsmann played like there was no tomorrow for his new team, and his enthusiasm on the field helped inspire several of his teammates to raise their games as well. Under the Argentine coach Ossie Ardiles, Tottenham went all out to score as many goals as possible with five forwards on the field at times, an unorthodox strategy fraught with risks. "I had a lot of fun and it was an exciting time," Klinsmann says, smiling at the memories of playing at Tottenham. "I played on a team that had real chemistry. Everything clicked. Fans always like to see goals, especially Spurs fans. I had never played on a team with five forwards before that like Ardiles lined us up. You worried for him, but what could you do?"

Klinsmann quickly fell in love with the cosmopolitan lifestyle of London and the city's great cultural diversity. He knew soccer had a proud tradition and special meaning for fans in England but was nevertheless amazed by the depth of their devotion to their team.

"When you talk about soccer in England, you have to talk about the environment and the atmosphere at those stadiums. It's incredible the way they sing their songs, the way the tension and the excitement during the game increases. It's something you just can't experience in other countries. It was always really special for me."

Klinsmann got an early taste of that special attachment of Tottenham fans to their club. His first game for the Spurs was a preseason exhibition match against a lower division side, more than three hundred miles away from home across the Irish Sea in Dublin. He was in awe of the Spurs fans' support: Thousands of fans made the journey to Ireland to watch the match against the Irish team Shelbourne.

"Tottenham is a way of life, and I didn't know that until I got there," says Klinsmann, who still feels a part of the club and regularly gets news alerts about Tottenham results. "I signed my first contract and thought, 'It's cool to be in London.' And then after two weeks I said to myself, 'Oh, my gosh, what is this here?' Before the friendly in Dublin I saw all these Spurs fans and said, 'Hold on, we just flew to Ireland.' I asked the other players, and they said, 'You're at Tottenham.' Tottenham is just so much more than a club. The supporters are special. They live and breathe for that club. You go to White Hart Lane and there are thirty-six thousand people singing. It's not just one section. It's the whole stadium singing. You go there and think, 'Wow.'"

Klinsmann says he saw the way that excitement from the crowds at Tottenham's stadium spilled over onto the field and pushed players to go beyond their limits, a spine-tingling experience that he found invigorating. The style of soccer that he played at Tottenham was often in the back of his mind when he was coaching Germany in 2004–06 and the U.S. Men's National Team from 2011.

"You walk onto the field and you sense all that energy there in the stadium. You just can't go slowly, you've got to give a hundred percent, you've got to give full pace all the time. You're so pumped up because of all the energy that the people are giving you. That's what's really special about soccer in England."

Klinsmann was impressed with how knowledgeable English spectators are. They cheered just about every notable effort on the field, and even a throw-in or corner kick won received applause. He especially admired their sense of honor and fair play. One of his lasting memories is the cheers he and his Tottenham teammates got from Liverpool fans after they outplayed the home team and after he scored the game winner in a 2–1 victory at Liverpool. Even though Tottenham had just knocked Liverpool out of the FA Cup tournament at the quarterfinal stage, the Liverpool fans stood and applauded Tottenham's strong performance.

"When you get asked about your best soccer memories, people usually talk about the trophies they won, the World Cup or the Euro or whatever," Klinsmann says. "One of the very most emotional memories that I have was winning at Anfield Road with Tottenham at that FA Cup game and scoring the winning goal in the last minute. As we were going into the locker room, our team was given a standing ovation. The fact that the people at Anfield gave *us* a standing ovation was really a special moment. Here are the famous fans of Liverpool standing up and giving a standing ovation to the away team. They were saying, 'Hey, you were the better team today.' It's not a trophy but it's something I'll never forget." Unfortunately, after beating Liverpool in the FA Cup, Tottenham lost the semifinal against Everton 4–1, with Klinsmann scoring the one goal. That loss destroyed hopes of a fairy-tale FA Cup final appearance for the club that at first had been barred from the tournament for the alleged transgressions of its previous owners before the ban was dropped on appeal.

Klinsmann's heroics for the Spurs and his popularity around

the country led to the coining of a new term, "Klinsmania." He was also referred to as "Cleansman" for the way he turned the spurious accusation he was a diver on its head. Klinsmann's popularity also helped change the antiquated image of Germans in England, a country that more than most others used World War II as a framework for its image of Germany even though the war had ended forty years earlier. It may sound like an overreaction—and was appalling to Klinsmann—that even as late as 1994 an exhibition game between England and Germany scheduled for Berlin had to be canceled because the date picked—April 20—was the 105th anniversary of Adolf Hitler's birth. English authorities feared trouble between small but significant numbers of English hooligans and German far-right extremists. Those fears are now long gone.

"I saw that season what soccer can do to bring a different perspective on attitudes that had been deeply held for years," says Klinsmann, who was also fondly remembered by Tottenham fans for driving around London in a dark blue 1967 Volkswagen Beetle convertible rather than a luxury sports car favored by many soccer players. "Soccer is a perfect tool to correct some false perceptions about different people and different cultures. Soccer shows us that we're all equal."

While playing in England, he was determined to learn from the German National Team's failure at the 1994 World Cup. He was on a personal scouting mission for the upcoming European Championships. As he had done before by playing in Italy in the 1989/90 season before the 1990 World Cup, Klinsmann was getting acquainted with England, its stadiums, its fans, and its mentality before the 1996 tournament that England would be hosting.

Klinsmann helped soccer regain some of its standing in the general public with his enthusiastic celebrations after goals and his unbridled love for the game itself. He was credited as well with helping make other players on his team better through his stamina and determination to succeed. Klinsmann's partnership up front with Sheringham was particularly successful and productive.

When Klinsmann arrived at Tottenham in 1994, soccer in England was going through a difficult period. English clubs, some of which were plagued by hooligan troubles, had been banned from all European competitions for the last five years of the 1980s after the Heysel Stadium disaster in Brussels in 1985. Thirty-nine Juventus Turin fans were killed at the European Cup final played there when a wall collapsed amid clashes started by Liverpool fans. A few weeks before that, fifty-six fans had been killed in a stadium fire at Bradford City. Then in 1989, ninety-six people died—many asphyxiated— and 766 were injured at the Hillsborough disaster when Liverpool fans pouring into the stadium crushed against each other before the FA Cup semifinal game.

On the field, England's national team suffered from the isolation as well. The team failed to qualify for the 1994 World Cup, a humiliation that reflected how cut off the country had become from the great soccer knowledge networks of Western Europe. There were hardly any top foreign players in England then, due to the league's poor reputation and tight quotas. That began to change after the Premier League was created in 1992 by breaking away from the Football League, Klinsmann's sterling efforts for Tottenham in 1994/95, and the Bosman ruling.

Klinsmann's sparkle and Tottenham's entertaining, high-scoring attack helped to rejuvenate the game in England. He was at the forefront of a movement of top foreign players who shifted from Italy's Serie A and other top leagues in Europe by the mid-1990s, along with Eric Cantona (1992), Dennis Bergkamp (1995), and Thierry Henry (1999). "When I came to England, there was Cantona but there were few other foreigners," Klinsmann says. "I don't know if I was a pioneer, but word spread out and soon you had Gullit, [Gianfranco] Zola, Bergkamp, and [Gianluca] Vialli," Klinsmann said in an interview with *FourFourTwo* magazine, mentioning players he knew in Italy who all went to Chelsea in 1995 and 1996. "I played with some of those guys and I was able to tell them 'this is cool, this is special.' And soon they came." He said he told them England was a fascinating place to play soccer.

"No foreign player had as much impact in one English season as Jürgen Klinsmann," wrote Andrew Anthony in the *Guardian*. He had written a famous anti-Klinsmann article titled "Why I Hate Jürgen Klinsmann" for the newspaper in June 1994 before Klinsmann arrived but several months later wrote an article with the exact opposite headline, "Why I Love Jürgen Klinsmann," after watching the impact he had at Tottenham. "The application, and the willingness to look elsewhere for innovation, are defining Klinsmann traits. And also bravery. He often put his head where other players would hesitate to place their feet."

Klinsmann was named Football Writers' Player of the Year in 1995, only the third foreign player so honored, after leading Tottenham to seventh place in the standings, the club's highest finish in five years. Klinsmann had also led Tottenham to the semifinals of the FA Cup. The number of foreign stars in the Premier League has soared since then, and it has become the most popular league in the world, broadcast to numerous countries.

"The time in England had a lasting impact on me," Klinsmann says. "I experienced so many wonderful moments over there, especially on the field, that really influenced me. The team spirit, the way everyone sticks together, the way everyone goes to the Players' Bar after the match for a beer—those are some of the things I'll never forget. I'd never have a problem going to England to deal with whatever issues the media have. Even if it's the most sarcastic thing, I'd just say okay."

A Tottenham teammate from Scotland, Colin Calderwood, who became a friend of Klinsmann's in London, said the German forward had a thoroughly positive impact on the whole team. "He was very humble and down to earth," Calderwood said in an interview with the London *Sunday Times* in 2004 just after Klinsmann agreed to coach Germany. "He was not somebody looking to go to premieres or be on the front of magazines. And he was obviously somebody who thought about the game. He knew what he wanted, the correct way to train, and you knew when he was unhappy with things. I think he found the game here easy to embrace, he liked the camaraderie, which was different to some of the places he had been."

Klinsmann still enjoys a towering reputation among Tottenham fans, and many hope he'll return one day as their coach. "Before he came to Tottenham, there was a lot of skepticism about him being a typical continental European—someone who would go down whenever there was an opportunity," said Trev Jenner, a London police officer and lifelong Tottenham fan. "But so many fans took him into their hearts when he made fun of himself by doing that dive after his very first goal. It was his style of play and his work ethic that Tottenham is all about. He made Tottenham better. It was the effect he had on the team, he raised them up, he was the personality on the pitch who inspired them. He always came across off the pitch as someone intelligent, articulate, and polite. He came across as someone who really understood what he was talking about, not just with football but with life in general—a very rounded and grounded person. He wasn't full of himself. He was an okay guy, a decent fellow, and a bloody good footballer."

When you talk to Klinsmann about that enduring admiration,

he smiles and says, "I'll always carry that club in my heart because it's a really special place. There's still a lot of appreciation both ways. We have the highest respect for each other. The Spurs fan is very, very emotional and a hard-core fan who wants you to work your backside off. But he also wants a certain spark to the game. They want players who make a difference, and I think they realize over time if you're a player who makes a difference, a player who's always trying and inspiring the others as well."

After that awkward start, the media quickly warmed to Klinsmann. "His elevation to Player of the Year reflects a remarkable achievement for a man who has totally changed the way he was perceived by the English, who for historical and sporting reasons are not always inclined to welcome Germans with open arms," wrote Mike Collett, soccer editor of Reuters in a 1995 article titled "Klinsmann Crowned Kaiser of English Soccer." "But outstanding team play, great goals, sportsmanship and a sharp sense of humor have enabled Klinsmann to win over the English. Even those who previously derided him as a cheat winning dubious penalties with theatrical dives now admit the German international captain has brought class, entertainment and quality to the English Premier League."

Klinsmann remembers his time in Tottenham as special. "It was probably the most exciting year I played in my career. So many things happened in the one season. The way people treated me, the way they welcomed me everywhere I went in England—I never enjoyed playing on a team that much in my career. I would never have a problem going to England."

He returned to London for the second half of the 1997/98 season, transferring from Italy's Sampdoria in December to try to help Tottenham avoid relegation. Spurs were stuck deep in the drop zone, in eighteenth place and in danger of being relegated, at a time when Klinsmann himself was looking to get his game together for the 1998

World Cup in France—his final tournament. Both Spurs in the Premier League and Klinsmann in Serie A were finding it hard to score until he arrived back in London. The reunion was a tonic for both. Klinsmann was no longer the overwhelming force he had been three years earlier, but he still gave the whole club a lift. He scored nine goals in fifteen appearances, and Spurs rose in the standings, finishing four points above the relegation zone, in fourteenth place. Six of his nine goals came when it mattered most—down the stretch in the final three games, including four in a spectacular 6–2 win against Wimbledon on May 2, 1998, which effectively secured Tottenham's place in the top flight. It was a brilliant performance that Tottenham fans still talk about decades later. The next week he scored his final club goal, a spectacular long-range blast against Southampton.

# BACK IN GERMANY

KLINSMANN WOULD HAVE liked to have stayed longer in England. But with the Euro 96 looming, he was feeling an urge to play in European club competitions again—the Champions League or the UEFA Cup. FC Bayern Munich president Franz Beckenbauer, aware of Klinsmann's escapades for Tottenham in England, was beckoning him to come back to play for Germany's top club. He said it was impossible to turn down Beckenbauer and called it an honor to be pursued by the "Kaiser." He had signed a two-year contract with Tottenham but with an option allowing him to leave after one year.

"It took me a while to decide," he says. "The people treated me so well in London that it made it difficult to say I'm leaving. But on the other hand, there was a chance to go to a club with the chance of playing for a title in Germany and to play in Europe in the next season, which was a big thing. I hadn't won a lot of trophies, and with Munich there were prospects to win titles. That was an important aspect. But there was another reason too. I wanted to find out if my wife and I could imagine living in Germany someday after living abroad for so long, and whether I'd be able to adapt to the German mentality."

After six years playing abroad for three different clubs in three different countries and learning three foreign languages, Klinsmann returned to Germany in 1995 as a conquering hero. He was suddenly seen as a multilingual ambassador for Germany, not only an outstanding player but also an articulate young man. Most German soccer fans understood by then that he had gone abroad not as a mercenary trying to make a fortune as some others had but instead to grow on the field and off. His soaring popularity in England had not gone unnoticed in Germany. It was the top story in the national media on the day he signed with Bayern, pushing politics and other news off the front pages and broadcast news.

He had left West Germany for Italy as a promising young national team player in 1989 and was now returning as an international star—one of the most popular Germans ever to set foot in England—and a stalwart on the *Nationalmannschaft* with less than a year to go before the next European Championship, which was to be played in England. Many Germans were surprised by what a thoughtful cosmopolitan character Klinsmann had become after his time abroad.

"Because he spoke the grammatically dubious Swabian dialect of his birthplace, people had once tended to write him off as simpleminded," *Der Spiegel* wrote. "Then he went off to the 1996 European championship in England and suddenly started giving news conferences in English. Once his accent was stripped away, his intelligence emerged. In the public eye, he became a cosmopolitan, a man smart enough to think beyond the next match."

A lot had changed in Germany during those six years Klinsmann was away, and he had changed a lot too. Even though Germany had so much going for it, with Europe's strongest economy and bright future after its peaceful reunification, he kept running into grumbling Germans and surprisingly negative sentiment in his home country, even though Germans had so much to be grateful for: The

Cold War that shaped the country for the last half century had ended peacefully, Germany was reunited, and the standard of living was one of the highest in the world.

"It surprises me to see so much moaning and groaning by some people in Germany," he told Horeni in *Klinsmann*. "There's such a fantastic social welfare system in Germany. There's far more poverty in Italy, but yet the people there are somehow happier. I'd wish there could be a bit more of that tolerance in Germany."

He discovered that the media in reunited Germany had also become more aggressive during his absence, resorting to increasingly unscrupulous methods to try to penetrate his private life. Klinsmann was always open and candid with the media about soccer questions, at the stadiums and after practice. But he had shielded his private sphere, and that was generally respected. In the late 1990s, however, the media were becoming more aggressive than ever before, and some journalists had no compunction about crossing lines.

"When I went back to Germany, people were expecting me to be a typical German," he says. "It caused problems when certain media and some people realized that I wasn't the same person I'd been when I left Stuttgart. I learned a lot abroad. It wasn't easy in Germany. A lot of Germans aren't as relaxed around well-known people as the English, the Italians, and the Americans. I kept feeling I had to justify myself for everything for Germans."

Klinsmann recalls one day when he bumped into a commercial TV network crew lingering outside a doctor's office, waiting to intercept him on his way to an appointment. Commercial TV networks had grown in size and influence in the years Klinsmann was abroad, and the media competition had greatly increased. The journalists were aggressively demanding answers from him, going much further than the press would have pursued their story in 1989. He said he had the feeling the journalists wanted him to strip down right then and there to show them his injury. "There was a pushiness that I hadn't experienced in Italy, France, or England," he says.

Before he signed with Bayern, he had to discuss a promise he had made to his father years earlier that he would never, ever play for FC Bayern Munich. Bayern Munich is Germany's most popular team, but it is also its most reviled team in many parts of the country, especially outside the state of Bavaria. Bayern Munich's perennial dominance of the Bundesliga—and its annoying habit of poaching the best talent from rival Bundesliga clubs—makes it a target of wrath for millions in Germany who will cheer for any team that Bayern happens to be playing against. It is a deep-seated animosity that drives the popularity of soccer in Germany, filling stadiums and boosting TV ratings whenever and wherever Bayern plays. It is that utter loathing of Bayern that makes their games so popular—even a tie or narrow defeat can be reason enough to cheer. The reaction is similar in England with Manchester United, in Spain with Real Madrid, and in Italy with Juventus Turin.

"When I transferred to Bayern Munich, I broke a promise I made to my father," Klinsmann says. "I had to talk to my father about it first and ask him to absolve me from that promise." Siegfried Klinsmann, who over the years had been hanging team pictures of whatever club his son was playing for in his bakery, gave him his blessings but said Bayern would nevertheless not become his favorite team.

Klinsmann was thirty-one when he started playing for Bayern, a veritable all-star team in Germany. He had seen a lot of the world but was eager to win championships as he entered the twilight of his career. He had helped West Germany win the World Cup in 1990 and Inter Milan the UEFA Cup in 1991, but there had been no trophies since then. He was hungry for more titles, and Bayern regularly battled for title in three competitions each year: the Bundesliga, the German Cup, and it almost always qualified for the Champions League.

"My reason for leaving the Spurs for Bayern Munich was only to play on a bigger stage," says Klinsmann. "I wanted to play top European soccer again." Later on, as the coach of Germany and then the United States, he would encourage his players to make similar moves up by telling those who were ready to strive to play for clubs that compete in the Champions League.

Ahead of the European Championships in England, Klinsmann helped Bayern Munich win the UEFA Cup in 1996, scoring a record fifteen goals in twelve matches. He also helped Bayern win the Bundesliga in 1997. He was the team's leading goal scorer in both seasons.

Bayern had not won any European titles since 1976 and seemed somehow content to dominate the domestic league, winning the Bundesliga with numbing regularity rather than trying to compete to win the Champions League against the clubs in Italy and Spain that were regularly spending enormous sums in the transfer market to acquire the world's best players. Klinsmann had experienced a lot of different coaching and management styles during his years playing abroad and saw many of the traditions at Bayern as counterproductive to success in modern soccer. He disagreed, for instance, with the practice of cloistering the players at a hotel ninety minutes away from Munich on nights before home games and challenged the prudence of making all their training sessions open to the public. He also raised questions about whether Bayern was truly hungry to succeed in the Champions League, noting Bayern hadn't pulled off any success at the European level in ages.

His criticism was at first dismissed, but it became clear that

Bayern executives were nevertheless listening. The prematch hotel confinement before home matches was quietly dropped, Bayern started closing some practice sessions to the public, and the club began aiming higher in Europe again—winning the Champions League in 2001 after losing a heartbreaking final two years before to Manchester United, a game in which they gave up two last-minute goals.

His two years in Munich were not free of turbulence. Klinsmann had a number of run-ins with Bayern captain Lothar Matthäus that filled the tabloid headlines. Klinsmann refused to take part in any kind of Faustian bargains, or "pacts with the devil," by abandoning principles for favorable coverage, with Germany's most powerful daily newspapers, such as *Bild*. That made him a target whenever things were not going well on the field.

In his second season in Munich, 1996/97, he was feeling somewhat stifled by coach Giovanni Trapattoni's defensive style of play, which the Italian coach whom Klinsmann had played for at Inter Milan had brought with him north over the Alps to Bavaria. Klinsmann, who had enjoyed the high-scoring attacking soccer in Monaco and London, complained openly about it, but nothing changed. His frustration erupted near the end of one game late in the season at home against Freiburg. With ten minutes to play in a scoreless draw, Trapattoni sent in Carsten Lakies, an amateur player from Bayern's third team in the regional league, to replace Klinsmann. It was the twelfth time in thirty-one games that Klinsmann had been subbed out. He jogged off the field full of anger. He was so furious that he kicked a hole in an advertising container behind the bench, a four-foot-high battery made out of particleboard. He later apologized to his coach and teammates for the outburst.

"We all make mistakes," he says. "I go out and kick a hole in the advertising barrel. I knew I made a mistake and was crying in the locker room to Trapattoni and apologizing for what I did. And he hugged me and said, 'Jürgen, it's all good, you lost it and it's okay.' We all make mistakes. For me it's important that you say you made a mistake. I said, 'Guys, I screwed up.'"

Bayern held on to win the league championship, but Klinsmann left Bayern at the end of the season after two campaigns in Munich, returning first to Italy to play for Sampdoria for half a season and then moving to London to play for Tottenham in December 1997. He had planned to stay at Sampdoria for the full season, but he suffered an injury early in the season and a change of coaches after that. With the 1998 World Cup coming up, Klinsmann was eager to get as much game experience as he could, so he returned to London, where he was welcomed with open arms. As he was thirty-two and his career was in its twilight, Klinsmann's next major focus was on playing for Germany in one last World Cup in 1998.

# WINNING THE EURO
# IN ENGLAND

ALONGSIDE HOSTS ENGLAND, Germany was among the favorites to win the 1996 European Championships played between Klinsmann's two seasons in Munich. It was seen as one of the last chances for Germany's golden generation, a group of players that had won the 1990 World Cup and reached the finals of the 1992 Euro in Sweden—and was expected to do better than it did in the 1994 World Cup. Germany's coach, Berti Vogts, had done some housecleaning after the 1994 disappointment, and one of the key changes was making Klinsmann his captain.

Vogts admired Klinsmann's fighting spirit and independent streak. He had seen how Klinsmann had raised his game in every tournament—the Euros in 1988 and 1992 as well as the World Cups in 1990 and 1994. He had seventy caps and the integrity needed to lead the team after the humiliation and division of the 1994 World Cup. Klinsmann had also been a close second in the European Footballer of the Year vote in 1995, behind George Weah of AC Milan, in a vote of journalists. He was also third in that year's FIFA Ballon d'Or (FIFA World Player of the Year) vote by coaches and captains. Including Klinsmann, there were only seven players left from the

1990 World Cup team who made up the core of the 1996 team play-ing in England.

Klinsmann knew England well and urged Vogts to let the team stay in the heart of London with all its hustle and bustle. German teams traditionally stayed in isolated villages away from fans, jour-nalists, and crowds. But Klinsmann had seen in the United States at the 1994 World Cup how important little things—such as the atmosphere—were to the team. He thought the energy of central London would benefit the team and, along with some other senior players, urged the DFB to base the team in the center of the pulsat-ing capital. Vogts agreed to a compromise: If the team reached the semifinals, they could move to a London hotel from their original base in the countryside.

With the right chemistry this time and several outstanding play-ers from formerly Communist East Germany on the united German team, such as sweeper Matthias Sammer in fine form, Germany started the tournament with a 2–0 win against the Czech Republic in Manchester that Klinsmann had to sit out due to a yellow card he had received in their last Qualifying game six months earlier. Klins-mann, who had been Germany's leading scorer in the Qualifiers with nine goals, was back on the field and scored twice in their 3–0 win over Russia, again at Old Trafford. Their third and final group match was a 0–0 tie against Italy at the same venue. Germany beat Croatia in the quarterfinal 2–1, again in Manchester, with Klinsmann get-ting his third goal but suffering a calf injury. The team collected its reward from Vogts for advancing to the semifinals and moved to a hotel in London for the semifinal game against England.

Klinsmann missed Germany's victory over England in a penalty shoot-out, 6–5, at Wembley Stadium in the semifinal, sidelined with the calf injury. Determined to play in the final against the Czech

Republic, he spent up to ten hours a day working with the medical team treating his injured calf, including up to six hours a day of massages. After five days of treatment, he was able to run again the day before the final and was fit just in time. Germany won 2–1 in overtime with a golden goal from Oliver Bierhoff.

"I think the European Championship was a great experience for us because there was a great camaraderie on the team," Klinsmann says. "We knew that with the team spirit we could compete with the other teams. We fought all the way through the tournament and played really good soccer. We might not have had the best team— Italy was probably a little bit better—but we had the strongest will." It was also the first championship for reunited Germany, and the victory by the team made up of players from both East and West may have helped the country overcome some of the lingering divisions. "I think soccer helped build a bridge between East and West Germany."

# FINAL WORLD CUP

KLINSMANN HAD HOPED to crown his international career for Germany two years later with another World Cup win—in 1998 in France. Germany got off to a bright start with a 2–0 win over the United States, with Klinsmann getting the second goal that sealed the win. Their second match was a 2–2 draw against Yugoslavia, and the third group game was a 2–0 win against Iran, with Klinsmann scoring his second goal of the tournament.

A shadow was cast over Germany after the second group game, in Lens, against Yugoslavia. A French policeman was savagely attacked and nearly beaten to death by a German hooligan. Horrified by the violence and the shame it brought to all of Germany, DFB leaders Egidius Braun and Gerhard Mayer-Vorfelder at first considered pulling the team out of the tournament. A shocked Berti Vogts announced he was ready to resign if that happened and was only talked out of it by Klinsmann, his captain. The attack against the policeman and the accompanying focus on fan violence had far-reaching reverberations back home and took the focus off soccer.

In the Round of 16 game against Mexico, Germany came from behind to win 2–1, with Klinsmann getting a late equalizer with a quarter hour left before Oliver Bierhoff scored the game winner just before the final whistle. Five days later, Germany was eliminated by Croatia by a score of 3–0 in Lyon, its worst World Cup defeat since losing to Hungary 8–3 in the preliminary round at the 1954 World Cup. It was a national humiliation. Germany had played well until defender Christian Wörns was sent off with a red card in the 40th minute. Robert Jarni scored to put Croatia ahead 1–0 just before halftime. Goran Vlaović (80th minute) and Davor Šuker (85th minute) got late goals to seal Germany's fate.

Klinsmann's dream of winning the World Cup had once again been dashed, and his talented team had failed to live up to its great promise and the pretournament expectations. He struggled to find the words to describe the depth of his despair. He did not talk in detail about the loss until several months later—to a group of journalists he invited for a meeting in Geislingen, where his career had begun some two decades earlier.

"I knew we didn't have quite as balanced a team as in '96 and that too many of the players had problems of their own," Klinsmann told the reporters. Several months before the tournament, he had announced plans to retire from both club and international soccer after the World Cup. "But that everything would be over so abruptly? Eleven years on the National Team, all finished and over just like that! After the final whistle, I was in a trance while waving to the fans together with Oliver Bierhoff. We felt ashamed. We were totally wiped out. It was a total shock in the locker room, for all of us. You're under all this extreme pressure and so full of energy. The emotions just explode. Everyone who came in would let go and just rip into everything, the referees and everything. It was like a world had collapsed. I remember the chancellor coming in and trying to console us. And, yes, I remember huddling and crying together with guys like [Jürgen] 'Koks' Kohler, [Thomas] 'Icke' Hässler, and Andreas Köpke. It took me days to get over all that."

It was Klinsmann's last game. From 1981/82 with the Stuttgarter Kickers to his club final game, for the Tottenham Hotspur in 1997/98, Klinsmann had played a total of 614 soccer games for his clubs and scored 277 goals. He'd won three club championships—the 1990/91 UEFA Cup with Inter Milan, the 1995/96 UEFA Cup with Bayern Munich, and the 1996/97 Bundesliga with Bayern Munich.

From December 1987 to June 1998, he played 108 games for West Germany and Germany, and scored a total of forty-seven goals, including eleven at three World Cups and six at European Championships. He was captain from 1994 to 1998. He won two titles as an international player—the 1990 World Cup with West Germany and the 1996 European Championship with Germany. He had no regrets. He had got everything he could out of his talent. He was satisfied. It was time for something new.

# PART III

# THE GERMAN REVOLUTION

# A JOB OTHERS
# WOULDN'T TOUCH

JÜRGEN KLINSMANN'S ENTRY into coaching was more a coincidence than anything else—thanks to a sequence of unlikely events
in quick succession that took place in Portugal, Germany, and California. It was triggered by a chance encounter that changed his life—
and his almost accidental entry into coaching helped revolutionize
the way soccer is played in Germany.

It was in the summer of 2004 when his path crossed with an old
friend from Germany, a former coach who happened to be traveling
through California. It was at the same time that the German Football Association was facing a monumental crisis after the German
*Nationalmannschaft* suffered yet another ignominious failure in a tournament, a rout exacerbated by Germany's demoralizing inability to
find a new coach.

When he retired as a player in 1998, Klinsmann was looking
for a total change of pace and a clean break. He had only just turned
thirty-four and was interested in doing something constructive
with the rest of his life. He was eager for new challenges and wanted
to make a mark in a new field. He was not necessarily interested in
coaching, a capricious and perilous occupation where the focus

seemed increasingly to be on the short-term results. He turned down several offers to coach, including to become a player-coach in what was then a four-year-old league in the United States, Major League Soccer.

Instead, he savored his quiet life in Southern California. He enjoyed spending more time with his young family and exploring fields away from the game after seventeen eventful years as a pro playing at the highest levels. In a country where soccer was still an exotic sport, few people he encountered in his new home had a clue about who he was. And that was fine with Klinsmann. "I wouldn't go to America to watch soccer—I'd go to get away from it," he famously quipped after the United States was picked to host the 1994 World Cup. And that was exactly what he was doing.

Most of his neighbors in the seaside town of Huntington Beach, where he and his family first settled in 1998, would not have recognized Klinsmann at the time. In Germany, England, and Italy, he still had rock-star status and would have trouble walking down a street without attracting a crowd of fans, autograph seekers, and well-wishers. In Germany, to this day he still has to wear a baseball cap and sunglasses if he needs to get anywhere in a hurry. He realized the futility of trying to launch a post-playing career in Europe, where whatever he did would inevitably be seen through the prism of his soccer-playing days.

There are few things less interesting to Klinsmann than living in, talking about, or dwelling on glories of yesteryear—and being a prisoner of his past was the last place he wanted to be. He usually waves off questions about his playing career with a short "That was a long time ago." Ask him why, and he says, "I'm just not the kind of person who looks back." The future is far more interesting.

For all Klinsmann's neighbors in Orange County knew, the tall, fit-looking blond guy from Germany spending so much time camped out at Starbucks on his computer was another one of those independently wealthy thirty-somethings, of which there was no shortage in the upscale beach towns south of Los Angeles. He was just another tanned face in the crowd who had somehow made a small fortune and was enjoying life.

Staying incognito in America wasn't always easy. Klinsmann had to politely turn down interview requests from local sportswriters who *did* know who he was. He told them he cherished the anonymity of America and, sorry, but he didn't want to jeopardize that. "Klinsmann the player doesn't exist anymore," he says. He wanted to be an ordinary dad who picked up his children from school and hung out at cafés.

Klinsmann stayed in shape. He worked out sixty to ninety minutes every day and sometimes for up to three hours—running, swimming, cycling, or in the gym. Weighing 170 pounds and standing five foot eleven, Klinsmann is as fit now as he was when he retired nearly two decades ago. "It's just an incredibly great feeling to work out and let off steam, tension, and aggression," he says. "Even as a kid I had an obsession about running around and playing. Even on vacation at the beach I feel like I have to go jogging, that my body needs it. If I don't go running or play soccer or get a workout, I can end up in a bad mood." He also plays in pickup soccer games that sometimes become spirited with local players and college students in Orange County. Aside from helping him stay in shape and providing an outlet for all his energy and competitive streak, the pickup games are a lot of fun and have helped him better understand the sport, quite literally, at the grassroots level.

Near the end of his playing career, when he was Germany's captain, Klinsmann might have started thinking and sounding like a coach—in soccer the captain is much more than the symbolic leader that captains tend to be in many U.S. sports. Because there are no breaks in the action and the noise in stadiums holding up to ninety thousand people can be deafening, the captain plays a vital linchpin role and is the brains on the field. But coaching, he thought, was just not in the cards.

"It was just a total coincidence that I got into coaching," Klinsmann says. It took the crisis in Germany and an unusual intervention from his former Germany coach Berti Vogts after a chance visit to his house in California to trigger a sequence of events that got him into coaching. He hasn't looked back since.

"It was all because of Berti," Klinsmann says. "He was on vacation traveling around in California in an RV with his son, and he called me up and said, 'We're going to be driving nearby and we just wanted to say hello.' I said, 'Are you kidding me? Come to my house and we'll have a barbecue.' "

The story began to unfold a few weeks earlier, in late June 2004, shortly after mighty Germany had stumbled badly, once again, in a major international tournament. Germany had been unceremoniously knocked out of the Euro 2004 in Portugal in the first round, after losing one and drawing two of their three Group Stage matches. The entire nation of eighty-two million felt pain, and a certain degree of shame, after the team lost their last Group game, 2–1, to the Czech Republic. That defeat in Lisbon on June 23 was all the more humiliating because the Czechs were not even using their strongest eleven players on the field. They had already qualified for the Knockout Stage and were resting several of their best players for that. Before that debacle, Germany had played two uninspiring ties—1–1 against the Netherlands and an eminently forgettable 0–0 against lowly Latvia—that were difficult for most Germans to stomach.

It was the second straight early exit from the Euro at the Group Stage, a nightmare for such a soccer-obsessed country. Germany's whole cultural identity and national self-esteem seemed in doubt when the national soccer team struggled so pitifully on the field. Even casual observers could see there was something terribly wrong with the team if it could not even make it out of the Group Stage for the second European Championship tournament in a row. It had become such a boring and predictable team, playing methodical, results-oriented soccer without panache or even the results.

German teams usually head into the big World Cup and European Championship tournaments brimming with confidence and expectations of winning the title, or at a minimum staying in the tournament to the semifinals. But not only did Germany get knocked out at Euro 2004 far too early, but the team also played abysmally in Portugal, with none of the style, determination, or even the grinding dominance that had been its hallmark in the 1970s and '90s. Germany had been a soccer power for much of the previous half century, consistently one of the world's best teams, winning three World Cups and three European Championships. But in 2004, the world seemed to be laughing at Germany and its steep decline to nineteenth place in the FIFA rankings.

It wasn't just the two quick exits from the European Championships in 2000 and 2004. On top of that, Germany had suffered a baffling and embarrassing four-year losing streak against the world's top teams. After beating England 1–0 in October 2000, Germany lost nine straight games to the top-ten-ranked teams: France (twice), England, Argentina, Brazil, the Netherlands, Spain, Italy, and the Czech Republic. It was another indication that something had gone terribly wrong with this once powerful team.

Before any heads could roll, Germany coach Rudi Völler stepped down. He fell on his sword less than twelve hours after the Euro 2004 debacle, to make way for a successor and a fresh start. He had actually been a desperation choice four years earlier. The DFB had plucked Völler from within its own search committee to find a new coach after the luckless Erich Ribbeck was forced out in the wake of the previous first-round exit from the Euro in 2000, held in Belgium and the Netherlands, after only two years in charge—the shortest reign for any postwar German coach.

Völler, originally hired as an interim choice, had long been popular with the fans for leading an erratic German team all the way to the final in the 2002 World Cup, which was played in Asia for the first time—hosted by Japan and South Korea. Germany had stumbled in qualifying rounds and only barely attained one of the thirty-two spots for the finals with a play-off win against Ukraine. But Germany's strong run at the World Cup was, in retrospect, due at least in part to an easy path to the final. After Group Stage wins against Saudi Arabia and Cameroon as well as a draw against Ireland, Germany was far from inspiring in the Knockout Stage. Riding on its reputation as a tournament team, Germany managed to grind out three straight colorless 1–0 wins against Paraguay in the Round of 16, the United States in the quarterfinals, and then cohosts South Korea in the semifinals.

Miraculously, Germany managed to avoid playing any top team until the final. The powerhouses of the game and pretournament favorites, such as Argentina, Italy, France, Spain, Portugal, Croatia, and England, had all already been busy knocking each other out. It wasn't until the final that Germany faced Brazil, one of the world's stronger teams—and lost 2–0 despite playing its best game of the tournament. On the surface, many in Germany thought it had a top team in 2002 because the team reached the final, but the comparatively trouble-free route to the final had only masked underlying weaknesses, shortcomings that were mercilessly exposed in 2004 in Portugal.

One of the enduring images of the 2004 tournament was of the once popular Völler being mercilessly booed by inconsolable German fans in Lisbon's Estádio Alvalade as he tried to thank the crowd for their support. Back home, fan frustration turned briefly violent when rioting broke out in Hamburg and angry fans rampaged in the country's second-biggest city after watching the game on giant outdoor television screens. Völler had a contract with the DFB through the 2006 World Cup, and in his first interviews after the debacle he said he wanted to continue. But he changed his mind overnight and resigned.

Bleak as it was, the situation got even worse in the weeks after Völler quit. The DFB first tried futilely to persuade Völler to stay in the job and then stumbled repeatedly in its attempts to find a replacement. No one was courageous—or foolhardy—enough to take on one of the most prestigious, if also most perilous, jobs in soccer. It came with a high price for failure: a reputation in tatters.

The DFB, the world's biggest federation of any sport in the world, with 6.8 million members, first got snubbed when its top choice, Ottmar Hitzfeld, unexpectedly turned them down. He had just left the coaching job at FC Bayern Munich, and had long been seen as the ideal candidate. He had won the Champions League with both Bayern Munich and Borussia Dortmund, and had for a number of years been interested in what was considered to be one of the plum posts in the soccer universe. Hitzfeld, who was fifty-five years old at the time, met with DFB president Gerhard Mayer-Vorfelder on June 27, but three days later turned down the offer, saying he needed a break after ten years of coaching in the Bundesliga. It was such a shocking rejection that Hitzfeld's decision was among the day's top national news stories, and it reverberated for days.

Another suitable candidate, Jupp Heynckes of Schalke 04, also unexpectedly had no interest in taking over the team that had been so badly beaten at the Euro in Portugal, as did Arsène Wenger, Arsenal's German-speaking coach from France. "The German team has a lack of technical proficiency and a lack of creativity," Wenger said at the time. "That's why it won't be able to keep up with teams like Brazil. That's the truth."

The DFB turned next to Otto Rehhagel, who had just led Greece to win the European Championship against long odds with an unattractive backward, destructive defensive style of play that few people in Germany wanted to see. But Rehhagel was a big name that summer after leading long-shot Greece to the title, celebrated in the tabloid press with a new Greek nickname, "Rehhakeles," for bringing glory to the country. He had never made it a secret that he wanted the top job in Germany. He toyed with the increasingly desperate DFB and its *Trainerfindungskomission,* its committee to find a new coach. Rehhagel was offered the job and thought about it for two days. But then on July 10 he too said, *"Nein!"* He simply wanted to be asked by the DFB before turning it down to stay with Greece.

It was incredible. Here was one of the world's top coaching jobs, vacant less than two years before the start of the World Cup, the world's showcase tournament to be played at home in Germany— and no one had the courage to take it. Certainly, it might have seemed like a *Himmelfahrtskommando,* a suicide mission, to many coaches after Ribbeck and Völler had both been eaten up in the job and seen their reputations all but ruined by the high media and public expectations. Their once sterling names had been irreparably tarnished for their troubles. The DFB had had only seven coaches in the previous fifty-four years, and yet there were no takers for this assignment. What had gone so wrong?

Other names were bandied about and discarded. Still others pre-emptively took themselves out of consideration. Several bowed out or begged off for one reason or another—including Werder Bremen's respected coach Thomas Schaaf, Felix Magath of VfB Stuttgart (on his way to Bayern Munich), and Freiburg's Volker Finke. Other names discussed and either rejected or unavailable included Hungary coach Lothar Matthäus, Cameroon coach Winfried Schäfer, Guus Hiddink and Dick Advocaat of the Netherlands, and Denmark's Morten Olsen. The notion of a foreigner coaching a great soccer power like Germany at the World Cup it was hosting was hard for many Germans to contemplate, but these were desperate times, and the DFB realized it might have to hire its first foreign coach—albeit one who at least spoke German—to lead the National Team.

The situation was looking increasingly ominous for the DFB when, out of the blue, they got an early morning phone call from California. Berti Vogts had been one of those seven postwar coaches, in charge of the *Nationalmannschaft* for eight years from 1990 to 1998 and at their last moment of glory in 1996 when they won the European Championship in England. He had a successful record, but expectations were impossibly high for the team from newly reunited Germany that was supposed to be even more dominant than the West Germany team that had won the 1990 World Cup three months before reunification.

"Thanks to reunification and the East German players on the team, Germany will be unbeatable for many years to come," former coach Franz Beckenbauer had famously predicted in 1990. Some Germans actually believed that. The East German players quickly integrated into and helped strengthen the pan-German team.

Germany's unification of the national soccer team was much faster, more thorough, and more successful than the merger of the two Germanys itself. After forty years of Cold War division and two completely different economic and social systems, eastern and western Germany struggled at times, in fits and starts, to grow together during the 1990s. There are still many East-West disparities in income, pay, and political outlook that fuel lingering resentments after more than a quarter century. The formerly Communist east is also poorer than the west, and with such limited financial resources in the east, no teams from any of the five eastern states have managed to stay in the top division, the Bundesliga.

The eight years of Vogts's reign in the 1990s felt short at the time and also disappointed the inflated expectations of a united Germany, as sketched out by Beckenbauer. Vogts had been the *Bundestrainer,* the national team's coach, when Germany won the Euro 96 in England eight years earlier, but he was blamed for losing the Euro 92 final to Denmark as well as for the two disappointing quarterfinal exits at the 1994 and 1998 World Cups. Some of the media in Germany had made life difficult for Vogts, in part because of his unwillingness to cooperate with the country's most powerful mass-circulation newspaper, *Bild,* as Beckenbauer had. Vogts refused to leak his starting lineups and other exclusive information to *Bild* and its *Sport-Bild* sister publication. He came under fire in the trendsetting tabloid-style newspapers when the results failed to match the lofty expectations. But Vogts, who was one of the key players on the legendary West Germany team that won the World Cup in 1974, remained widely respected in soccer circles as a *Fachmann* whose expert opinion was still valued at the DFB headquarters in Frankfurt. So he picked up the phone in California and called Horst R. Schmidt, the general secretary at the DFB headquarters in Frankfurt.

"I've just found your next *Bundestrainer* for you," Vogts told an incredulous Schmidt from nine time zones away. "Seriously, I've just found the next German national team coach for you, someone who's got exactly what you need—Jürgen Klinsmann. He's the only one who can save you now. You don't have a lot of time before the World Cup, and he's your man. He's the one to change things that need to be changed. He'll put things on the right track. Trust me."

Schmidt laughed out loud at first, dismissing the suggestion of picking a recently retired former player without any coaching experience living in the United States for one of the prime jobs in sports—for many Germans, the job of *Bundestrainer* is almost as important as, if not actually more important than, *Bundeskanzler,* the chancellor of the German government.

It seemed ludicrous at first. Klinsmann had made plenty of enemies at the DFB with his direct, open, and critical style. But Vogts wouldn't back down, displaying the same trademark tenacity that had led to ninety-six international caps in his career as a defender for West Germany, earning him the nickname *"Der Terrier"* for his doggedness on the field.

Vogts urged Schmidt and then his boss, DFB president Gerhard Mayer-Vorfelder, who joined the phone call a few minutes later, to at the very least give Klinsmann serious consideration. Vogts argued that his former captain was exactly the kind of breath of fresh air the DFB needed for its World Cup at home—an open-minded, hardworking, ambitious, headstrong, disciplined, and creative reformer with integrity who was already well known outside Germany. On top of all that, Vogts said, his optimism could help show the world what modern Germany was about. "If you don't have a coach yet, then just sit down and talk to him. You'll see what I mean."

# BARBECUE BRAINSTORMING

VOGTS HAD IN FACT only been passing through Southern California on his way to Las Vegas when he stopped to call Klinsmann, who persuaded him and his sixteen-year-old son Justin to stop by. They had their barbecue and talked for hours over red wine in Klinsmann's backyard overlooking the Pacific Ocean. It was a lively discussion *auf Deutsch* that stretched into the evening. Like a pair of Monday-morning quarterbacks, they agonized over the direction of soccer in Germany and talked about what the *Nationalmannschaft* needed. And they talked about the coaching job that, bafflingly, no one seemed willing to take on. There was no dwelling on the past; the conversation was focused on Germany's future—even if neither realized how far their brainstorming by the beach would actually take them.

As former World Cup winners for West Germany, both had been pained by the rout at Euro 2004 and the general malaise in Germany. But being pragmatic Germans, Vogts and Klinsmann saw the crisis as an opportunity. They were full of constructive ideas about reforms that were needed. It was an analytical chat around the barbecue, not unlike the myriad conversations German fans were having around the world that July.

But this barbecue ended up becoming much more. It's tempting to step back for a moment to contemplate whether the fate of German soccer might have been different and to wonder whether Germany would have won the 2014 World Cup without the exciting style of soccer Klinsmann introduced in 2004—or whether this book would even have been written—if Vogts hadn't made that phone call. "It's one of those stories that you get with soccer," Klinsmann says with a smile. "A lot happens by chance."

Klinsmann had no coaching experience at any level but had gotten his pro coaching license four years earlier at a special seven-week DFB training course, a *Sonderlehrgang,* set up for distinguished former international players who had at least forty caps and had won a World Cup or European Championship. It was a onetime opportunity. The crash course, first proposed by Vogts, compressed seven months of lessons into seven weeks, with 240 hours of classroom lessons instead of the 560 hours normally required. After all, Vogts reasoned, anyone who had won a major title with the *Nationalmannschaft* had seen and learned a lot about the game and thus deserved at least partial credit toward the license. The license is a requirement for any coaching job in Germany.

Vogts's idea was to try to ensure that his "golden generation" of players would stay connected to the game and the DFB as coaches, and be able to pass along their wealth of experience to younger players. A total of nineteen participants—a veritable who's who of German soccer at the time—took part in the course in Hennef, a hamlet on the Sieg River near Bonn. Among those attending alongside Klinsmann were former Germany internationals Matthias Sammer, Andreas Köpke, Jürgen Kohler, Andreas Brehme, Stefan Reuter, and Guido Buchwald, as well as Doris Fitschen—from the women's national team with 144 caps. Joachim Löw, who had coaching experience in Switzerland, Stuttgart, and Turkey without having a pro license but who had nevertheless been allowed to coach Karlsruhe

SC with special temporary exemption from the DFB, also took part. Hennef is where Klinsmann got to know Löw, who would later serve as his assistant coach—and become his handpicked successor as Germany's coach from 2006.

Klinsmann says he had never really given much serious thought to one day becoming a coach after he retired as a player in 1998. "Coaching was not something I had on the radar," he says, although he adds he hadn't ruled it out either. "But I knew I wanted to stay connected to the game. I love it. It's been my life."

At the time, Klinsmann was more interested in spending as much time as possible with his family. He'd met Debbie Chin through friends when she was living in Italy, and they got married in 1995. Their son, Jonathan, was born in 1997, and their daughter, Laila, in 2001. As a player in his final season in 1997/98, Klinsmann wasn't happy about missing out on so much of his young son's life because of the traveling, training, and games away from home for his clubs and country.

He and his wife decided in 1998 to settle down permanently, to put down roots in a place where his son could grow up feeling a sense of belonging. "Our thought process was, 'Where should he grow up?' And we said, 'Well, he has to grow up close to family.' We thought he needs to have his cousins, uncles and aunts, and grandparents, so that leaves us with just two options: Stuttgart, where my family was, or Orange County, where her family was."

Klinsmann yearned for a lifestyle for himself and his family that was as "normal" as possible, unencumbered by his past fame. He certainly did not want to end up like his childhood idol, Gerd Müller, regaling German tourists with stories of his glory days at a roadside steak house somewhere. "We knew they could grow up as normal kids here in California," he says. "In Germany, they would have always been seen as the kids of the former player and would always be connected with the name and the past—and I didn't want to live in the past. I wanted to start a new chapter of my life. In Europe I couldn't have gone to a local college and taken classes, but here that was all possible. It made it easier to get back to an ordinary life where I wasn't always confronted with my past. My past wasn't important to anyone here."

He dove into the computer courses at a nearby university, learning about the powers of the Internet before it was ubiquitous, and started taking Spanish lessons—learning his fifth language after German, Italian, English, and French. He also served as an ambassador for Germany's 2006 World Cup bid, accompanying Chancellor Gerhard Schröder on trips to promote Germany's World Cup application and discussing all kinds of political and social issues with the German leader. Schröder was, as it happened, a former striker himself on his hometown club TuS Talle in the *Bezirksliga,* the seventh division in the German soccer pyramid.

Klinsmann had also been busy as a driving force behind a charity for underprivileged children called Agapedia, Greek for "Love for children." He had founded the charity in Germany, Bulgaria, Moldova, and Romania with several close friends. All the proceeds from his farewell match in 1999, attended by fifty thousand fans in Stuttgart, were donated to charity.

Despite all he was doing in California, Klinsmann reluctantly agreed to take part in the 2000 training course for coaches. He was gradually opening up to the idea of one day becoming a coach, or at least having an option to coach. Vogts and the DFB had urged Klinsmann to help round up some of the former National Team players, as an erstwhile captain, for the crash course.

Coaching qualifications are taken seriously in Germany. It's not quite the same as graduating from the military academy in West Point, but there is the Hennes-Weisweiler Akademie in Hennef, which is affiliated with the University of Cologne's sports department. Coaching candidates have to complete rigorous training in a wide range of fields to get their *Fussball-Lehrer Lizenz,* or coaching license. But Klinsmann, living happily with his growing family in California, said at first he didn't want to take part in the course.

"Berti said we need to keep this generation in the game, and that was his thing," Klinsmann says. "The federation agreed with Berti, but they asked me to organize it. I said, 'Okay, I can call up some of the players but, guys, it's your thing. I'm good. Life is okay.' And then they said, 'Okay, you organized it so now you have to take part too.' I said, 'Me? Coaching license? I'm just getting my head around life in America. I'm good.'" But Vogts and the DFB wouldn't let up and finally persuaded Klinsmann to take part in the course.

Two years after retiring, Klinsmann reasoned it wouldn't be such a bad idea, after all, to have another option open for down the road. In any event, he always enjoyed learning something new. Klinsmann got the *Fussball-Lehrer Lizenz* and even helped create an innovative social project and Internet portal for young soccer players and children as an extracurricular project together with his classmates and their eight instructors at the DFB training course. It was called *FD21—Fussball in Deutschland im 21. Jahrhundert* (Soccer in Germany in the Twenty-first Century)—and is a platform designed to get children interested in soccer.

Even after obtaining the license, Klinsmann still wasn't looking for a coaching job. He had done his internship for the DFB license at the Los Angeles Galaxy under the tutelage of their coach, Sigi Schmid, and enjoyed it. However, he stayed focused on his family and aspects of soccer other than coaching—until Vogts stopped by for that fateful barbecue. Listening to Klinsmann's critical analysis of Germany's weaknesses, it dawned on Vogts that his former captain would be the ideal candidate for the Germany job, exactly the catalyst for change that the team so urgently needed.

"We sat there talking for hours, and at one point Berti says, 'Could you ever consider coaching the German National Team?'" Klinsmann says. "I said, 'I think you're kidding.' I said anyone should be interested, and who wouldn't be excited about a job like that? But I'm not sure the DFB was ready for my ideas. And so I told him I couldn't imagine the DFB would ever go for that."

Klinsmann and Vogts both knew the DFB well. There were some powerful barons inside the stodgy organization whose creativity was limited to guarding their fiefdoms. There are more than two hundred officials and functionaries at the DFB's Frankfurt headquarters alone, many of them entrenched in a ponderous old way of doing things. Klinsmann sensed they would resist such a revolutionary idea as turning over the reins to an outsider and neophyte. Not only did he lack coaching experience, he was also living halfway around the world in a country where soccer was considered a minor sport. That was the probable response under normal circumstances, but the DFB was in crisis mode after so many of their coaching choices had given them the cold shoulder.

"I told him that if I ever did take a job like that, I'd do it based on all the things that I've learned in all the difference places I'd been— and that a lot of that knowledge comes from the United States," Klinsmann says, fully aware that would normally not go down well with those in power, who at the time didn't take the United States seriously when it came to soccer. Vogts nevertheless kept offering enthusiastic encouragement. "Berti told me that is exactly what Germany needs—a totally different direction because the old direction isn't working anymore."

Vogts assured Klinsmann he wasn't kidding at all, that he was dead serious. The day after Vogts made the call to the DFB, Klinsmann got a call from headquarters. Horst R. Schmidt, one of the DFB's officials in charge of its operations, was on the line.

"He said he was just talking to Berti, and Berti said they might be able to talk to me," Klinsmann recalls, a smile spreading across his face at the memory. "I thought, 'Are you kidding me?' But he said, 'We'd just like to sit down with you and explore the issue with you.' And I said, 'Okay, but I'm not going to fly all the way to Frankfurt for a coffee.' He said he understood. I told him I could obviously read about what was going on in Germany right now and understood all the stress and pressure they were having after Hitzfeld and then Rehhagel said no. So I said, 'Why don't you fly to New York and I'll fly to New York, and we can meet sort of halfway at a place near the airport—in and out.' And that's how it happened."

Klinsmann turned to his two business partners, Mick Hoban and Warren Mersereau. They had formed a sports marketing and business development company called SoccerSolutions about five years earlier, not long after Klinsmann moved to California. It was a consultancy created to help soccer clubs and companies succeed with branding, strategic planning, research, event management, business development, and networking. "I learned to think more strategically," Klinsmann says of his experience with SoccerSolutions. Loath to rest on his laurels or live idly off his name, Klinsmann was instead determined to take on challenges and learn new things. He got to understand the business aspects of soccer in America, in the areas of youth development, training camps, and designing soccer facilities. Through SoccerSolutions, Klinsmann worked as a technical adviser on the design of the stadium that became the home of the Los Angeles Galaxy. Klinsmann urged Tim Leiweke, the president of Anschutz Entertainment Group, which owned the club, to include a roof over the grandstands, even though it almost never rains in Southern California, to give the stadium a more authentic soccer feeling.

Klinsmann was quickly warming to the idea of coaching after the meeting with Vogts and the call from Frankfurt. "I hadn't really thought about coaching before that," he says. "But it was nice to have the coaching license and that experience. Obviously, I had a lot of experience getting to know about different coaching methods over the years as a player. You play in Italy and learn about things there, and then France and then in England—and obviously you knew the German coaching approach. I got to learn about the American approach to coaching too. It was a nice mixture of knowledge to have, but at the end of the day it comes down to the practical side."

He talked to Hoban and Mersereau about the DFB meeting set for New York and how to prepare for it. "I said, 'I think they are actually serious, so we need to put together a paper, we need to be prepared.' They said that's no problem—we've been talking about these things for years. We'd been talking about all those issues like, What would you do if you were running a team in a professional environment? How would you do it? How would you structure it? What's your vision and how would you execute it? What's your philosophy? And things like that. We put that all down to paper in an hour or two. I modified it a bit after we talked and then presented it in New York to Mayer-Vorfelder and the DFB."

Klinsmann flew to New York with his pitch, and they spent five hours at an airport hotel on July 21 talking candidly about the coaching job. Mayer-Vorfelder and Schmidt seemed surprisingly open to his ideas and point-blank criticism of the way the national soccer team in Germany had been falling behind other nations. But the conversation wasn't limited to soccer and the team's poor performance on the field. They also talked about what the tournament could mean for Germany, as a showcase for the nation that gives an inordinate amount of thought to its image in the world. Klinsmann discussed Germany's soccer traditions and how to revitalize them, and how he saw a strong, confident soccer team as an essential part of the country's postwar heritage. Showing up at the World Cup at home with a team that could get knocked out at the Group Stage was just not acceptable.

Germany had come a long way since World War II ended in 1945, a long way since the Berlin Wall fell in 1989 and the country reunited in 1990. There were many in the DFB, the government, and industry as well who were hoping the World Cup could be a showcase for Germany to exhibit what a modern, efficient, and exciting country it had become. In some countries in Europe and elsewhere, Germany's entire history was still often unfairly reduced to the twelve years of the Nazi reign, Adolf Hitler's crimes against humanity, and the destruction of World War II. But Germany was far more than its Nazi past, and the World Cup could be a once-in-a-lifetime chance to show what modern Germany was all about.

Klinsmann's presentation focused on soccer, but it also touched on the larger social, political, and historical aspects of what winning the World Cup could mean. He dove into areas that went far behind the kind of conversations that Mayer-Vorfelder and Schmidt were accustomed to in job interviews with coaches. Klinsmann talked about creating a team that played to Germany's traditional strengths, a team that could become better than its constituent parts and inspire a wave of healthy patriotism in a country that had long feared too much national pride. Having played for top clubs in Italy, France, and England, Klinsmann had spent much of his life abroad. He was able to convincingly explain why Germany's standing in soccer had fallen in recent years, dropping behind other more dynamic countries. Its methods were outdated and its cautious style of play was woefully out of step with the modern play of the best teams in the world. He was also confident a strong team playing exciting soccer could be propelled forward with the kind of patriotic support that he had seen in Italy, France, England, and the United States.

"We're making ourselves look ridiculous as a soccer association," Klinsmann told them. "We can't allow that to happen as a nation because we're hosting the 2006 World Cup, which is going to be the biggest event in Germany for decades to come. It's the chance to show the world a new image of Germany. We have the opportunity to create a national brand."

Klinsmann offered the DFB leaders an unvarnished truth. It hurt. He was only telling them what, deep down, they already knew but had not wanted to admit: that Germany had cut a poor figure in recent years and had had one miserable, subpar showing after another. It was time to change all that with decisive, painful reforms, and he outlined his plans for a modern coaching structure and strategies.

"They just said, 'Whoa, where does this come from?'" Klinsmann recalls of the meeting. "I said this is just coming from a different angle, this is just a different way of looking at things. And I said if you would take on a project like that—I called it a project, which a lot of people didn't like—then you need to understand the bigger picture of the World Cup 2006 in your own country. And I'm living outside the country; I'm looking at it from the outside. I said, 'Maybe you want someone looking at it from the inside. If that's the case, that's okay, but then you've got to find someone else inside Germany to do that. I'm not going to live in Germany 24/7. I love Germany, but I'm half American now and half German. My kids are growing up in the United States.'"

Klinsmann's hard-hitting presentation had convinced the DFB bosses—especially Mayer-Vorfelder. He just wasn't used to that kind of a multidimensional presentation from a prospective soccer coach. Klinsmann had outlined his plans, explaining what he had in mind, what he had learned in the United States over the last six years, and how, if he were coach, he would assemble a team of experts in various fields to be part of his team. "MV," as he was sometimes called, had known Klinsmann as a player since the 1980s when he was the president of VfB Stuttgart and had tried—in vain—to keep him in Germany before he moved to Italy. Mayer-Vorfelder had long been a senior minister in the regional Baden-Württemberg state government and had seen a lot of presentations over the years, but nothing like what Klinsmann had put on the table.

"Mayer-Vorfelder was especially into all this," says Klinsmann. "He looked at me and said, 'Do it your way! Do it your way! I'll back you up.' I think the DFB didn't know anything about how much my life had changed after I stopped playing. But one thing they did know was that I had the courage to take this on."

Mayer-Vorfelder notes in his autobiography, *Ein Stürmisches Leben: Erinnerungen* (A Stormy life: Memories), that he was surprised by Klinsmann's willingness to consider the Germany job because he had repeatedly failed to get Klinsmann involved in coaching in the past. "I was already full of hope when we met in the New York hotel," Mayer-Vorfelder writes. "Then Klinsmann handed us a detailed master plan with a precise list of how he would run the team as coach." He was impressed but adds, "I could tell right away that Klinsmann and his ideas and methods would run into a lot of resistance at the DFB, with all its traditions. But I was sure that it'd be worthwhile to support him. German soccer needed a man with his kind of engagement and élan, with his enthusiasm and his drive. I promised him that I'd push his wishes and demands through at the DFB."

Klinsmann flew back to California and consulted with his wife about the job possibility, conferring with her and his "family council," the same way he had talked with his father as a fifteen-year-old while weighing the pros and cons of signing his first professional contract with the Stuttgarter Kickers or staying in school. He was certainly interested in the challenge, but he was enjoying his life in California and didn't need the job in Germany. Debbie asked him what would happen if he didn't take it. He told her that he would probably have regrets for the rest of his life if he didn't have the courage to give it a try. In that case there was only one answer: She told him he should definitely take the job.

Klinsmann phoned Vogts. "Hey, it looks like I'm going to be the new Germany coach, can you imagine?"

# NO TIME TO WASTE

Jürgen Klinsmann didn't waste any time implementing the sweeping changes at the DFB once he was hired—one day before his fortieth birthday, on July 29, 2004. There was an air of both excitement and apprehension in Germany about his hiring: enthusiasm from those who remembered his exuberance as a player as well as fears from some who fretted about his lack of experience. Germans are, even in the best of times, loath to experiment and prone to worry. And there were certainly risks involved in hiring an inexperienced coach two years before their home World Cup. His appointment, after another week of more detailed negotiations in Stuttgart about structures and his coaching staff, ended an uncomfortable five-week interregnum for Germany, an awkward void that followed the June 24 resignation of Völler, who had been a teammate of Klinsmann's on the West Germany team that won the 1990 World Cup. It marked the start of a new era for Germany—one of revolutionary reforms that transformed a plodding *Nationalmannschaft* that had been living off past glories into a dynamic, insatiably goal-hungry squad playing an entertainingly fast-paced, attacking style that the country would soon fall in love with and the world would come to admire.

Appearing at his first press conference as Germany's *Bundestrainer* as a young man in a hurry, Klinsmann announced his ambitious goal for the team—winning the 2006 World Cup. It was an improbably bold target for a team that had just gotten knocked out of the European Championships without a win in three games. He also said he wanted to reestablish German soccer as a brand the world would admire and made it clear that he wouldn't hesitate to identify the problems. He outlined his plans to overhaul the DFB, which in his eyes had become complacent, lethargic, and too set in its old ways of doing things, and to introduce state-of-the-art methods and performance analysis. The inertia at the DFB itself had become a part of the problem.

"The fans in Germany have the great hope and aspiration that we'll win the World Cup in 2006 at home—and that's my goal too," Klinsmann told the press. Deep reforms were urgently needed, he said, and warned that past successes wouldn't mean anything going forward: "We've got to open ourselves up and take a look at what's going on outside our borders. You can learn something from everyone."

His appointment was both exhilarating and controversial, for he had already run into a buzz saw of resistance and skepticism from parts of the German media, Bundesliga coaches, and even the DFB. Many could not fathom how the DFB could pick a newcomer for such an important job. It was bad enough in their eyes that he had never coached a team in the Bundesliga, but Klinsmann had no coaching experience at all. In fact, he had even spent about half of his playing career outside Germany, with only seven years' experience in the Bundesliga. Many, especially those who felt threatened by his plans to challenge the status quo, wasted no time in second-guessing him. If they hadn't seen the writing on the wall before he was hired, they heard Klinsmann's unmistakably clear message: "We've got to build up a new structure at the DFB." He said a free hand to open up the stuffy atmosphere at the DFB was an essential condition for taking the job.

Sportswriters and soccer experts alike viewed Klinsmann's trumpeted goal of winning the World Cup in 2006 as extraordinarily optimistic, if not downright foolhardy, in light of the embarrassingly poor run at the Euro 2004 and Euro 2000 before that. On top of that, there was a nagging angst that Germany did not have enough talented players on the team or in the pipeline for a good run in a tournament that was by that point less than two years away. The DFB and Germany's thirty-six professional clubs in the first and second divisions had started developing academies to improve the training for young players after the 1998 World Cup debacle. The programs, designed to improve as well as standardize coaching and opportunities for talented players, were expanded with a new sense of urgency after the dreadful showing at the 2000 European Championships. The number of full-time professional, licensed coaches increased from about one hundred in 2000 to about four hundred by 2014, according to Raphael Honigstein in *Das Reboot: How German Soccer Reinvented Itself and Conquered the World.*

But those programs were just getting off the ground in 2004, and it would take another six years for those players to have an impact on the senior national team. By the 2010 World Cup in South Africa, nineteen of Germany's twenty-three-man squad came through the academies into which the thirty-six pro clubs had invested more than half a billion euros since 2002. "They are largely responsible for producing Germany's dazzling and young World Cup team," wrote Karolos Grohmann in a Reuters article in 2010 titled "Germany Reap Benefits of Youth Plan," noting that hundreds of players had been trained for the clubs by their own academies. "Players such as Thomas Müller, Mesut Özil, Sami Khedira, Jerome Boateng, Holger

Badstuber and keeper Manuel Neuer, who are now household names worth millions of euros, emerged from this system."

Klinsmann was nevertheless confident in 2004 that if his reforms were given the time to take hold and he had the freedom to do what was needed, he could succeed in putting a competitive team on the field in 2006. "Winning the World Cup was part of our goal—but at the same time we wanted to get people in Germany excited about the National Team again," Klinsmann says, explaining why he set such a lofty target at the outset. "I kept saying, 'We have to start with the end in mind.' Germany is a soccer nation, and it's only logical for the coach to want and dream about going to the final. We also wanted to show that we could build an identity, one that everyone could identify with—fans, players, and everyone working for the team."

Among the barons of the Bundesliga who didn't like the idea of an outsider coming in and telling them how to do things was Schalke 04's old-school commercial manager, Rudi Assauer. He began attacking Klinsmann from the outset and dismissed his hiring as "a job-creation measure for a former National Team player." The cigar-chomping manager remained a die-hard skeptic. Schalke's coach, Jupp Heynckes, also bemoaned Klinsmann's lack of experience, even though he had been among the candidates who wouldn't take the job.

Klinsmann said Heynckes was "absolutely right about that." But he pointed out that he had a strong coaching team around him and a willingness to learn. He said he welcomed the constructive criticism. "The critics have the right to express their opinions and that's totally okay with me. Maybe we'll have the chance to meet and talk about it. Criticism can help you improve."

Klinsmann had anticipated the skepticism and tried to take it all in stride. "I knew coaches in Germany would raise their eyebrows and question what we were doing," he recalls. "They said I was crazy, they said that I was *'Der Amerikaner.'* But that was only part of the job. I made it clear when I took the job that I'd have a different view of things and was going to be thinking outside the box."

Having had a strong bargaining position because of the dearth of candidates and the DFB's dire predicament with just twenty-two months left until the start of the World Cup, Klinsmann felt empowered with a strong mandate from the top echelons of the association to push through the painful reforms that he felt were needed. He had no intention of compromising on the reforms that he had outlined in his talks for the job. "I didn't have time for diplomacy," he says.

Klinsmann was especially adamant on having the freedom to form his own coaching staff. Not only did he succeed in thwarting an attempt by Franz Beckenbauer on the *Trainerfindungskommission* to foist upon Klinsmann his own former assistant coach, fifty-five-year-old Holger Osieck, as a sort of watchdog, but he also got the DFB to agree to his plans to create a new position: *Teammanager.* It would be a new general manager post designed to free the coach from commercial, sponsorship, and some media duties so that he could concentrate more on the players and the team on the field. Klinsmann appointed his former Germany teammate and ally Oliver Bierhoff. With aplomb, Bierhoff took over many of the time-consuming responsibilities that had in the past piled up on the coach's shoulders—a position that Klinsmann has worked to create in the United States for the Men's National Team. "The general manager role was extremely important because he deals with all those day-to-day issues that could overload a coach. He worked with the media, the sponsors, and the federation."

Klinsmann picked Joachim Löw as his assistant coach. He had

gotten to know Löw as a classmate at the coaching academy in Hennef in 2000 and was impressed with his abilities to break down and succinctly explain even the most complex aspects of the game. "I was a pro for seventeen years and I'd never seen a coach who could bring those things across like Jogi," Klinsmann says. "I knew I needed to bring in high-quality people around me who would be strong in specific areas. I felt that because I didn't have any previous coaching experience, I needed an assistant coach who was strong in that area, and Jogi Löw was a very experienced coach, very good at practices, focused, and good at explaining things."

Three months into the new job, Klinsmann caused a stir in Germany with another revolutionary idea imported from the United States—hiring a sports psychologist, Hans-Dieter Hermann, from the University of Heidelberg. It was a radical idea for soccer in Germany at the time, fraught with stigma and eschewed by the self-appointed guardians of the game. Klinsmann encountered more than a little derision for the concept that a soccer player could benefit from a psychologist. But he prevailed.

"The developments in many of the other countries we played against were advancing further in some of these areas, but we hadn't moved forward at all," Klinsmann says. "The German National Team still had just a head coach and one assistant coach before who were responsible for just about everything. No one ever challenged that structure before. Everyone kept carrying on the same way. It was important for me to give the team a professional support system from the start. So that's why we had a co-coach, a general manager, a sports psychologist, a fitness coach, a chief scout, and a specialist for the media. I wanted a professional environment with a group of people I could trust blindly. This was one point that I wasn't going to compromise on, and told the DFB, 'If you want me, then we're going to do it that way or not at all.' If they didn't agree to that, I wouldn't have taken the job."

Klinsmann did not exactly endear himself to DFB functionaries beneath Mayer-Vorfelder, putting his finger on the wound of the Euro 2004 debacle. He pointed out that too many people had been asleep at the wheel for too long while other nations were catching up to and overtaking Germany. "Basically the whole thing needs to be taken apart," Klinsmann had said of the DFB in a German newspaper interview shortly before being hired—a devastating and painful analysis from an outsider about what had long been one of the country's most respected institutions. That, Klinsmann added for good measure, would be the recommendation of any consultancy looking at the DFB. "We need to question every single ritual. We need to do that continuously. Reforms don't happen in phases. Reforms need to be part of an ongoing process."

And that is exactly what Klinsmann did from 2004 to 2006. He set out on his program to change the mentality of the DFB and brought in his new ideas on coaching, training, nutrition, and fitness. In his quest to turn things at the DFB upside down, if not completely take it apart, he challenged everyone to push themselves for higher goals and to be open to new ideas no matter where they came from. His goal was to get the country behind the team again by playing a captivating style of soccer.

"To inspire those fans emotionally, we realized early on that we needed to play a type of soccer that would excite people," Klinsmann says. "We can't play a fearful style, we can't hang back and play counter-break soccer and hope for a set-piece goal. We have to take it to them, we're going to attack, we're going to be doers. That's what this country is about. We're reunited, it's amazing. We're Germany. We're a country of doers. So I said we have to shake things up, we have to give our players the belief we can do it, we have to become better in every aspect of the game, we have to throw it all out there. We have to provoke the people who think we can hold on to the old ways. Hold on to what? The old ways weren't working anymore. They didn't work in Portugal. If our way doesn't work, at least we tried to do it the way we thought was the right way to go, and then they'll kick us out."

He was also at pains to empower the players and encourage independent, feisty thinking. Remembering his own experiences about what he liked and didn't like as a player, he took steps to keep top DFB officials as well as important sponsors away from team gatherings as much as possible, ending the long traditions of sponsors mingling with the players. Sponsors and some at the DFB grumbled, but the changes were welcomed by the players, who found those elbow-rubbing gatherings at best a nuisance.

Some of those ideas he imported from the United States—to the shock and chagrin of the German soccer establishment. What on earth, they thought, could a major soccer nation like Germany possibly have to learn from a soccer minnow like the United States? Klinsmann knew the answer to that—plenty.

He caused more anguish at the DFB within his first few months by installing not only a sports psychologist but also a Swiss scout, Urs Siegenthaler, alongside the American fitness trainers from a company called Athletes' Performance. Weren't German scouts and fitness trainers good enough? DFB officials bemoaned. Klinsmann was upsetting German pride left and right in his quest to find the best for his team. He also invited motivational speakers from different fields outside soccer to come to team meetings to help his players envision the prize of winning the World Cup at home. As part of the efforts to expand their minds and way of thinking, players went to museums, watched PowerPoint presentations, gave archery a try, played table tennis tournaments, and were handed lists of recommended reading that included a book of rules for team conduct. Klinsmann was upsetting the status quo—and was in the process opening himself up for criticism from the media, Bundesliga coaches, and DFB officials, all of whom had been leery of his methods in the first place.

"The American fitness trainers were criticized in Germany before they even had a chance to start," Klinsmann recalls, still somewhat astonished by the narrow-mindedness. They were brought in to help improve his players' performance, fitness, and strength, and to reduce susceptibility to injury. "Over the years they've specialized in individual training programs for athletes, no matter what sport they're in. I think there's a lot more potential in this area. If you can improve the jumping ability of a center forward, that could lead to maybe two or three more headed goals per year—and one of them could be in the World Cup."

The fitness trainers from Athletes' Performance were ridiculed by some at first, but they have long since become an integral part of the German team, playing an important role in helping the country win the 2014 World Cup and to reach five straight finals or semifinals in big tournaments. In a tacit acknowledgment of the wisdom of Klinsmann's ideas, most Bundesliga teams now have fitness and mental trainers as well.

"We'd stopped moving forward in our thinking with soccer," Klinsmann says. "But we had to open up and take in information from other areas. I think you can learn a lot from Americans, from the French, and even from the Japanese. It doesn't matter at all if the people who share knowledge are from Germany, America, or South Africa."

Long before he returned to coach Germany, Klinsmann had met Mark Verstegen, the founder and president of Athletes' Performance, while doing consultancy work for the Los Angeles Galaxy. Always open to an eclectic mix of ideas, Klinsmann was instantly fascinated by the specially tailored training methods and grasped their potential, perhaps remembering his own extracurricular sprint training for the VfB Stuttgarter Kickers two decades earlier that had helped him cut his time for one hundred meters by nearly 10 percent. Klinsmann often talks about the possibility that an extra 5 to 10 percent can make the difference between winning and losing. Verstegen's company had been working with a variety of different athletes since its founding in 1999, including NFL, NBA, and MLB players.

They designed fitness and training plans with the aim of bettering stamina and performance to meet both the needs of the individual players as well as the team's high-paced style of play. Verstegen even taught players yoga to improve their flexibility and focus, training that was seen at the time as blasphemy to skeptical German sportswriters.

An important aspect of the training was encouraging players to take responsibility for improving strength and endurance on their own rather than relying on others to get them or keep them in top shape. "We tried to educate the players, saying, in a way, 'You decide your own future,'" Klinsmann says, a philosophy he has pursued as the U.S. coach. "We said, 'We'll give you the tools, but you have to decide yourself if you want to get to that next level.' It's not those on the outside who will decide how their future or their career goes. It's the players themselves who decide how far they can go."

The German media was downright hostile when they first saw the muscular American fitness trainers with crew cuts, looking perhaps more like Marine drill sergeants than soccer coaches, barking orders at the nation's *crème de la crème* while the players went through their odd-looking paces. The media's thinking was: Americans?

*Absurd!* What could Americans possibly know about soccer that Germans didn't know already?

" 'Get your J Lo up!' a trainer barked at players during a pre–World Cup workout in 2006," wrote Scott Reid in the *Orange County Register* in an article titled "Ever the Realist, Klinsmann Pushes U.S. Soccer Team Forward." " '*Wie bitte?*' one confused player asked. What? The trainer responded, 'Your (rear),' referring to the singer's famous derriere."

There was a press conference in Germany with Verstegen shortly after he joined the team in 2004, where more than one hundred German sportswriters—a typical German media pack following the *Nationalmannschaft*—grilled him mercilessly about his qualifications, indignantly demanding answers about what they referred to as silly-looking training methods. They had just been watching Germany's elite players seeming to struggle to move forward with giant rubber bands tying their ankles together, doing sprints with the elastic bands around their waists, and heaving heavy medicine balls.

That's not the way German soccer teams had trained before, even though the players themselves quickly grasped the benefits of the tailored workouts. German soccer workouts had not changed much in the previous decades, often enough just a jog through the forest followed by tactical training and ball-handling skills. That might have been enough in the 1950s, '70s, and '90s, the decades when mighty West Germany teams won their three World Cup titles and two of their three European Championships. But the game had advanced and was much faster now. And the game Klinsmann wanted his team to play would be even faster. He said adjusting Germany's training sessions was long overdue.

Klinsmann looks back at that criticism of and resistance to change as typical of Germany at the time. "In a certain way there was the jealousy factor involved because they thought, 'How can we have Americans working with our best players? It's a country with little soccer history,'" Klinsmann says. "But it wasn't about history. It's about quality. They're top-class quality. It split people in Germany. Some had open minds and said, 'This is great, this is cool, we should look abroad and see what's going on out there,' but there were other, conservative-minded, people who said, 'We've already won the World Cup three times so why change?'"

As part of Klinsmann's efforts to modernize the training and improve as many aspects of his players' performance as possible, players started wearing high-tech cardio and GPS gadgets from Athletes' Performance to constantly monitor their heart rates and speed during workouts. They recorded players' sprint times and data about their ability to change direction. They sent off any players the computer determined needed remedial work to train with separate groups.

They were able, for instance, to compare data on an identical drill from week to week to see if the players were getting more or less done in the same amount of time—a sign of waxing or waning fitness. They could also follow the players' recovery by studying how quickly their heart rates recovered after high-intensity phases. In between watching and sometimes even playing directly with his team on the field, Klinsmann could be seen darting over to the sidelines in the middle of workouts to peer at a computer that was compiling real-time fitness data.

Klinsmann brought another tool from the United States that radically changed the landscape of locker rooms in Germany—ice baths. The large plastic tubs filled with cold water into which players climbed after games and workouts became a fixture in the dressing room, with some players swearing by the virtues of the cold-water plunges and others swearing *about* standing in barrels of water with a temperature of a chilly fifty to sixty degrees Fahrenheit.

"It comes from American football originally, and Athletes' Performance started it in soccer with the German team in 2004," says Klinsmann. "It helps you regenerate faster, pulls out the inflammation from training and games, and it makes your recovery easier. But it's a pain in the B for at least ten to fifteen minutes. Some players don't mind, others hate them." He also introduced those regeneration methods and monitoring devices to FC Bayern Munich when he returned to Germany to coach the country's premier club. "We put some built-in ice baths into the performance center at FC Bayern in 2008. Really nice! It definitely wakes you up! We use ice baths as well with the U.S. teams."

Klinsmann brought other ideas about best practices with him from the various stops in his playing career. He had watched and learned from more than twenty coaches, including some of the masters of the game: Arie Haan at VfB Stuttgart, Giovanni Trapattoni at Inter Milan, Arsène Wenger at Monaco, Otto Rehhagel at Bayern Munich, Argentina's César Luis Menotti at Sampdoria, and Ossie Ardiles, another Argentine, at Tottenham, as well as Franz Beckenbauer and Berti Vogts for Germany. "You never stop learning," Klinsmann says. "Things I learned then are still flowing into my work now."

Some of the ideas also came from coaching seminars and workshops he attended around the world. With an eye on the long term and a desire to help lastingly turn soccer around in Germany, he had new ideas on the organization of the DFB, youth training, and standardizing training and systems.

Aside from his internship with the Los Angeles Galaxy in 2000, Klinsmann has spent short periods of time as a visiting coach studying the methods of Phil Jackson and the Los Angeles Lakers, Pete

Carroll and the University of Southern California football team, and Duke basketball coach Mike Krzyzewski. He picked the brains of those American coaches and brought some of those ideas with him back to Germany. Ironically, Klinsmann is sometimes criticized in the United States for importing too many ideas from Germany and Europe into the uniquely American system, but he bristles at the notion there is anything wrong with borrowing good ideas from elsewhere.

"I don't use the best practices found in the United States or Germany," he says. "I use the best practices from around the world. If I see something in Australia or China or Europe that is extremely good, I put my nose into it and want to learn about it. I've been at coaching symposiums in Brazil and other places around the world, and there's often interesting stuff you can pick up there, too."

As the new Germany coach, he vowed to bring in younger players and redoubled efforts to find new German talent that might have been off the radar in the past—especially Germans who had gone abroad as youngsters. With all due respect for the Bundesliga, Klinsmann noted with some concern that there was only one player on Germany's Euro 2004 team—backup goalkeeper Jens Lehmann—who was earning his salary playing on a club in England. Fourteen years earlier there had been nine players on the 1990 World Cup–winning team on clubs abroad, himself included. It was yet another sign of Germany's decline as a great soccer nation. Within two years of Klinsmann's arrival, there would be half a dozen Germany players on the rosters of top foreign clubs in the best leagues in England and Spain.

"We gave a lot of thought to what the German National Team should stand for: What are our strengths and what are our weaknesses?" Klinsmann says. "What does the outside world think of it now and how do foreigners look at us now? Our strengths are aggressiveness, taking it to the other teams, and playing offensively with a willingness to take risks. That's the game we wanted to show the world but also in every workout until it was automatic. We needed to get that into our heads and hoped that word would get out to our opponents that that's the way we're going to play."

# NEW STYLE

Jürgen Klinsmann's main aim at first was to revamp the team's style of play and change their image as unimaginative drones. He wanted his team to be on the attack from the start and not to play cautiously as in the past. "I always liked to score goals and take risks," Klinsmann says. "My aim was to have a system set up for attacking soccer." He is an unabashed advocate of an offensive, high-scoring style of play. A former striker himself with an insatiable appetite for goals, he wanted his team to play at a higher pace with zonal marking defense combined with increased pressure. He wanted to cultivate a hunger for goals so that his players would keep pushing for more goals even when they were already comfortably ahead.

It would be a notable departure from the old-school style of soccer where teams defended deep in numbers in their own half of the field and tried to wear down and destroy the other team's offensive game, hoping to score a lucky goal first off a counterattack or set-piece goal—a goal scored following a rare stoppage in play as the result of a foul or the ball going out-of-bounds—from a free kick or corner kick, and then try to sit on their lead, protecting a 1–0 advantage until the final whistle. That traditional German grind-it-out style of unattractive soccer featured a sweeper, in the mold of Franz

Beckenbauer. The sweeper would roam in front of the back line to anchor the defense and then, after winning back possession, try to slow the game down if necessary by deliberately walking the ball forward, looking to make an incisive pass and waiting patiently for an opening downfield.

Open, attacking soccer was the kind of play that Klinsmann had always enjoyed when he was on the field himself, especially under Ardiles at Tottenham, and is a style he is convinced that most players themselves enjoy. It is certainly the game the millions of spectators watching in the stadiums and on television prefer.

"I'd rather win a game 4–3 than 1–0," Klinsmann says without hesitation. "At the end of the day, that's what the fans want to see— attractive and attacking soccer. They want to see excitement. They want to go to the stadium and see goals. Yes, there can be an exciting 0–0 game too. But at the end of the day it's all about scoring goals."

At the same time he was eager to empower his players and get them on board for such a high-paced, high-risk style of play. He first offered his National Team's players a choice on which direction the team should go—in part because the offensive, attacking approach demands a far higher level of fitness and far more running.

"It was important right from the start to clarify what we wanted to stand for," Klinsmann says. "We sat down with the team in September 2004 and asked, 'What kind of soccer do we want to play? What kind of style do we want to develop, and who are we?' We said we wanted to attack, to create pressure, to be very aggressive and fast paced, and to make things happen instead of waiting for them to happen. We asked the guys if they thought that suited us, and the answer was, 'Yes, that's exactly what we are.' The most important thing is that the players believe in what they're doing. This wasn't something developed by the coaches. It was influenced by what's going on around the world, by the top teams competing in the Champions League. So that was our road map and everyone was on board: We're going to attack, that's our style."

Instead of the seemingly endless lateral passing back and forth around the midfield in a patient, often tedious, search for a crack in the other team's defense that had been a hallmark of past Germany teams with their sweepers, Klinsmann's players were encouraged—and drilled—to push the ball forward with quick vertical passes and flood into the other team's half of the field. Instead of the conventional results-oriented style that earned past teams the unflattering nickname "Tanks" in other countries, the Germans were suddenly playing a delightfully creative, high-energy attacking style. The goal was to swarm out on the attack the instant they won possession of the ball.

"We worked step-by-step to make our game more offensive, getting the ball forward quickly and pressing our opponents in their own half," he says. "We drilled it into everyone's heads that we wanted to attack. Forwards score goals when they feel confident, so we tried to give them that confidence."

Klinsmann wanted to build the tactics around quick attacks with quick feet and quick thinking, exhorting his players to take more risks going forward while at the same time being willing to run far more than in the past to cover for each other, cleaning up defensively more often for each other when necessary. They were taught to put pressure on the opponents in their end of the field and speed up the transition to attack whenever they regained possession. Toward those aims, he shifted his team to a 4-4-2 formation from the more cautious, defensive-minded 3-5-2 formation. The defenders were also encouraged to push farther up the field to pressure the opponent in their own half, with especially the fullbacks expected to support the attack.

The language of players' post-match interviews changed, too. The forwards, midfielders, and defenders suddenly started sounding like a much more fully integrated team with the offensive players speaking of a shared responsibility for letting in goals because of their own errant passes in the forward third of the field, and defensive players talking, with a twinkle in their eyes, about their newfound scoring opportunities.

Klinsmann wasn't afraid to shake up the hierarchy of the team that had so ingloriously crashed out of the Euro less than two months earlier. He set the tone for the new era on his first day with the team, August 16, 2004, with a demotion that reverberated for the next two years and still upsets some people in southern Germany: He took away the captain's armband from thirty-five-year-old goalkeeper Oliver Kahn, in the twilight of his career, and gave it to twenty-seven-year-old midfielder Michael Ballack, who was heading into the prime of his career for Germany. Klinsmann also stripped Kahn of his starting guarantee, throwing open the goalkeeping job to competition with Jens Lehmann in the belief that competition for the job would make both goalkeepers, and the entire team, better.

The tragic hero of Germany's strong run to the 2002 World Cup final, Kahn had five clean sheets—five games without giving up any goals—and allowed in only three goals in six games. But, unfortunately, Kahn blundered when it mattered most in the final. He fumbled a long-range shot from Rivaldo in the 66th minute with the score still tied at 0–0. The loose ball was tapped in by teammate Ronaldo for Brazil's opening goal on the way to a 2–0 victory. Kahn might have still been at the peak of his powers in 2004, and he certainly would have been a mainstay on any other Germany team led by one of those more experienced coaches who turned down the job. But to Klinsmann, Kahn represented an old-fashioned style of soccer, staying planted on the goal line, which he wanted to break away from with his more offensive-minded team.

Klinsmann did more than just strip Kahn of the captain's armband he had held for two years under Rudi Völler. He wanted the captain of this new dynamic team to be in the heart of the action, a better-connected linchpin between the forwards and defense. Klinsmann also made it clear that the goalkeeping job, and *every* position on the team, would be an open contest for 2006. There were no job guarantees anymore. Kahn was still the first choice, but he was going to have to share duties in rotation with his backup, Lehmann, and a final decision on who would play at the World Cup would be made later—much to the annoyance of the coaches and executives at Bayern Munich, who represent a powerful lobby in German soccer.

But Lehmann, who played in the Premier League for Arsenal, had developed into the more modern type of goalkeeper who clearly fit better into Klinsmann's offensive strategy. Lehmann could spark the attack with quick, crisp passes forward, and he possessed a fearlessness about leaving the box more often—a sort of hybrid between a goalkeeper and sweeper that has become the prototype for Germany keepers ever since. A new style of *Torwart*, a goalie whose skills were honed in the fast-paced Premier League, Lehmann was an important part of the offense and helped initiate the attacking game, whereas Kahn represented the old school of thinking where the keeper digs in on the goal line.

It was a courageous, if controversial, decision coming right at the start, but it set the tone for Klinsmann's two years in charge. In an instant, he had emphatically made clear that he was throwing open the competition on the team for every position, if even one of the most senior and respected players' jobs was no longer set in stone.

Klinsmann was not only challenging Kahn, who had been something of a folk hero in Germany after the glorious run to the final in the 2002 World Cup, to either raise his game a few more percentage points or get out of the way. He was also running the risk of provoking Kahn's club, FC Bayern Munich, which not only wields a lot of clout in the Bundesliga but can also hold considerable sway over parts of Germany's mass-circulation media such as *Bild*. Indeed, Klinsmann's decision to challenge Kahn at the start would later be part of the critical background noise against Klinsmann a year and a half later when the results weren't going Germany's way for a while. Kahn's demotion was likely one of the reasons that Bayern's commercial manager, Uli Hoeness, later started his attacks against Klinsmann's decision to continue living in California and commuting to Germany, ostensibly an issue of trifling importance, which *Bild* nevertheless turned into a campaign against the coach.

Yet on the team itself, Klinsmann's moves to break up the pecking order at the start of the World Cup cycle was a welcome signal that competition for every position would indeed be open. Klinsmann made it abundantly clear that he was starting from scratch and past performances didn't mean anything anymore. That had been his own personal conviction, and now he was applying his philosophy to his players in the hopes it would raise everyone's game. The clear message was that those who worked hardest, both with the National Team and, more important, on their own and with their clubs, would be rewarded for their efforts. "Sports is all about not standing still," Klinsmann says. "You have to prove yourself again and again."

With a decade of experience as a player himself and 108 caps to his name for Germany, Klinsmann fully understood and appreciated the dynamics that followed whenever the *Leitwolf*, the leader of the wolf pack, had retired, been dropped from the team, or emasculated. From the point of view of the fans and the cut player himself, it can often appear to be a hardship when once highly regarded and distinguished players are unceremoniously dropped from a National Team headed to a tournament. But for many of the other players on a team, it represents a golden opportunity to move up the hierarchy or onto the starting team. Seasoned veterans can usually read the writing on the wall and more often than not opt to retire from their national teams before they are forced out.

There was hardly a better moment to unleash new creative energy from players than at the start of a new two-year cycle leading up to the next big tournament. Klinsmann knew how positive energy could have a trickle-down effect on the players who had been starters eager to fill the void at the top, or among players on the bench seeing a chance to move up into the starting team. The public and media might harbor feelings for their sentimental favorites or a meritorious established player cut down or cut out, but for younger or other players on the team, the smell of fresh blood in the water was an opportunity not to be missed.

"Competition always has a stimulating effect," says Klinsmann, who despite fierce opposition from Bayern Munich and its acolytes stuck to his policy of rotating the country's two superb goalkeepers until picking Lehmann just two months before the World Cup started. The competition seemed to make both of them better. "That's what sports is all about—performance, competition, and mutual respect. It made Ollie better because he had to go out there and try to defend what he had built up over the years. It was an open position, like every position on the team."

Klinsmann was determined to turn his lack of coaching experience—which he never made any bones about—into an asset. He pointedly elevated the status of his assistant Joachim Löw and relied heavily on input from other coaches on the staff and external experts, like the fitness trainers. That model was still in place on the team when it won the 2014 World Cup. At workouts, Klinsmann trained with the forwards while Löw worked with the defenders, and the goalkeepers trained with their specialist coach, first Sepp Maier and then his successor, Andreas Köpke.

"As a player, I was used to the head coach having everything under his control and he would only sometimes ask his assistants for advice," Klinsmann says. "For the sake of learning quickly, I had to act differently and handed decision-making responsibilities over to my staff. It eliminated hierarchies and had an overall positive effect."

The new Germany team under Klinsmann got off to a flying start in the second half of 2004 with five wins, two draws, and just one defeat in its first eight games—the newly offensive-minded team scored twenty goals, or 2.5 goals per game. It was a refreshing change of pace. The strong run included impressive draws against two of the best teams in the world, Brazil and Argentina. The only blemish was a 3–1 loss at South Korea just before Christmas. It was a quick and powerful turnaround for the team that had scored just two goals in its four matches—or 0.5 goal per game—before Klinsmann took over.

And it was a welcome change in style for long-suffering fans who were used to the team hunkering down after taking a 1–0 lead. The 2.5 goals per game scored in those first eight matches were also more than ten times as many as Germany had scored in each of the last two European Championships. In 2000 Germany scored just once in three games (0.33 goal per game), and in 2004 it got only two goals in three games (0.66 goal per game). That new offensive style of play captured the zeitgeist of the Klinsmann era and has become a trademark of Germany teams over the last decade. This statistic perhaps helps illustrate the change better than any other: In Klinsmann's forty games as coach, Germany was held to one or zero goals only eleven times, or just over one in four games; in Germany's forty games before he took over, the team was held to one or zero goals twenty-four times—in more than half their games.

"Part of our mentality was always that we liked to attack and add a second or third goal," Klinsmann says. "I think that with the excitement of the fans, the full stadiums, and the great atmospheres it inspires everyone around to try things out and take more risks. If you're playing in front of eighty thousand fans in a stadium like in Dortmund, and you score the first goal, all you want to do is score the second goal and the third goal. It's just the nature of it. That's what's been driving English soccer for generations. It's a real joy to go to a game in Germany now and be part of that atmosphere. That creates an environment where people want to see things happen. You don't want to just sit back and defend. The German mind-set is very different from the Italian. They want to play the tactical game. They don't want to lose. One goal is enough. We're pretty much the opposite of that in Germany."

Klinsmann thought it was also essential to foster a climate that encouraged independent thinking and strong-minded personalities on the field—attributes that he always aspired to as a player. He wanted to empower the players, equipping them with the confidence to make the important split-second decisions, any one of which can win or lose a game. His philosophy on coaching is that once the game starts, it is almost entirely up to the players what happens on the field. It is the players, not the coaches, who have to make the countless instant decisions. Unlike other mainstream American sports, in which the coaches can have a more direct impact on the flow and tactics of a game from the sidelines, coaches in soccer can prepare teams for games, but there is little they can do after the opening kickoff aside from using their three substitutions as judiciously and shrewdly as possible.

When the initial resistance to and criticism of Klinsmann finally died down, many Bundesliga club coaches and general managers quietly became converts to the high-scoring philosophy, winning over new fans with the more exciting style of play. There was a small handful of coaches at the time also advocating the attacking, pressing style, such as Ralf Rangnick. The German clubs also became more successful in European-wide club competitions, including UEFA's Champions League and Europa Cup. The standing of Germany's clubs rose steadily in the UEFA five-year rankings from fourth place in 2004 to second place, behind Spain, four years later, overtaking Italy and England in the process. Because its clubs had stronger records in the European-wide club competitions, Germany earned the right to send four teams, the same number as Spain, to the Champions League instead of three in 2008.

"There are many coaches in Germany who are now fans of the attractive and attacking style, who are willing to take risks," says Klinsmann, pleased that the *Nationalmannschaft* turned into a trendsetter for the league. "They're willing to give players the chance to try things out and therefore making the game really attractive. That's really cool."

It was hardly a coincidence that there were two Bundesliga teams playing against each other in the 2013 Champions League Final. It was an all-German matchup in London at the final of world's most important club tournament between Bayern Munich and Borussia Dortmund, a riveting game that Bayern won 2–1. In less than a decade from its nadir in Portugal, soccer made in Germany had become among the most successful brands played in Europe. In that season there was an average of 2.87 goals per match scored in the Bundesliga—up from an average of 2.68 in the 2002/03 season before Klinsmann took the helm.

The foundation and attacking style that Klinsmann introduced in 2004 paved the way for the international team's success, leading to its fourth World Cup win in 2014 in Brazil. The offensive style of play culminated in Germany's epic 7–1 thrashing of the hosts in the semifinal. It is also worth noting that in an increasingly competitive world, Germany made it to at least the semifinal in the five straight major international tournaments from 2006 to 2014 in the wake of Klinsmann's reforms, a record of achievement that also included two final appearances in those eight years, at the 2008 Euro and 2014 World Cup. His philosophies were introduced to the youth teams in Germany, which began playing with a similar focus on attacking. In 2009, Germany's three youth teams claimed the European Championship in their respective age groups: Under-21, Under-19, and Under-17. Many of the players on those three teams were on Germany's 2014 World Cup team.

"Klinsmann gave German soccer the reforms and fresh blood it urgently needed," says Philipp Köster, the editor of the popular and respected highbrow soccer magazine *11 Freunde* (Eleven Friends). "Soccer in Germany was stuck in a rut in 2004 with outdated structures—that was especially the case for the *Nationalmannschaft* and the Bundesliga. The training methods and coaches training in Germany had fallen behind the international developments over the years. Reforms were overdue, and there was no way Germany could have continued on as before after the disasters of the Euro 2000 and 2004."

Köster says that Klinsmann played an important role in bringing about the changes Germany needed and that it didn't take long for Bundesliga clubs to silently adopt many of his ideas that they had first belittled. "I doubt the reforms would have been carried out with such thoroughness without Klinsmann. His big advantage was that he wasn't contaminated by the existing structures. Someone from inside the DFB couldn't have pulled it off like that. Klinsmann's reforms were hugely important from a psychological point of view. He showed that in soccer you can quickly change things with a lot of drive, engagement, and conviction. That encouraged a lot of Bundesliga clubs."

# "MADE IN AMERICA"
# FOR GERMANY

Jürgen Klinsmann didn't expect the changes he introduced to please everyone. They weren't designed to make everyone happy. After a strong start in his first game with a win in Vienna against Austria in August 2004 and 1–1 draw against Brazil in Berlin in September, Germany traveled to Tehran in early October for an important friendly against Iran in front of an enormous crowd of 120,000 male spectators—women were barred from the Azadi Stadium, although some reportedly managed to sneak in disguised as men.

Germany won an exciting game 2–0 thanks to some brilliant saves by goalkeeper Lehmann, making the most of his chance to shine after long being Kahn's understudy. Klinsmann also used the game to test out two little-known and previously overlooked new players he had called up—defender Per Mertesacker of Hannover 96 and midfielder Thomas Hitzlsperger of Aston Villa, both of whom went on to have long careers for Germany. Consciously casting a wide net for new and untapped talent, Klinsmann had already called up three other new players in his two matches: Robert Huth from Chelsea, Andreas Görlitz from Bayern Munich, and Werder Bremen's Frank Fahrenhorst.

"I saw Robert on television playing in the Premier League, and he came on for the last twenty or thirty minutes with such tenacity, so much power and energy," Klinsmann said at a news conference in Berlin after Huth made an impressive debut against Brazil. "Robert got his chance and used it. It was super the way he demonstrated so much self-confidence."

By the time the World Cup started, Klinsmann had given twelve new players their first chance on the German National Team. Including veterans, he tried out a total of thirty-nine players. His final World Cup squad had twenty-three players. Several young players, including Bastian Schweinsteiger, Lukas Podolski, and Philipp Lahm, came into their own and flourished for Germany under Klinsmann's tutelage and drive for youth, while players like Mertesacker and Hitzlsperger, whom he plucked from obscurity, became mainstays on the team.

Klinsmann's changes went beyond the game on the field. He wanted to push not only the players' bodies but also their minds—and even switched the colors of the team's away jersey from its traditional black to red. Studies in the United States had found that red promotes positive thinking and an aggressive style.

Klinsmann called upon his experiences in the United States to expand their horizons. He encouraged his players to read, assigned them to take a basic computer course, and then linked everyone by e-mail—even though it took a while for some of the players to learn how to open e-mail documents. The players were also given looseleaf binders with the schedule of games leading up to the World Cup, the birthdays of everyone on the team, and the code of conduct that spelled out reminders such as to refrain from criticizing teammates in public and to be friendly to journalists and fans alike. Another notable rule was right out of Klinsmann's own personal code of conduct: If players have to break an appointment with a journalist, they should make sure they cancel it well in advance, instead of just not showing up.

One of his first acts when he met his team in a hotel in August before the Austria exhibition game was to show the players a film of the most emotional moments of the country's proud soccer history, with clips from the 1954, 1974, and 1990 World Cup wins accompanied by Eminem's song "Lose Yourself." *11 Freunde* observed that the film had a powerful impact on the young players: "The message was clear, and the players stood there watching it with their jaws dropped." The scenes from those victories had had a galvanizing effect on the entire country and helped cement Germany's standing in the world as a top soccer power.

Adding sports psychologist Hans-Dieter Hermann to the team in December 2004 further ruffled feathers in Germany—especially among the traditionalists. It was a delicate decision, just before a three-game road trip of exhibition matches to Asia, and the static Klinsmann got about it illustrated just how backward-thinking so much of Germany's conservative soccer establishment was, even though mental training was already becoming an important part of so many other sports. It came not long after the arrival of the at-first widely ridiculed American fitness trainers. Among the Bundesliga general managers expressing doubts about the sports psychologist was Dieter Hoeness of Hertha Berlin, who complained of the increasing "Americanization of the DFB" under Klinsmann. There were also skeptical articles in some tabloids about the new "shrink," and a headline in *Bild* wondered rather primitively if a player like hardened veteran goalkeeper Kahn would ever end up going to the "psycho doc."

But Hermann's assistance was invaluable at the World Cup, and—like the fitness trainers who joined shortly before him—he has been an integral part of the Germany coaching staff ever since, often sitting on the team bench. Hermann, who wrote his dissertation on overcoming stress, had earlier worked with Olympic athletes, including Austria's downhill skiing gold medal winner Hermann Maier, German Olympic gymnasts, and boxers.

Hermann's focus was on helping the Germany players and coaches cope with the enormous expectations, criticism, and stress of playing the World Cup at home while getting the most out of their abilities. A decade later, it was clear that some of the players on the team hosting the 2014 World Cup, Brazil, could have benefited from a sports psychologist. Before Brazil was crushed by Germany 7–1 in the semifinal, some of the Brazil players wept openly after earlier games they *won* and appeared to be at the breaking point under the weight of all the expectations on their shoulders long before they were eliminated by Germany.

England's coach at the 2006 World Cup, Sven-Göran Eriksson, wrote in his autobiography, *My Story,* that one of his biggest regrets was that he did not add a psychologist to his team, if for no other reason than to help the players overcome penalty shoot-out phobia. England had one of the best teams at the 2004 European Championship in Portugal but lost to the hosts on penalties, 6–5. It was their fourth exit in a row from a major tournament on penalties. Two years later, at the World Cup in Germany, England and Portugal met again in the quarterfinals and were again forced to go to penalties. England lost 3–1 after three of their best players—Frank Lampard, Steven Gerrard, and Jamie Carragher—had their penalty shots blocked by Portugal's goalkeeper, Ricardo. "When penalties arrived, I was still certain we would prevail, even though England had never won a penalty shootout in a World Cup. I was wrong," Eriksson writes. "I should have brought in a coach to help us prepare psychologically for penalties. I know that now." England's penalty shoot-out record was especially dismal: They had lost all three World Cup penalty shoot-outs (1990, 1998, and 2006) and two of their three European Championships (1996 and 2004). "I should have done it after the exit from the 2004 Euros. Why did I not do it? Maybe I thought that players such as Gerard, Lampard and Beckham, who had been there before and took penalties for their clubs, had the experience to handle the pressure. Perhaps I did not want to bring in a specialist to prepare us for something that may not happen. Whatever the case, I had made a mistake." After Eriksson left in 2006, England lost another penalty shoot-out, to Italy, in the quarterfinals of the 2012 European Championship.

Yet two years before the same 2006 World Cup in Germany, Klinsmann sometimes had to defend the decision to add the sports psychologist and pointed out to a skeptical media that it was a voluntary offering for anyone interested. "He'll be a useful asset for us in coping with stress and getting out top performances. It's entirely up to the players and coaches on whether or not they want to talk to him about coping with stress or improving concentration. I'm convinced he can help us. The mental aspects of the game are just as important as the fitness, where we still have room for improvement."

Klinsmann says that Hermann, who was integrated with the team in practice and in the locker room, also helped both him and his coaches. "He wasn't there only for the players—he was there for the coaching staff as well. He would say to me things like, 'Your talk to the team had too much tension in it or maybe not enough tension,' or maybe he would tell me things about my body language or energy level in the team talks. These guys had a good eye for all these things. It was fascinating. It was a learning process for all of us."

Step by step, Klinsmann was enacting the changes and modernization efforts that he had told the DFB would be part of his reforms. But there was pitched resistance from the DFB when he said he wanted to scrap the plans to have the team's World Cup based in the small western provincial town of Leverkusen, near Cologne. Franz Beckenbauer and DFB president Gerhard Mayer-Vorfelder had already agreed in 2002 to base the Germany team in a luxury hotel there and train at Bayer Leverkusen's grounds. It was a gesture to chemical company Bayer, which sponsors the Bundesliga club and had helped support the DFB's bid to win rights to host the 2006 World Cup. Its 22,500-seat stadium was far too small to be a World Cup venue, but the DFB gave Bayer some consolation by offering to base the *Nationalmannschaft* there and use the stadium as its training grounds.

The decision was made before Klinsmann took over, and he opposed it from the start. He persuaded the DFB to tear up the agreement. He knew his players would rather be in a big city like Berlin for the World Cup, where the final would be played, rather than more than 340 miles to the west in the provinces of North Rhine-Westphalia. Being based near the venue for the final was an important psychological signal for Klinsmann and his players. It was another power struggle that the players took note of with tacit approval.

Remembering what he liked and didn't like as a player, he had already banned sponsors and DFB functionaries from luncheons with the team and had even gone so far as to create areas for players where even he and his coaches were not allowed. His players could clearly see that Klinsmann was out there fighting for their interests and subjugating absolutely everything else to the goal of Germany winning the World Cup. The base in Berlin turned out to be ideal, in a luxury hotel on the edge of the Grunewald forest, furthering the team's concentration yet offering enough distraction to prevent anyone from going stir-crazy during the monthlong tournament. It was a brilliant move—creating a quiet haven conducive to concentration but not cut off from the outside world—that Germany took with it when picking its base for subsequent tournaments.

More important, the team hotel was near the top-quality Hertha Berlin training grounds and Berlin's Olympic Stadium, where the final would be played, and it was only a ten-minute ride from the bustling Ku'damm section in the heart of west Berlin. Being near the venue for the World Cup final for the duration of the tournament would, above all, send a subliminal message: This is where the roads to this tournament lead, this is where we want to finish the World Cup. "That wasn't just about the 2006 final," Klinsmann says. "It was all part of the changes we wanted to make that would stay in place beyond 2006. The structures that we were putting in place were designed to ensure long-term success."

# CONFED CUP

YEARS AGO, THE CONFEDERATIONS CUP was not considered to be an especially important tournament in most countries around the world. An eight-team tournament held since 1997, it used to be seen as so irrelevant that Germany twice opted not to take part when it had qualified as Europe's representative—in 1997 after the Euro 96 win, and in 2003 after its run to the 2002 World Cup final.

Since 2001, however, the Confederations Cup has been held a year before the World Cup in the country that will host that tournament the following year—and its standing has been elevated into an important dress rehearsal. Not only for the host country, to see if its stadiums and infrastructure are ready for the thirty-two-team World Cup, but also for teams with aspirations of winning the Cup a year later, to get a glimpse and feel of the country and some of the stadiums they will be playing in.

Jürgen Klinsmann identified the 2005 Confed Cup at home in Germany as a priceless opportunity to help get his team ready for the World Cup in 2006, and by doing so he also added more prestige to the Confed Cup. Germany, as hosts, had qualified automatically for the World Cup and did not have to go through the rigors of qualifying like most other nations around the world trying to win one of the other thirty-one spots available for the finals. Instead, Germany was consigned to a long run of friendlies—aside from the Confed Cup—leading up to 2006. Klinsmann kept pointing to the tournament as Germany's only chance to get competitive games and tournament experience during those two years.

The Confed Cup in 2005 was made up of the top team from each of FIFA's six confederations: Greece from UEFA (Europe) after winning the 2004 European Championship; Argentina representing CONMEBOL (South America) as the runner-up to Brazil in the 2004 Copa América; Mexico from CONCACAF (North America, Central America, and the Caribbean) as the winner of the 2003 Gold Cup; Tunisia from CAF (Africa) as the winner of the 2004 African Cup of Nations; Japan from AFC (Asia) as the winner of the 2004 Asian Cup; and Australia from OFC (Oceania) as the winner of the 2004 OFC Nations Cup. Also at the 2005 Confederations Cup were World Cup holders, Brazil, and the 2006 World Cup host country, Germany.

Playing the exciting, attacking style that was winning over its fans, Germany was victorious in two of its three group games, against Australia (4–3) and Tunisia (3–0), before playing a thrilling 2–2 tie against Argentina. Klinsmann's team was beaten 3–2 in the semifinals by Brazil, which was ranked as the world's best team. Brazil went on to win the tournament by defeating Argentina in the final. Germany took a strong third place by beating Mexico in a riveting game in Leipzig—winning 4–3 in extra time and ending the long winless streak against top teams.

It was in any event a successful tournament for Germany and an amazing turnaround for the team. Just one year after scoring a meager two goals in three games in its devastating first-round exit from the Euro 2004, Germany had erupted for a total of fifteen goals in five games at the Confed Cup and showed the world it could play an exciting brand of fast-paced soccer. "It was a valuable experience," Klinsmann says. "We showed we could compete against the best in the world again. I was positively surprised how far we'd come in a year, even though we still had a long way to go."

Klinsmann had managed to build an attacking team with a confident fighting spirit—led by players like captain Michael Ballack but also increasingly by young players flourishing on his squad, such as a trio of talented twenty-year-olds: Lukas Podolski, Bastian Schweinsteiger, and Per Mertesacker.

In Klinsmann's first full year, Germany won ten of its sixteen games, with four ties and only two losses. The team scored forty-two goals—or 2.6 goals per match. In the year before he took over, Germany had only six wins in its fourteen games, with three ties, five losses, and a total of twenty-two goals—seven of which came in a lopsided 7–0 win over tiny Malta. Excluding the win against Malta, Germany scored just 1.2 goals per game that year. It was clear to Germany fans, and not just statisticians, that something powerful had changed under Klinsmann's coaching.

# CRITICS COME OUT

AFTER KLINSMANN'S PROMISING FIRST YEAR, which helped restore national pride in the team and made Germans feel complete again, the next eight months—from August 2005 through March 2006—proved to be difficult. Germany managed to win only two of the next seven games—beating South Africa and China while losing to Slovakia, Turkey, and Italy with ties against the Netherlands and France. The 4–1 loss to Italy on March 1 in Florence was especially bitter, leading to some media calls for Klinsmann to be fired even though the start of the World Cup was three months away.

The criticism was led by an unholy coalition of erstwhile enemies from newspapers like *Bild* as well as the formidable Bundesliga club Bayern Munich, which had an ax to grind with Klinsmann over Kahn's demotion. There were also many former players now working as TV pundits and newspaper columnists, most of whom had played at Bayern Munich at some point in their careers, eager to pounce on Klinsmann and extract revenge for the way he was shaking everything up, challenging their beliefs and many of the things they had represented. Their uninformed criticisms reflected not only a troubling impatience after such a major shake-up but also were lobbed from afar—without trying to understand what Klinsmann and his coaches were trying to do. It proved to be a major distraction.

"I underestimated how long it would take some people in Germany to realize we had a lot of problems to work on when we began," Klinsmann says. "It wasn't only with the team's fitness but also with speed and tactics. We had a lot of work to do in a lot of areas. The people who were criticizing us, like Günter Netzer, Franz Beckenbauer, and Lothar Matthäus, in my eyes didn't have any insight into the work we were doing. It was a lesson for me to see people wanting to get rid of me just because we lost the one game to Italy. There were people out there who wanted to destroy nineteen months of hard work."

Klinsmann was accustomed to criticism as a player and was not going to let the detractors get to him or his team, especially so close to the World Cup. "That's all just part of the job," he says. "We told the players there'd be setbacks along the line, and we'd get bopped on the head when games go badly. It's another question whether it's justified or not. But my advice to everyone on the team was always to just take a glance at the newspaper criticism and then forget about it. You just have to absorb what people are saying. The coaches aren't exempt from the criticism. We're self-critical ourselves. The important thing is to ensure that everyone keeps improving, all the time."

Klinsmann was sometimes raked over the coals, in particular for the circumstances surrounding how thirty-four-year-old defender Christian Wörns of Borussia Dortmund was dropped from the team in February 2006. He had been a stalwart on coach Rudi Völler's 2002 team, and like any red-blooded German soccer player, he dreamed of playing for his country in the World Cup, especially at home.

But Wörns was part of the older generation and had even been Klinsmann's teammate in the 1990s. Some blamed him for the quarterfinal exit at the 1998 World Cup; Germany had played well in a scoreless first half but after he got a red card in the 40th minute, Croatia scored just before the break and beat ten-man Germany by a score of 3–0. Wörns had earned sixty-six caps, but he was an old-school defender and no longer an automatic selection for Klinsmann, who was happily experimenting with younger, more attack-minded center backs like Mertesacker and Robert Huth.

Wörns was unhappy about that, reluctant to acknowledge that at thirty-four he no longer had the speed of his younger rivals, and had obviously not paid enough attention to his code of conduct handbook and what happens to those who publicly speak out against decisions. Wörns opted to challenge Klinsmann in public, saying that it wasn't performance on the field that counted anymore in picking his team. By not only breaking the code but also casting aspersions on his teammates' abilities, Wörns had shot himself in the foot. Klinsmann could handle the criticism directed at himself but was incensed by disrespectful comments toward the other defenders on the team. He dropped Wörns and said he would never play for Germany again while he was coaching.

The string of sobering results after such a brilliant run the previous year had also fueled an increasingly acrimonious public discussion during the winter of 2005–2006 about, of all things, where Klinsmann was living. He had decided from the start in July 2004 to maintain his residency in California and see how that worked. "Living in the United States gave me a different perspective," he says. The experiment of commuting to Germany for longer stays about twice each month was working better than he'd expected at the outset, and there was nary a complaint about it at first. He was getting the job done.

Because national teams, which are in effect a nation's all-star team, practice together only in brief spells of a week or so sporadically a dozen times a year and have only a game or two each month in between the monthlong tournaments, it normally doesn't matter where a coach lives the rest of the time. Other top international coaches at the time commuted from afar and without any to-do: Japan coach Zico from his home in Brazil; Greece coach Otto Rehhagel from Germany; and Cameroon coach Winnie Schäfer shuttling between Germany and Cameroon. And during Klinsmann's first year it was not an issue either.

He was certainly plugged in to what was happening in Germany, following it from afar much more intensively than other foreign coaches could keep track of their players. Klinsmann also synchronized his daily routine to Germany when in California, rising before dawn, usually at 5:30 A.M., to make phone calls or take part in thrice-weekly teleconferences with his staff in Frankfurt, where it was 2:30 P.M.; watching Germany and other league games on satellite television; and staying in touch with his players by e-mail or phone. Klinsmann actually found it useful to keep some distance from Germany and had been settled with his family in California since 1998. His head was nevertheless in Germany for most of the day even if he was physically some six thousand miles away. He and his staff kept the operation running full speed ahead with Löw and ten scouts from the DFB going to Bundesliga games every weekend, and reporting their findings to Klinsmann.

Appearances, however, sometimes count more than anything else, and Klinsmann had ruffled many feathers and rubbed some people the wrong way with his direct style in his first year. As soon as the results weren't going as well in 2006, some of his old-guard adversaries came out of the woodwork, seizing on the temporary slump to try to use his commuting as an indication that he wasn't committed to the job. "They said things like I had spent 'too much time in the California sun' and 'He's probably lying on the beach' while I was actually working up to eighteen hours a day," Klinsmann says.

It was a classic *Nebenschauplatz,* a secondary issue, which Germans can be particularly fond of at times, but when the attacks from the powerful trendsetting tabloids added their weight, it became part of the public narrative in early 2006. Most of the critics chose to turn a blind eye to any upside of Klinsmann's commuting: Having a bit of distance to the situation in Germany enabled him to observe and monitor global developments ahead of the World Cup. There is also an inherent envy by many Germans, especially during their long, dark winter months, of compatriots who manage to escape to a warm, sunny climate like in Southern California. There are an average of just 160 hours of sunshine in Germany from December to February, compared to about 713 hours in Los Angeles. If Klinsmann had been commuting from Minnesota or Iceland, with winter climates as dark and cold as Germany's, it's unlikely there would have been such a commotion about his residency.

"I didn't fly back home because the weather in California was nicer but to recharge my batteries," he says. "You can only give your energy to others if you have it yourself. In Germany I'd have been consumed by petty things and unable to focus on the bigger issues. Some people might have preferred to see me in Bundesliga stadiums, but I had other priorities. It was an advantage to keep a bit of a distance. It helped me to keep a clear view of the bigger international picture." At one point, when the criticism of Klinsmann living in California was reaching a crescendo, he was actually in South America at a coaching conference arranged by Brazil's coach Carlos Alberto Parreira to talk about building team spirit on a national team filled with so many different personalities. The criticism of his commuting was not universal, however, and FC Bayern Munich's

chief executive Karl-Heinz Rummenigge went out of his way to defend Klinsmann by quipping, "It's good that Jürgen gets away from
Germany so quickly so he doesn't have to read all the nonsense that
gets printed in the newspapers here."

Klinsmann made forty-two trips to Germany during his two
years as coach, flying some five hundred thousand miles, roughly the
equivalent of twenty circumnavigations of the Earth. But he never
once complained about the long-distance travel, the eleven-hour
flights between Frankfurt and Los Angeles, the nine-time-zone difference, or the accompanying jet lag. He tried to fight the inexora-
ble and unpredictable jet lag by hitting the gym or doing work in the
middle of the night at either end of his journey. In general, Klinsmann spent about two weeks each month in Germany.

"At the end of the day, the only thing that matters is the quality
of work you deliver," Klinsmann says. "The world has changed with
modern communications, so it doesn't matter where you are physically. Commuting like that was no different from what thousands of
people in other professions do. Wherever I was in the world, I could
stay hooked up with Germany. What difference did it make if I phone
a player from California or Frankfurt? I had no problem with that
criticism and respected those who had differing views. But I had to
decide what's best, and in my view it was a setup that benefited the
team."

The pressure on Klinsmann nevertheless worsened in the spring
of 2006. He had tried in vain to hire a new technical director at the
DFB alongside the general manager role being filled by Bierhoff. He
offered Berti Vogts the job, but he turned it down. Klinsmann's next
choice was Bernhard Peters, the successful coach of Germany's two-
time Olympic gold-medal-winning field hockey team. He was
impressed with Peters's ideas and his ability to think outside the box.
"I thought we should have more respect for other sports," Klinsmann

says. "I thought we'd been asleep for the last ten or fifteen years in Germany while other sports have overtaken us."

Peters was an advocate of "tactical cross-pollination" between soccer and field hockey, as Raphael Honigstein notes in *Das Reboot*. German field hockey had long been a "hotbed of innovation," he writes, with Peters observing, "Hockey is very similar to football in tactical terms. I can pick up inspiration from football, and also provide an impulse for football, too." But this was Germany, where soccer is king and field hockey is a minor sport. Hiring a field hockey coach was just a step too far for the traditionalists. DFB executives vetoed the move, which led to a brief feeding frenzy in the German media. The DFB instead installed Matthias Sammer, a former Germany international and ex–Borussia Dortmund coach. Sammer was a grim taskmaster whom the media assumed could, if necessary, be called upon to step in and take over if Klinsmann had to be sacrificed in the few months remaining before the World Cup.

The winds were turning against Klinsmann in early 2006. He had acquired a number of adversaries at Bayern Munich and in the tabloid media, and not only because he was a catalyst for change that made the self-satisfied soccer establishment uncomfortable. Other reasons for the growing animosity included Klinsmann's decision to make Kahn compete against his former understudy Lehmann for the goalkeeping job. Soccer in Germany is, among other things, a place where some people look to settle old scores, where there is sometimes a yearning to get even that is splendidly summed up by the word *nachtreten,* "kicking back."

Klinsmann was once again a target of criticism from *Bild* because of his steadfast refusal to cooperate with the newspaper and because he wouldn't leak internal team information to the mass-circulation daily with its twelve million readers. The newspaper, which calls itself the largest in continental Europe, was also still galled that it had been beaten in July 2004 on the scoop that Klinsmann would be the next Germany coach—a story first reported by its rival *Süddeutsche Zeitung*. Klinsmann had eliminated privileges of access for *Bild*, discontinuing the unseemly practice of giving *Bild* exclusive access to the players or his roster a day before games, and he emphasized to his players the perils of leaking internal team information to the media. *Bild* did not appreciate being treated like any other newspaper.

Years before, as a player for Germany at the 1996 European Championship, Klinsmann had successfully sued *Bild*—and donated the proceeds to charity—after it refused to retract a bogus allegation that he was among a group of Germany players who caused a stir in the team's hotel in England for going into its sauna as people in Germany do—naked—rather than the English way: with a swimsuit on or wrapped in a towel. So his detractors, including some of those players, pundits, and functionaries who lost out with his reforms, were bent on revenge, lurking and ready to pounce upon any semblance of a reason to attack Klinsmann. The 4–1 loss to Italy one hundred days before the start of the World Cup provided the opportunity they were aching for.

"4–1, Mamma Mia, we're bad!" *Bild* wrote, blaming Klinsmann for the debacle by saying the team "would drown at the World Cup," while another newspaper, *Frankfurter Allgemeine Zeitung*, called it the "Fiakso von Florenz" (Fiasco in Florence) and said, "Germany has been shrunk to dwarf-size in soccer." The *Süddeutsche Zeitung* described it as a "90-minute blackout."

Several days after the numbing Italy defeat, Klinsmann faced further criticism from *Bild* and Beckenbauer for flying home to California instead of taking part in a World Cup technical workshop in Düsseldorf. Löw attended in his place. Klinsmann was surprised and dismayed by the increasingly negative sentiment in Germany—instead of any visible pride that the team was, in general, playing much better and more inspired soccer than it had eighteen months earlier. But that's the way Germans can be when they vacillate so completely between hot and cold: *Himmelhoch jauchzend, zu Tode betrübt*—"On top of the world, to the depths of despair," as Germany's most famous writer, Johann Wolfgang Goethe, described the mood swings of his compatriots with such immortal words in his 1788 play *Egmont*.

"They wanted to chop my head off," Klinsmann says. The copresident of the DFB, Theo Zwanziger, admitted years later that there was indeed a clandestine backup plan to replace Klinsmann shortly before the World Cup if the situation worsened after the Italy loss. "All of Germany, myself included, feared for the worst for the World Cup," Zwanziger writes in his autobiography *Die Zwanziger Jahren* (The Zwanziger Years). "I have to admit that I also began to have doubts about our coach. I continued to express my loyalty to Jürgen Klinsmann in public pronouncements and in letters back to all the 'experts' out there giving me advice about the coach, but internally we did draft a plan B. If it looked like a disaster was looming for the World Cup and Klinsmann couldn't be saved anymore, we decided that Matthias Sammer would take over the controls. But only four people knew about it—Horst R. Schmidt, Franz Beckenbauer, Wolfgang Niersbach, and me—not even Sammer himself. Fortunately, it never came to that."

Three weeks after the Italy game, the outlook suddenly brightened again when Germany crushed the United States—of all teams—by a score of 4–1 in an exhibition game in Dortmund. It was an important match and an important win for Klinsmann, silencing the naysayers who wanted to fire him just three months before the start of the tournament. It was also a victory that sparked a nine-game winning streak for Germany that took the team all the way to the semifinals of the World Cup at the same stadium in Dortmund where they beat the United States. There, in front of sixty-five thousand frenzied spectators, Germany lost 2–0 to Italy in overtime, a heartbreaking defeat that knocked out the hosts just one game before the final in Berlin. After beating Portugal four days later, 3–1, in the game for third place on July 8, everyone—even many of his naysayers—was begging Klinsmann to extend his expiring two-year contract. Klinsmann at first left the question unanswered—even though he had already made up his mind—because he first had some important business to deal with.

# AMERICAN-STYLE PATRIOTISM

It IS HARD TO exaggerate the euphoria of patriotism that swept Germany during and after the 2006 World Cup. The tournament will by nature always dominate the host country's attention, and capture the public's imagination in soccer nations, but the enthusiasm reached unimaginable levels in Germany and changed the country in profound ways—probably more than any other World Cup before or after it. It forever altered the way the world looked at Germany and, perhaps more important, it changed the way the Germans viewed themselves.

Eager to be good hosts under the official motto "*Die Welt zu Gast bei Freunden*" (A Time to Make Friends), Germany did a superb job of organizing the World Cup. That wasn't surprising for a country with a knack for organization. What was surprising was the way Germans transformed themselves into a nation suddenly so comfortable with their patriotism, a country no longer reluctant to wave the black-red-gold flag for their team, a country no longer hesitant to sing their own national anthem. The two million soccer fans from abroad got to see the best of Germans: their meticulous planning, their fantastic infrastructure with modern, comfortable high-speed trains, and their newly renovated stadiums. They also got to see the friendly side of Germany with millions in buoyant moods, aglow over their team's snowballing success as the tournament progressed. On top of it all, the weather in June and July 2006 was nearly perfect—more Mediterranean that summer than the Icelandic it can feel like in some especially cold and wet summers. Towns and cities throughout the nation had created spirited open-to-the-public fan zones in front of giant high-definition TV screens. It was a new kind of collective viewing experience for which they invented a new meaning for the old English term "public viewing." The public viewings in Germany had nothing to do with funerals but were instead gathering spots for large crowds—up to five hundred thousand at the Brandenburg Gate in central Berlin—to watch the games together. Some twenty million people watched each of Germany's seven games at the open-air fan-fest venues. Getting Germans enthusiastic, even patriotic, wasn't part of Klinsmann's assignment, but it was certainly a collateral effect of the World Cup that he had shaped with such perspicacity.

"Throughout the two years leading up to the World Cup, we kept talking about what it could mean for everyone involved, for the people in Germany and the image of the country," Klinsmann says. "Obviously, we needed to get the soccer side right and play a style that would excite people. But at the same time, this was the first time the whole world would be looking at Germany since reunification. It was the first chance to present a new picture to the world, coming some seventeen years after the Berlin Wall fell, to show how Germany was able to rebuild eastern Germany and how the country reunited. We always kept saying, 'This is the opportunity, this is it, we've got to get our act together on the field, but the important thing is that the people in Germany embrace it as *their* World Cup. We should show the world how we really are: being open, being multilingual, being multicultural, being happy, and being able to party. Just show them there is a completely new Germany.' "

There was a nervous air of anticipation among German fans at the start of the tournament and, as is their nature, fears that their team would suffer a similarly discouraging fate as in 2002 and 2004 when they were knocked out in the first rounds. But that angst started to dissipate after Germany won a thrillingly high-scoring opening game against Costa Rica, 4–2. The enthusiasm from the Black Forest in the south to the Baltic Sea in the north grew when Germany beat Poland, 1–0, five days later, thanks to a dramatic last-minute goal by Oliver Neuville. By the time Germany routed Ecuador, 3–0, to win its group, hopes for greater glory were soaring. Klinsmann's team then defeated Sweden 2–0 in the Round of 16 in Munich— after playing an awe-inspiring first thirty minutes of attacking brilliance that had the whole world watching admiringly—and got past Argentina in Berlin's Olympic Stadium, winning a dramatic quarterfinals penalty shoot-out 4–2. Germany teams are always good at penalties, having won four out of their four times when World Cup games went to the nerve-racking shoot-outs. Having team psychologist Hans-Dieter Hermann on the squad was controversial in 2004 when Klinsmann brought him on, but it seemed to give the players added confidence in the World Cup. Goalkeeper Jens Lehmann, who stopped two of the four Argentine shooters, appeared to rattle the Argentine penalty takers by pulling a crumpled-up slip of paper out of his sock and studying his crib sheet on the habits of the Argentines between each kick—as if he knew their penalty-shooting secrets. All four German players scored their penalties.

A dream that had seemed impossible less than two years ago when Klinsmann first outlined his goal of winning the World Cup to a skeptical news conference in Frankfurt was suddenly just two tantalizing wins away from becoming reality. A country famous for its naysayers, skeptics, and doubters—as reflected in their own self-mocking slogan of compound negatives *"Gibt's nicht, geht nicht, haben wir nicht"*—had become a nation of believers in the optimism that Klinsmann had brought back to Europe from America. Crowds of tens of thousands cheered the team bus and the players at every opportunity.

But the fairy tale ended in the semifinal game against Italy. Klinsmann's team gave up two goals late in overtime in front of a frenzied but ultimately heartbroken crowd in Dortmund. Germany won the consolation game in Stuttgart, beating Portugal 3–1, to take third place. Nevertheless, riding on the excitement of the team's riveting performances on the field, and its five stirring wins in a row during the monthlong tournament, something powerful changed in the nation and how it viewed itself. Germans not only fell in love with their team again, but they also started to embrace patriotism for the first time in their postwar history.

Even though the team had lost to Italy in the semifinal, there were some 25,000 cheering fans crowded into the center of Stuttgart, bringing traffic in Klinsmann's home town to a standstill, to cheer the coach and his team when they arrived at their hotel on the evening before the game for third place against Portugal, to be played one day before the final between Italy and France in Berlin. It was an astonishing outpouring of support and many fans were chanting, "Stuttgart is better than Berlin, better than Berlin, better than Berlin" to cheer up the players who had had their hearts set on playing the final in Berlin, while others held up banners reading, *"Weltmeister der Herzen"* ("World champions of the heart") and *"Klinsmann muss bleiben"* ("Klinsmann must stay"). German filmmaker Sönke Wortmann, who made a documentary film about the 2006 team called

"*Deutschland, ein Sommermärchen,*" and wrote a diary to accompany it, felt the frenzy himself and noted that many newspapers wrote that there had never been such a celebration for a Germany team before that. "That was sort of true," Wortmann wrote. He pointed out that there were more people cheering in 1954 when the team that won the country's first World Cup in Berne returned home by train. "But we came the full circle in 2006. In 1954, a German national soccer team had given the young nation its first real bit of self-esteem. In 2006, another German national soccer team was able to help the nation start to like itself."

For decades, Germans had been extraordinarily uncomfortable with displays and symbols of national pride and patriotism, an understandable reaction to their Nazi past more than a half century earlier, even though many Germans felt it was time to move toward a more relaxed patriotism. But of all the elements of America that Klinsmann brought with him back to Germany, none was more intense than his healthy and wholesome attitude toward patriotism. Before his very first game in August 2004, against Austria, Klinsmann stood on the sidelines and sang the German national anthem with remarkable American-style gusto. His singing of the national anthem gradually caught on with his team, then the crowds, and ultimately almost the entire nation. It was an American thing to sing along. Many Germans at first struggled with the lyrics to their own *Nationalhymne,* simply called the *Deutschlandlied.* The once controversial third stanza beginning "*Deutschland, Deutschland über alles*" (Germany, Germany above all) was banned after the war. But that lingering German angst about excessive patriotism didn't stop Klinsmann, who had admired the uninhibited outpouring of patriotism he had experienced in the United States.

Because so few Germans actually knew the lyrics, the German DFB began, helpfully, flashing the words as subtitles on giant video screens set up in stadiums before games in 2004 to accompany the music, and by 2006, many of the fans were singing the words along with Klinsmann and most of the players. It wasn't quite the same level of intense goose-bump-filled enthusiasm that stadiums filled with England or Italy fans generated before international games. But it was a sea change for Germany.

By the time the World Cup started, millions of Germans were wearing Germany flags on their shirts, hanging the flag from their balconies and houses, and even attaching miniature made-in-China *schwarz-rot-gold* flags to their car antennas. Shops were sold out and flag makers struggled to meet the demand. Young children suddenly wanted to wear T-shirts with German flags on them, untainted and oblivious to the Nazi past, and teenagers painted German flags on their cheeks—an incredible sight in a country that had long been so conflicted about its past.

"I think it really helped coming from the United States, because the patriotism here is hard to beat," Klinsmann says. "What happens here on the Fourth of July is just unbelievable, and it's unheard of in Germany the way Americans show their pride in the flag. Americans give off this patriotism and a sense that we're the number one country in the world. Whether that's true or not isn't the point. It's about, 'This is the United States, this is the world's melting pot, it's the greatest country in the world.' I kept saying in our discussions before the World Cup, 'We've gotta have the people in Germany really embrace their team, we've got to try to give them something to be joyful about, and then maybe something we can't even imagine will happen.' That's how we kept pushing and pushing it."

The newfound patriotism caught on quickly. "I think it's great that I'm not the only one with a German flag attached to my car anymore," President Horst Köhler quipped about his official car, which had always had a German flag attached to it. "People are now getting to experience Germany as a happy, optimistic country. They're feeling good and are identifying with their country and their national colors—I think that's just great." Foreign visitors who had been expecting to encounter dour, unfriendly, and grumpy Germans based on the antiquated stereotypes were astonished to discover their friendliness, humor, enthusiasm, and relaxed patriotism.

Klinsmann did not set out to change Germany, but was pleased to see so many of his compatriots finally able to show an affinity for their flag and country in an unstrained way and give the world new impressions about Germany. "I always said when we were starting out, 'Start with the end in mind,'" Klinsmann says, referring to meetings with his general manager Oliver Bierhoff, co-coach Joachim Löw, and goalkeeper-coach Andreas Köpke. "Oliver, Jogi, and Köppi looked at me and thought, 'What do you mean?' It was something that Mick Hoban taught me," he says, referring to his U.S. business partner. "He always said, 'Where do you want to be at the end, when the World Cup is over?' So you start with the end in mind and define it." Klinsmann's main goal was to improve the quality of the *Nationalmannschaft* in a short period of time and get the country excited about their team again, and let the rest take care of itself. "We wanted to show that we could build something that everyone could identify with—the fans, the players, and those who worked for the team. We wanted to develop an attacking style on the field that required courage and conviction. And it was our job to show that could be done. It was a change in culture and it was great to see how the people identified with our work."

He and his coaching staff tapped into their own experiences as players on the Germany teams of the late 1990s. "I have a lot of pride in my roots, about my heritage, and about a lot of things that I was able to experience in sports, mainly through the German national team—that is deeply anchored inside me," Klinsmann says. "Our goal was to use the tournament to show the world a new picture of Germany, but we didn't know that the effect it would have on Germans would become that important. This love of our country, this positive patriotism, developed to the point where people were saying, 'I really feel good to be German.' I think that shows once again that soccer, and sports in general, can bring people together and allow us to look at ourselves in a different light. I think Germans have been thought of more highly around the world ever since then."

Klinsmann does not in general like to look back at the 2006 World Cup. He has moved on. But if you press him about it, he will tell you that he is pleased with the way the team improved, the way the reforms he helped initiate took hold, and that Germany is back among the world's top teams, playing an exciting brand of soccer. "One of the best things to come out of the World Cup is that Germans are seen differently in the world now," he says. "They've got a new image of Germany, they saw a country with people partying and having a great time at the World Cup, they saw a country that was a great host and open to the world. They also got a new image of the German team, that we were able to play really good soccer."

What is important, he says, is that Germany's *Nationalmannschaft* ended up being an important agent of change that pushed the development of soccer forward in the ensuing decade. "The thing that matters is that a lot has happened since then," he says. "The clubs in Germany started to be aggressive and forward-thinking, introducing fitness coaches and sports psychologists and specialists all over the place. Those were things that we tried out during the World Cup. It's great."

It was a magnificent experience to see and feel Germany rallying around the team and giving the world a new impression about the country. "People still talk to you about the 2006 World Cup wherever you are abroad. They don't talk to you about how we played and against which teams we won or the loss to Italy in the semi-finals or how Italy beat France in the final. Instead they talk about what the Germans did in that World Cup. And that's pretty cool. And that's what the game can do."

# TIME TO MOVE ON

KLINSMANN DECIDED NOT to extend his contract with Germany even though his players and the country were almost universally urging him to stay. Even his erstwhile critics like Franz Beckenbauer and *Bild* were exhorting him to continue, to finish what he started. Whether Klinsmann would stay on as coach of the *Nationalmannschaft* or not was one of the most pressing questions of the day in Germany in the early summer of 2006, filling not only the sports pages but the front pages as well. An opinion poll by the Forsa Institute, a leading German pollster that normally focuses its surveys on politics and major social issues, found that 93 percent of Germans wanted him to continue and 95 percent were proud of the team's World Cup performance. But Klinsmann had already dropped subtle hints during the latter stages of the World Cup that he would not extend his contract. He began openly praising the qualities of his assistant coach Joachim Löw at conference, which is not something that head coaches usually take the time to do, and telling reporters near the team's base in Berlin that it felt like he had already accomplished his mission: "We've started a reform process that is independent of any trainer—me or anyone else. It's a philosophy that will carry on no matter who is in charge."

There was even a *"Klinsmann muss bleiben"* (Klinsmann Must Stay) campaign building in the media led by many of the same newspapers that had previously wanted him fired. Amid the frenzy in Germany that came to be known as "Klinsmania," the thirty-nine-year-old Volkswagen Beetle convertible with its 44-horsepower engine that he had driven in 1994 and 1995 while playing at Tottenham was auctioned for more than €300,000, even though Klinsmann had given it away more than a decade earlier because it was rusting.

So why did he choose to leave? Klinsmann said he was flattered by the compliments after the months of criticism but added he was simply exhausted after two grueling years on the hot seat and facing so much resistance along the way.

"Nobody could imagine what that was all like," Klinsmann says. "It was wonderful the way it all ended, but it was just a lot, a lot of work over those two years. It was a lot of banging into walls, and it was exhausting. I just had the feeling that we need to go home and for us, as a family, that's California. The next friendly was scheduled for three or four weeks later, and I just said to Debbie, 'I can't imagine being back on that bench in three or four weeks.'"

Klinsmann said he was not physically exhausted, that even during the stress of the World Cup he managed to maintain his daily workouts, but mentally and emotionally he was drained. "I just needed a break," he says. "Once I make a decision, I just go with it and don't look back. It was pretty much at the end of the tournament, after the Italy game. You want to see the outcome of everything, but after Italy I thought, 'It's been an extreme ride, something I could never have imagined and something I'll never forget.' But I felt like, 'You've got to cut it now, you got to cut it off.'"

Klinsmann delayed announcing his decision for several days until after the tournament ended and while he tried to persuade Joachim Löw to take over. It wasn't easy at first and Klinsmann had to track him down in the Black Forest. "We went to the Black Forest because I first had to convince Jogi to take it over," Klinsmann says, adding that he and his family spent three days in the Hotel Engel in Baiersbronn recuperating from the World Cup and waiting for Löw to agree to accept his job. "I said, 'Jogi, I'm sitting here at the hotel, and I'm not leaving until you agree to take over the team.'" Klinsmann wanted to relax and unwind with his family, go for quiet hikes in the forest for a few days. But when word got out that he was in town, the serenity was shattered.

"I knew he could do the job, but he just badly wanted me to stay on," Klinsmann says. "It was not that he wasn't comfortable enough, he just said, 'Jürgen, don't do that now. We've built everything together and all four of us are such a great team.' I said, 'Jogi, I need to go home, my home is California, I need to move on. Maybe it's wrong, but it's just how I feel and I know you can do it, you're good and you have an amazing team with you, you just need to take over that ship.'"

Three days later Klinsmann met Löw again in the Black Forest and he agreed to accept the job. Klinsmann then called Mayer-Vorfelder who, after a brief attempt to talk him out of leaving, also realized that it was pointless to try to persuade Klinsmann to stay. They called a news conference in Frankfurt, and Klinsmann said farewell just before boarding a jumbo jet home.

"It was anything but an easy decision, but one I had to make," he told a news conference that was nationally broadcast live on several German TV networks, on July 12, 2006—almost exactly two years to the day after the barbecue with Vogts in Huntington Beach. It was not entirely surprising, but nevertheless it was disappointing for millions of German fans who had hoped he would continue and finish the job he started by winning the next big tournament. In his 712 days as coach, Germany had won twenty games, with six defeats and eight ties. His team had outscored opponents by 81 to 43 goals and his winning percentage was better than three of his four predecessors: Franz Beckenbauer, Erich Ribbeck, and Rudi Völler. Only Berti Vogts had a slightly better winning record. Germans clearly loved their new high-scoring soccer team and were overjoyed about their newly discovered patriotism. Klinsmann was the one who brought that all together. How could he possibly leave now?

Klinsmann's voice quivered at times during the farewell news conference and he had to fight off tears at one point. "My great wish is to go home to be with my family, to return to a normal life with them," he said, before adding with the same disarming candor that had marked his whole career: "Another important reason is that, as a result of these two years, I've lost a lot of strength having to deal with the functionaries. I feel empty and internally burned out. I owe it to myself to take a six-month break now. I won't do anything else."

Four years later, Klinsmann was sitting in one of his favorite cafés in California overlooking the Pacific Ocean. He was pleased that two Bundesliga teams, Bayern Munich and Borussia Dortmund, were about to play each other in the Champions League final and excited about the attacking style of play that had infected the entire German league following the 2006 World Cup, and that the stadiums in Germany were filled with soccer fans, families, women, and children. He had been in the stadium in Vienna for the final of the 2008 European Championship game, cheering for Germany and the team filled with many of the players he had groomed together with Löw. And he had been in South Africa in 2010 at the World Cup, working as a color commentator for TV networks in the United States, Germany, and Britain, where Germany made it to the semifinals before being beaten once again by Spain, which went on to win the Cup. Klinsmann was clearly thrilled and pleased that Germany had once again become one of the world's top and most feared teams, consistently reaching the semifinals and finals of big tournaments. But he waved off taking credit for the changes.

"I was extremely happy that things fell into place at the World Cup in 2006 after two years of work, happy that all those risks we took and all those things that we tried out actually worked," he says. "You never know beforehand when you try something new whether it will work or not. But it all worked out, and the wonderful thing is that the people embraced it, the people of Germany really identified with it. Hopefully, it stimulated a lot of other people out there to try things and to take risks and to just go for it. What matters is that the developments didn't stop and a lot has happened since then. Soccer is always an environment of change. It's like life. That's why I love it so much. You never know what's going to happen next. There are no guarantees."

# RIGHT TIME, RIGHT PLACE

Jürgen Klinsmann made waves in Germany, lasting waves that helped turn the *Nationalmannschaft* back into one of the world's best—and put it on course to the World Cup semifinals in 2010 and to winning the tournament in 2014, for the fourth time, with an exhilarating style of attacking soccer that attracted new fans around the world. He was determined to do what he thought was right for soccer in Germany even though he created more than a few enemies in the process. Klinsmann is happy to be candid for those who listen to what he says with an open mind; he speaks directly and without any hidden agenda. For those hostile to his ideas and methods, he is an easy target because he is anything but tight-lipped about his ambitious goals.

"I regret that he stepped down because he started something in Germany and didn't finish it," said none other than Franz Beckenbauer in a December 2006 interview with *Sport Bild*. Beckenbauer had first called up Klinsmann to the *Nationalmannschaft* in 1988 but had been one of his chief critics in the difficult period right before the World Cup. "He wanted to win the World Cup and didn't accomplish that." Beckenbauer had tried to persuade Klinsmann to stay right up to the moment he resigned. The "Kaiser" praised Klinsmann for having the courage of his convictions. "In my mind, the methods he brought from the United States were good. He brought in a fresh breeze even if he upset a lot of people."

Another former coach, César Luis Menotti at Sampdoria in Italy, was also full of praise for the way Klinsmann revived Germany's National Team at the World Cup. "I had heard a lot about Klinsmann's new style, but what I saw was a revolution of historic dimensions," said Menotti, who led Argentina to the 1978 World Cup win. "The rhythm and the attack made this team so incredibly good. It's amazing how much this Germany team has changed in such a short period of time."

As fate would have it, eight years later, at the 2014 World Cup in Brazil, Löw's Germany team ended up getting drawn into the same Group G that Jürgen Klinsmann's United States team was playing in. And the two countries were set to square off in the final group game on June 26 in Recife—with one of the two teams emerging as the winner of the group. It loomed as a showdown for supremacy and was important for both teams' hopes of advancing to the Knockout Stage. Germany won the game 1–0, but the United States played as an equal.

At the news conferences before the game at Germany's World Cup base at Campo Bahia, one player after another stood up to praise their former coach for his courage, vision, and determination to push through the reforms eight years earlier and give the team the attacking style of play that had become Germany's signature—and for giving so many younger, untested players a chance.

"He was the first coach to give an entire generation of young players a dream and played a major role in bringing a gust of fresh air into German soccer," said defender Per Mertesacker, a six-foot-six center back discovered by Klinsmann. He had phoned Mertesacker on his twentieth birthday on September 29, 2004, to call him up for the game against Iran that would be the first of 104 caps. "Klinsmann infused a lot of confidence into an entire generation of young players, and that's still there today. He's a very motivating coach who built up a lot of players on our team. A lot of coaches who came into the DFB with Klinsmann are still here today, and we're still benefiting from fruits of what he started back then. We're still on the path that Jürgen started us out on, even now eight years later."

Löw, too, never hesitated to give Klinsmann credit for his team's success. At an unusual joint news conference televised nationally from Cologne before a Germany-USA friendly on June 10, 2015, the two coaches spent an hour answering questions about their respective teams, and on their experience working together. Löw went out of his way to make sure the more than one hundred German sportswriters recognized Klinsmann's role in Germany's success.

"We'll always remember the enormous role that Jürgen played in helping us win the World Cup in 2014," said Löw. "There were a lot of serious problems at the German DFB when Jürgen and I started back in 2004. Times changed after that. A lot of people on our team recognize all that, and we're extremely grateful for all he did. What I've always admired about Jürgen is that he knows in which direction he wants to go and he goes there. He's responsible for a lot of the decisive changes that we made, with the general manager and the fitness coaches. Without those changes we wouldn't have had such a successful phase as we've had. He's played a large part in our winning the World Cup. What I've always admired about Jürgen is that he's always so straightforward, that he knows where he wants to go and has the confidence to overcome all kinds of resistance when he's convinced about something."

Löw also praised the work Klinsmann had done with U.S. soccer. "We've seen a strong improvement in every aspect of the U.S. team's style," he said. "When you look back at the developments over the last three or four years, you can see a lot has happened. The U.S. team has advanced tremendously. It's a completely different team than four years ago. They play at an enormously high pace now. They're playing a much stronger style of soccer than they did a few years ago. They exude an aura of courage, and especially mental strength, that they didn't have in the past. I was really impressed." As if to prove the point, the Americans beat world champion Germany 2–1 the next day. It was the second time in their last three games since 2013 that the United States had beaten Germany.

Even though his entry into coaching in 2004 was the result of an improbable sequence of events, Klinsmann was clearly the right man with the right ideas in the right place at the right time. "He disappeared as suddenly as he came," wrote soccer magazine *11 Freunde*. "After his final news conference, Jürgen Klinsmann took off with a one-way ticket home to California with an elated feeling that he accomplished the job he set out to do. He was sapped of strength from his 'Project 2006,' and the goal of winning the World Cup, and exhausted by trench warfare with journalists and troublemakers at the DFB. He was zapped by his own ambition and living up to his own goals. He didn't win the World Cup, but he had nevertheless accomplished something very extraordinary indeed in Germany."

# PART IV

# FC BAYERN MUNICH

# A DIFFERENT VIEW OF
# BAYERN MUNICH

AFTER SHAKING THE German Football Association out of its deep slumber and leading the German *Nationalmannschaft* to third place at the 2006 World Cup, Jürgen Klinsmann was hired by FC Bayern Munich eighteen months later, in January 2008, for a similarly challenging assignment: to reinvigorate the top German club's approach and achieve more consistent success internationally in the Champions League.

His clearly defined aim this time was to turn the club into a more aggressive, exciting, and attacking team that would score more goals on the field—and to give it an even more professional, modern organization off the field with state-of-the-art facilities. He put an emphasis, above all, on making Bayern more successful in the Champions League, where the club had struggled to gain traction in the previous six years. Although Klinsmann coached FC Bayern Munich for just under one season, the reforms he implemented had a lasting impact on the club. He was unceremoniously fired after just ten months, even though Bayern Munich was still in the thick of the Bundesliga championship battle, only three points behind league leaders VfL Wolfsburg. Yet an objective and deeper look at the bigger picture shows that FC Bayern Munich became a stronger team in European competition in the six seasons after Klinsmann's reforms were introduced than in the six seasons before his time in Munich. The post-Klinsmann team reached the Champions League's final or semifinals in five of those six seasons after failing to reach even the semifinals in the six years before he arrived.

Klinsmann was one of the world's most sought-after coaches in 2007 and 2008, after leading Germany's campaign in the 2006 World Cup, an accomplishment that earned him Coach of the Year in 2006 in Germany and respect in soccer circles around the world as an energetic reformer. His name was mentioned almost every time a high-profile coaching job opened—from the national teams of the United States and Australia to club teams like Chelsea and Liverpool. But he was in no rush to jump right back into the game. Instead he spent more than a year meticulously cataloging, analyzing, studying, and digesting what had worked well and what hadn't during his two years coaching Germany. Klinsmann also worked diligently on improving his Spanish-language skills, saying he was waiting for the "right cause" with the right team, the right people, and the right situation.

FC Bayern Munich was delighted to win the sweepstakes in January 2008 by beating out other top clubs and countries pursuing them. Bayern celebrated Klinsmann's surprise appointment—not even his mother in Stuttgart was aware of the pending deal—as a major coup. The news was announced without fanfare on the Bayern Munich Web site on a Friday morning shortly after 10:00 A.M., much to the chagrin of the country's scoop-hungry tabloids that once again would rue the missed opportunity to break a major story about Klinsmann. Mass-circulation newspapers like *Bild,* which live off of newsstand sales and beating the competition with hot news, never forget losses like that. They would renew their love-hate relationship with Klinsmann for his steadfast refusal to enter into any kind of Faustian bargains with them—favorable coverage for scoops and more cooperation. His surprise, but welcome, return to Germany was once again the top item on the evening news and the front pages of newspapers.

The expectations had risen sharply when Klinsmann arrived. In the 2007/08 season before he went to Munich, FC Bayern Munich was knocked out of the UEFA Cup by Russian club Zenit St. Petersburg in the semifinals by an aggregate 5–1 score.

Klinsmann, who had played for FC Bayern Munich for two seasons from 1995 to 1997, went to Germany's premier club as its coach in 2008 full of energy and élan. He was also eager to try living in Germany with his family and still had a lot of friends in Munich. Using state-of-the-art technology and training methods, he wanted to awaken the slumbering giant, raise aspirations, and turn FC Bayern Munich into a top contender for the title in Europe's premier competition—rather than settle with being the near-perennial winner of the domestic league. Being the big fish in a small pond was never good enough for Klinsmann, and his grand plan for the international stage was music to the ears of Bayern Munich executives.

He set out to make the team better in every way possible. He strongly encouraged his foreign players from Brazil, Argentina, France, and Italy to learn German and offered German tutors to make that easier, but he also installed interpreters at team meetings to make sure they would understand everything being discussed. His concern was that if the foreign players who didn't speak German were able to understand only 85 percent of the instructions or communication with teammates, it could lead to misunderstandings on the field that might cost the team at a crucial moment. Klinsmann also created a cutting-edge *Leistungszentrum,* performance center, for a reported €15 million—complete with gym equipment, lounges, a yoga room, computers, and a library—where players could do more individualized work on their bodies and minds. He put an end to the "doorstepping" arrangement where reporters had to hover outside by the parking lot, waiting to talk with players on their way to their cars, and instead invited reporters into a designated area in the center for briefings and interviews. Klinsmann was mainly concerned with the equipment and facilities inside the performance center. The interior architect Jürgen Meissner, who had also done design work for the German national team at the 2006 World Cup, installed four white Buddha figurines in the rooftop lounge. Klinsmann later faced criticism for the Buddhas after German newspapers turned it into an issue.

Working toward making Bayern one of Europe's top teams, Klinsmann used his simple, understated, and straightforward approach to get the most out of his players. "We want to measure ourselves against the best in Europe," he said at a nationally televised press conference in Munich to announce his signing, on January 11, 2008. "The goal is to make every player better—every day." That goal stuck.

Klinsmann's aim was to implement an aggressive pressing style of defense and high-scoring attack that would make every team dread playing against Bayern. "We've got to play faster and be quicker with our passes," he said at the time. "We want to show a dominating and proactive style." It was similar to the theories of modern soccer that he had applied to the German *Nationalmannschaft* four years earlier— and is the basis of the style Bayern has used to dominate opponents ever since. Klinsmann had a problem with complacency. That led to one memorable exchange with forward Luca Toni, who was coasting in workouts in his second season at Bayern under Klinsmann after a brilliant first season when he scored a total of thirty-nine goals. At one point, an exasperated Klinsmann went over to the towering Italian, who had helped his country win the 2006 World Cup with two goals, and told him that he needed to put all those past glories behind him and start raising his game for Bayern again. The coach's message at a practice one day was as simple as it was typical Klinsmann: "Okay, Luca, we've both won World Cups. Now let's get to work."

Klinsmann had had two full years and complete control as the Germany coach. But at Bayern, which had long been successful in the domestic league while burning through sixteen different head coaches in twenty-seven years, he had less time to get results and was given less control—because Bayern Munich executives insisted on having a say in many of the technical decisions. Bayern's commercial manager, Uli Hoeness, even sat alongside Klinsmann on the bench during games, his practice for thirty years. He moved up into the stands the season after Klinsmann left.

Even though Klinsmann's ten months of coaching Germany's premier club ended abruptly, they were marked by sweeping changes and the introduction of an exciting attacking style of play that put Bayern Munich firmly on track for greater glory. But they were also marked by misunderstandings, turbulence, and tensions with club executives, and criticism from some of the media and fans. Klinsmann's run at Bayern Munich is sometimes fallaciously viewed as a failure because he was dismissed early, with five Bundesliga games left, and because there were two bitter defeats near the end—a 4–0 loss in the Champions League quarterfinals to Barcelona four days after a 5–1 loss in the Bundesliga away at VfL Wolfsburg. But a closer look at Klinsmann's time at Bayern Munich shows that he actually succeeded in putting the club on a trajectory toward greater success in the Champions League, more goal scoring and even stronger domination of the domestic league.

Despite German tabloid-media-fueled suggestions that Klinsmann stumbled at Bayern, an examination of the record shows that not only did they have strong runs and a number of outstanding performances in all three competitions they took part in under Klinsmann—the Champions League, the Bundesliga, and the German Cup—but more important, some of the changes he introduced have contributed to the club's enduring success, especially in the Champions League.

There was one especially fascinating Bundesliga game between Hoffenheim, the league leaders at the time coached by a similarly attack-minded coach, Ralf Rangnick, and Bayern shortly before the league's annual five-week midseason Christmas break, an unforgettable top-of-the-table showdown that left fans, journalists, and the TV audience in awe after ninety minutes of pulsating high-speed soccer. In what was called one of the best Bundesliga games ever played, Klinsmann's team came from a goal down to prevail 2–1, thanks to a late goal from Luca Toni. "Every once in a while there's a soccer game where the final score doesn't really matter," wrote sportswriter Ralf Köttker in the *Die Welt* newspaper of the game that was televised to 167 countries around the world. "The 69,000 fans in Munich saw such a game yesterday. Bayern won 2–1. But the real winners were German soccer and its fans. Seldom before had a showdown between two of the league's top teams lived up to the lofty expectations as this one did. Both teams went into overdrive; it was a fast-motion film. It was athletic, dynamic, modern soccer anno 2008." Bayern Munich chief executive Karl-Heinz Rummenigge and Germany coach Joachim Löw chimed in with praise, saying the game was one of the best the league had ever seen. "Why can't games in the Bundesliga be like that all the time?" wrote *Die Zeit*. Even the usually critical soccer magazine *Kicker* was enthusiastic: "It was a hugely entertaining, wide open duel of the highest quality. Both teams spoiled the audience with high-paced, attacking soccer and every player seemed to run beyond their breaking point." Klaus Hoeltzenbein wrote in the *Süddeutsche Zeitung*: "It was only a game. But it was the best game of the year."

Bayern Munich followed up that December win against Hoffenheim with a 5–1 thrashing of VfB Stuttgart in the Round of 16 in the German Cup in January after the winter break. Yet those stirring victories were all but forgotten in April after the two heavy defeats to Wolfsburg and Barcelona. These losses, near the end of Klinsmann's reign, eclipsed his otherwise solid overall record of twenty-nine wins, nine losses, and nine ties. That first-year record also included a winning streak of eleven games in a row in the Bundesliga. Bayern were in third place (with sixteen wins, six ties, seven losses) in the league when he was fired in April. They had won all but one of their games in the Champions League (six wins, three ties, one loss, and a record-breaking 12–1 aggregate win against Portugal's SP Sporting in the Round of 16) and were unlucky to get knocked out of the German Cup (with three wins, one loss) in the quarterfinals. Bayern had gotten off to a slow start to the season in the Bundesliga, winning only three of their first eight games and falling to eleventh place in the eighteen-team league. That can be attributed, at least in part, to the time needed to adjust to Klinsmann's extensive reforms. Another factor hurting Klinsmann's start was the 2008 European Championship tournament. Bayern's players made up the core of the German *Nationalmannschaft* that had gone all the way to the final, where they lost to Spain 1–0 on June 29. As a result of Euro 2008, many of Bayern's players on the Germany team were still on vacation for weeks after their club teammates and other Bundesliga players had reported for duty. Bayern Munich's Germany team players didn't report back until nearly a month later, just before the Bundesliga season started on August 15. Compounding the woes, the team's star player, Franck Ribéry, who suffered torn ligaments in his ankle in France's 2–0 loss to Italy at the European Championships, missed the first six weeks of the season.

Despite being eliminated in the quarterfinals of the Champions League and German Cup competitions, Bayern was only three points out of first place with five games to play when Klinsmann was fired. Four of the five remaining games were against teams in the bottom half of the league standings. The championship, in other words, was still wide open.

Looked at another way, Klinsmann's win-loss record is all the more impressive considering that Bayern Munich did not spend any money at all on new players in the transfer market before the start of the 2008/09 season. The club actually earned a net €10 million that season by selling Marcell Jansen to Hamburg SV and Jan Schlaudraff to Hannover 96. At the time, Bayern was busy rushing to pay off a €340 million loan for the construction of their home stadium, the Allianz Arena, at an accelerated pace. It was originally a twenty-five-year loan from 2005, but Bayern retired all debt on the stadium in about nine years, sixteen years ahead of schedule. Klinsmann also had to do without the services of veteran goalkeeper Oliver Kahn, an anchor of the team's defense for fourteen seasons, who had retired at age thirty-nine at the end of the 2007/08 season. Kahn's longtime understudy, Michael Rensing, was unable to fill his shoes, and struggled at times. He was replaced the following season by reserve keeper Hans-Jörg Butt and released by Bayern in 2010.

Unlike many of its Champions League rivals, such as Barcelona, Real Madrid, and Manchester United, Bayern Munich had long had a reputation for thrift and had accumulated massive reserves in its *Festgeldkonto,* a war chest filled with some €150 million. It was only after Klinsmann left that Bayern cracked open its "piggy bank" and started spending serious money for top talent in the transfer market. For instance, in the season after Klinsmann's departure, Bayern spent €80 million on transfers to obtain stars including Arjen Robben (from Real Madrid) and Mario Gómez (from VfB Stuttgart). Klinsmann said in a German television interview after he left Munich that he let Bayern executives persuade him before the season that the team didn't need any reinforcements from the transfer market. "That was a mistake I made," he said. Bayern Munich could nevertheless still have won the Bundesliga championship, he added. Yet there was no bitterness, and Klinsmann is pleased with what he learned at Bayern and the changes he was able to implement.

"It was absolutely a good experience," Klinsmann says today. "It was a tremendous experience to work with different people in a different environment. It didn't end the way we wanted it to end, but you know what the reasons for that were so you just move on. It was a priceless experience. I thought I'd be able to break through some of the structures that were cemented in place, but the only one who shared that belief with me was Karl-Heinz Rummenigge. Obviously, with hindsight, I'd do some things differently. But there were many things that I started at FC Bayern that were adopted by my successors."

Klinsmann had faced criticism by some of the same newspapers that had made life difficult for him at times when he was coaching Germany. Their drumbeat of faultfinding had turned some of Bayern Munich's demanding fans against Klinsmann as well. Disappointed though he was at not being able to finish the season, he left Bayern without any regrets.

"We've laid the foundations for the future," Klinsmann said in a statement issued on the day he was fired. He even offered a "heartfelt thanks" to Bayern Munich, the fans, coaches, and players "for an exciting time" in Munich. He added that he thought Bayern could still win the Bundesliga championship. The team managed to keep its strong run going by winning four of their final five games, with a tie against Hoffenheim the only blemish, to move up a notch to second place behind champions VfL Wolfsburg.

Klinsmann did indeed put his stamp on Bayern Munich. In the six years after he coached them, the club became more successful in the Champions League and more offensive-minded in the Bundesliga, scoring more goals than before. After he left, Bayern Munich made it to the semifinals of the Champions League five times in six years and to the final three times, winning it all in 2013. In the six years before Klinsmann coached in 2008/09 and introduced his reforms, Bayern never made it past the quarterfinals.

In his 2008/09 season, FC Bayern Munich was unbeaten through the Round of 16 in the Champions League and a dominant force with six wins and two ties before the quarterfinals—outscoring their opponents by a lopsided 24–5 margin. But they suffered their one and only Champions League loss in the quarterfinals, losing 4–0 at Barcelona before playing a 1–1 tie a week later in Munich. A slew of injuries had weakened Bayern in the game against the team that went on to win the Champions League: top striker Miroslav Klose, their best fullback Philipp Lahm, and their best center back Lúcio all missed the game in Barcelona.

Philipp Köster, the editor of *11 Freunde,* says that Klinsmann did a remarkable job modernizing soccer in Germany as coach of the *Nationalmannschaft* from 2004 to 2006, breaking down barriers and resistance to reforms at the DFB and at Bundesliga clubs. But Klinsmann was not given the same time, resources, and authority at Bayern.

"There was a big misunderstanding about Jürgen Klinsmann's work at FC Bayern," Köster says. "He wanted to apply the same recipes at Bayern that he used for the national team. But he overlooked the fact that the management structures at FC Bayern are completely different than at the DFB. The national team was without any leadership when Klinsmann arrived, and he could implement the changes he wanted with relatively little interference. But at FC Bayern, he had to deal with powerful club leaders who didn't want to relinquish control."

Raphael Konigstein writes in *Das Reboot* that even though Klinsmann struggled at Bayern, he nevertheless laid the foundation for the club's subsequent success. "Bayern had explicitly wanted change, but change on their own terms and without an annoying let-up in wins. Klinsmann's personnel decisions were resisted because they didn't fully trust his judgement." Bayern executives were especially doubtful, he adds, about Klinsmann's decision to bring in Landon Donovan to Munich on a two-month loan from the Los Angeles Galaxy during the MLS's off-season winter break. Konigstein said that at the end of the day, Klinsmann had put Bayern on the right track to the benefit of his successors. "The performance center as well as some of the fitness staff he had left behind soon helped Bayern regain their place among the European elite under Louis van Gaal and Jupp Heynckes over the next few years."

Klinsmann also promoted promising young players to Bayern's first team from the second and third teams, including Thomas Müller, Holger Badstuber, and Mehmet Ekici, giving the talented amateurs their first professional contracts. Müller, nineteen years old at the time, made his debut for Bayern under Klinsmann as a substitute in the Champions League, scoring his first goal in his first game against SP Sporting Lisbon in the Round of 16. Just over a year after making it onto Bayern's first team under Klinsmann, Müller won the Golden Boot at the 2010 World Cup as the tournament's top scorer, with five goals and three assists.

Sometimes it takes a while for reforms to have an impact. Karl-

Heinz Rummenigge, Bayern Munich's chief executive, said in 2015 that he thought Klinsmann had made positive changes at Bayern during his ten months in Munich. He also accepted some of the blame for Klinsmann not having more success. What is clear to those who follow the Bundesliga is that post-Klinsmann Bayern teams are far hungrier for goals than the teams of the earlier, more cautious era. While Bayern Munich teams from the late 1990s to Klinsmann's era often seemed content to sit on their lead once they got one or two ahead, post-Klinsmann teams seemed rabid for more goals even once they opened a two- or three-goal lead. A look at the statistics confirms that. In the six years after Klinsmann's 2008/09 season, Bayern Munich teams scored an average of eighty-four goals per thirty-four-game Bundesliga season, 2.47 goals per game, compared to sixty-seven goals, an average of 1.98 goals per game, in the six seasons before Klinsmann.

Klinsmann soon returned to California—disappointed about not being able to finish the job in Munich but without any bitterness and more knowledge than he had before he arrived. He felt he had put Bayern on the right track for the long run, and called it all a learning experience. He also decided to use the unexpected free time on his hands to fulfill a lifelong dream—getting a pilot's license. With some encouragement from his wife, he signed up for a course and started learning how to fly helicopters. "I was always fascinated by flying," he says. "I always loved going to airports, I loved the take-offs and the landings. I always wanted to be a pilot, right up until I was sixteen and got my first pro contract in Stuttgart." He flew a lot as a soccer player and over the years he sometimes got the chance to ride with the pilots in the cockpits of jumbo jets. He always enjoyed the experience. "After Bayern, I just said I always wanted to see how difficult it would be to get my license," he says. "I felt I needed a challenge for my brain, I needed something different than soccer."

He found a helicopter flight school near his hometown and went back to school, taking theory and flight classes. "After five or six lessons I began to think it was a crazy idea, that it was too complicated. But one of the instructors told me, 'Jürgen, if it were easy, then everyone would be a helicopter pilot.'" He decided to stick with it. It took more than a year for him to get his private license and he has since been enjoying privately flying helicopters around Southern California. "Now I'm working on my commercial license." Why that? "I just want to get better. It's the same as if you have a B license as a coach you want to get an A license and once you get that you want a pro license. It's the same in any field: you want to get the higher qualification."

# PART V

# THE RISE OF SOCCER IN THE UNITED STATES

# A VISION FOR SOCCER
# IN AMERICA

JÜRGEN KLINSMANN HAS a clear vision for soccer in the United States: He wants to help the country be more successful at the World Cup than it's ever been before, and to build a world-class program with a team at the top of the pyramid that is strong enough to one day win the world's most important tournament. Klinsmann has been the head coach of the U.S. Men's National Team since 2011 and was given the added responsibilities of technical director in 2013 to oversee developments of the entire program.

Considering that the World Cup has been dominated by a handful of European and South American nations, Klinsmann's goal is an ambitious undertaking by any measure. Some might even call it impossible. There have been twenty World Cups since 1930, and only eight countries have ever won it. Three nations—Brazil (five), Germany (four), and Italy (four)—have won thirteen of those twenty tournaments. But Klinsmann is an incorrigible optimist, a believer in the power of change, and an unabashed admirer of America's fighting spirit.

In the increasingly competitive global game where a number of nations in Asia, Africa, Central America, and South America that were once considered "small" in soccer are taking giant leaps forward, his first aim is to make the United States a top-ten team. That is no small order considering the U.S. Men's National Team's average FIFA ranking since 1993 has been nineteenth. He has also set the bar high for the next World Cup, in 2018 in Russia—making it to at least the Final Four, the semifinals.

Klinsmann believes the United States has the potential to break the lock that European and South American countries have on soccer, and even one day win the World Cup. He has a broader mandate and additional responsibilities as technical director—he is in charge of raising the level of the entire U.S. soccer program.

But winning the World Cup will require extensive reforms that not everyone will like, considerable patience that Americans aren't exactly famous for, more self-motivated players capable of competing against experienced professionals from other countries, and above all an honest self-evaluation of where the United States is in relation to the rest of the world.

"The USA needs to face one essential fact: we are the equivalent of a developing third-world nation in the world of soccer," wrote Robert Wilson in a sharply worded analysis for *The Huffington Post.* "We have no reason or justification for swagger. Much less be arrogant. The USA has accomplished very little, outside of staging the 1994 World Cup."

It is an uphill battle. Because soccer is by far the number one sport in most of the rest of the world outside the United States, it will take more than wishful thinking and pompous pronouncements to become a World Cup contender against competition that never sleeps and against nations where highly driven youngsters starved for success are juggling soccer balls, kicking them against walls, and working on their skills for countless hours every week.

Klinsmann is determined to put the U.S. Men's National Team on track to rise into the top ten and get to the World Cup's semifinals at least in 2018. To get Americans more comfortable and confident against the world's best teams, Klinsmann has gone out of his way to schedule difficult friendlies, or exhibition matches, against the best opponents possible—even at the risk of losses piling up. He's doing it to make American players better prepared to meet again in a World Cup one day, which for Klinsmann is the goal that matters.

"The only way to get better is to play against the better teams," Klinsmann said after the United States came from behind to beat the Netherlands 4–3 in Amsterdam and Germany 2–1 in Cologne in two memorable friendlies played within a six-day span in June 2015.

It's an extraordinarily complex challenge considering so much of the way the United States plays soccer is out of sync with the way the rest of the world plays the game. The U.S. pro and college leagues play a different seasonal calendar, its leagues are closed off without the highly competitive promotion-relegation system that the rest of the world follows, and playing soccer is an expensive proposition for most young players in the United States whereas elsewhere it is a game for the masses and working class. But Klinsmann believes the country he is so fond of and has made his home is on the right track.

The popularity of soccer at the youth, high school, and college levels keeps growing every year. In some parts of the country soccer has replaced football as the main fall sport as concerns about football-related head injuries increase. That and rising costs have led some high schools and colleges to drop football. At least nine high school and youth football players died from injuries suffered in the 2015 season. The number of high school students playing football tumbled by more than 25,000 between 2010 and 2015, according to a CBS news report.

Soccer is growing rapidly in American schools. The National Federation of State High School Associations reports there were

805,250 boys and girls playing soccer at nearly 9,000 high schools across the country in the 2014–2015 school year. That was up from 759,907 at just over 8,000 high schools in 2010–2011 and far above the 49,593 at 2,200 schools in 1969–1970. By comparison, the number of football players dropped from 1,109,836 at 14,279 schools in 2010–2011 to 1,085,182 at 14,154 schools in 2014–2015.

"Overall, the game has grown tremendously at all levels in the United States," Klinsmann says, smiling as he reflects on the exponential progress over the last two decades. "It's growing at the youth level, the high school and college level, and the amateur level for adults. The fact that Major League Soccer is now twenty years old, getting stronger and bigger by the year, is absolutely fascinating. Soccer has made it in the United States. It's recognized. It's accepted. People like it. It's mainstream. And like it is in other countries, it's the national team that is the locomotive driving all that growth."

Klinsmann wants to keep that momentum going and hopes to see soccer become a major sport in the United States led by a strong national team. The 2014 World Cup gave millions of Americans a tantalizing glimpse of how exciting a major international soccer tournament can be, connecting the country to the rest of the world like never before, as millions of Americans enthusiastically followed the tournament. Some twenty-four million Americans, a record television audience for soccer, tuned in to watch the U.S. team play to a 2–2 tie against Portugal, and twenty thousand fans crowded into a fan zone in Chicago's Grant Park, creating a rousing atmosphere to watch the 2–1 win against Ghana. American followers of the team in Brazil were the largest and loudest fan contingent. "We were able to make an emotional connection to the people," he says. "This is the real thing, these are the best players in our country, and this is how we measure ourselves with the rest of the world. It's totally emotional."

"Soccer got another really big boost in the United States—both emotionally and in the media—because we made it out of the Group of Death at the World Cup in Brazil," Klinsmann says, referring to what most soccer experts said was the most difficult of eight groups of four teams in the first round of the 2014 World Cup. "Soccer has made a huge leap forward, but there's still a long way to go to become a top-ten team. That's still a lot of work to do. We're at the point now where our goal is to break into the top ten and stay there over the next five to ten years." And the long-term goal is to win the world's most important tournament even though it might take a while to achieve that: "It will definitely be the goal to win the World Cup, many years down the road," he says.

The United States is still disconcertingly disconnected from the way the rest of the world plays the game in a number of areas. While many of the major sports in the United States are focused on the domestic championship, soccer is different: It's an international competition. The Super Bowl winner is the best football team in the country; the NBA champion is the best basketball team. But the best soccer team is the winner of the World Cup.

"It's a bigger puzzle in the United States than in other countries, but that's also what makes this so exciting," says Klinsmann, referring to the project of making the United States a global soccer power. "We're putting the pieces of the puzzle together now. It's important for Americans to remember that we're not competing in a domestic environment with soccer. Americans are used to the competition being within America, like with the NBA, the NFL, or the NHL. It's all America-driven, and the top players in those sports from around the world want to be part of the NBA, the NFL, or the NHL. It's not easy for Americans to understand that with soccer it's the other way around: Soccer is a globally driven sport. Your competitors are around the globe and your way of thinking has to be in a global way. It's a big transition, and these kinds of changes take time. That's just the way it is."

Klinsmann is fascinated by the chances for soccer in the United States. There are about 4 million Americans registered but more than 13 million who play soccer—a huge increase compared to 100,000 players in 1967 and 4 million in 1984. FIFA reported in 2007 that there were 2.5 million men in the United States on registered teams, making it the second-largest soccer country in the world behind only Germany (6.3 million) and ahead of Brazil in third place (2.1 million). In women's soccer, the United States has the largest number of players registered: 1.7 million. That is twice as many women as the next largest country, Germany, with 871,000. Worldwide, FIFA said that there are 265 million people who play soccer regularly or occasionally. The world's governing body said that women make up about 12 percent of that total. According to an ESPN Sports Poll conducted by North Carolina scientist Rich Luker in 2012, pro soccer already ranks as the second most popular sport in the United States among twelve- to twenty-two-year-olds—behind only the NFL but ahead of the NBA, MLB, and college football.

"We can be extremely happy with the way soccer is growing," Klinsmann says. "It's an evolution, not a short-term process. The foundation of the game is always going to be the youth sector, the kids. But there are still many things that aren't connected the right way," he says, referring to the need to develop a clear pyramid structure that offers a transparent path from the bottom to the top.

U.S. Soccer, the official governing body, had launched massive efforts to expand the youth development even before Klinsmann started in 2011. The U.S. Soccer Development Academy was founded in 2007 to improve the landscape for elite player development by adopting practices that bring the game more in line with international soccer. The Academy, funded primarily by U.S. Soccer, has grown to more than 100 clubs across the country. This model was preceded in 1999 by the establishment of the Under-17 Residency Program in Bradenton, Florida. The full-time residency has up to thirty-five players year round in an immersed environment which includes both sport and schooling. The inaugural class included players such as Landon Donovan, DaMarcus Beasley, Kyle Beckerman, and Oguchi Onyewu who went on to play for the United States in World Cups.

U.S. Soccer now spends about $14 million a year on youth national teams and player development—for men *and* women. Major League Soccer spends about $20 million a year on youth academies. By comparison, the German DFB spends more than $23 million on its 366 regional performance centers, and the German pro league, the Bundesliga, spends another $135 million per season on its youth academies. Money might not buy happiness, but it can help make countries better in soccer. The prosperity of a country and the amount of its wealth that it devotes to soccer are important determining factors for long-term success, as Kuper and Szymanski note in *Soccernomics*: "We have also seen that rich countries are best at finding, training, and developing talent. In short, it takes experience, population, and wealth to make a successful soccer nation." They believe the United States has many of the right ingredients to become a major soccer power in the long run.

Pep Guardiola, a former Bayern Munich coach and Barcelona coach who led the Spanish club to two Champions League titles in three years, says he has seen major growth in soccer in the United States and believes there is vast potential for success. Americans' enthusiasm for soccer has been growing in recent years, and the strong run at the World Cup in Brazil galvanized that long overdue development. Guardiola, who got to know the United States well while spending a year on sabbatical in New York City in 2012 after leaving Barcelona, is impressed with the development of the U.S. Men's National Team under Klinsmann. "The United States is making a lot of steps forward in their concept about soccer," he says. "They play so aggressively and are physically stronger. The United States is a reality in world soccer. In the next few years, they will be stronger in the World Cup and can make it better and better." One of the world's best forwards Neymar, who has excelled for both his club Barcelona and Brazil, also noted the rapid growth in the United States and said that he could see himself playing soccer for a US club one day. "I would also like to play in the United States," he said in an interview with RedBull.com in early 2016. "The US is a place where the game is growing and attracting a lot of interest of lots of players who are becoming more and more popular there. So this makes me curious, it makes me interested to see it closely."

Klinsmann talks often about self-motivation and how he wishes American players could do more on their own to improve their games. That, he says, is the key to success for the top soccer players everywhere in the world. "There are a lot of fundamental questions that we still have to talk about more. How much drive is there? How many hours a day, or how many hours each week, are the kids playing soccer? What drives them at the end of the day to make themselves better? Are the coaches properly trained and educated? Yes, the game is growing, millions of kids are playing it, but I sometimes fear a lot of that doesn't make it through the channels of communication, or it gets lost in things like the pay-per-play model in the youth sector. There are so many things that aren't yet connected the way they should be connected. America is such a huge, fascinating place. I think it's going to take years to get it all right."

If he had a magic wand, that would probably be the one aspect of soccer in the United States that Klinsmann would like to change the most over the long run: getting young children to be as hungry to improve their soccer skills as their contemporaries in soccer nations around the world.

To become one of the world's best in the World Cup, Klinsmann believes the United States needs to develop a culture where youngsters have the drive to play soccer in their neighborhoods or on a team for three or four or more hours every day of the week, year-round. It's been a positive development in recent years that serious youth soccer players are now devoting at least ten months a year to the game. Yet in general, American children play lots of different sports, and that means they might have only a few months a year to devote to soccer. What does that mean for the United States' longer-term prospects in soccer if children in Germany, Brazil, Italy, and Argentina are playing *only* soccer year-round?

"I think that's the missing ingredient compared to what's happening in the best soccer nations around the world—the drive and the amount of time that kids are out there playing the game," says Klinsmann, who ended up becoming one of Germany's best players ever through countless thousands of hours of practice, practice, and more practice. He's convinced it was mainly because of drive and diligence, although he also had a modicum of talent to start with.

Klinsmann isn't the only top player to emphasize it was hard work and endless hours of practice, more than anything else, that made his success in soccer possible. England forward Wayne Rooney writes in his autobiography, *Wayne Rooney: My Story,* that it was mainly work and discipline that were responsible for his soccer success. "I would put hard work first, then natural ability—and then luck. Some people have somehow got it into their heads that I've been an overnight success, come from nowhere, so I must be a bit stunned by all the things that have happened to me. That's not how I see it. All I see is ten years of hard work, of practicing, and training, and discipline. It's been a long long time, all my life really, so I don't look around and think I'm dreaming."

Some of the world's best players admit, however, they reached plateaus and stagnated earlier in their careers, after reaching a certain level of comfort before raising their game at some point thanks to a timely jolt or a wake-up call from a club coach, national team coach, or even their own agent. Sweden's striker Zlatan Ibrahimovic describes in his entertaining bestselling 2011 autobiography, *I am Zlatan,* that he was coasting once he had made it onto a top Dutch club, Ajax Amsterdam, and was frustrated that he couldn't transfer to a top club in Italy. His agent Mino Raiola told him when he was still a young player that he just wasn't good enough and not getting any better with just five goals in twenty-five games in 2004. Raiola used a series of four-letter expletives to shake him out of his lethargy, telling Ibrahimovic, "You're nothing." He told him that he would have to work three times harder in practice and do things like sell his luxury watches if he wanted to move up to the next level. "He was right, wasn't he?" writes Ibrahimovic, who later on became one of the most effective goal scorers ever for clubs in Italy and France as well as for the Swedish national team. "I had been too pleased with myself, thinking I was all that great. It was the wrong attitude. It was true that I hadn't scored enough goals and I'd been too lazy. I hadn't been motivated enough. I began to give everything I had in practice and matches. . . . It got me going and it got me more of a winner's mind-set."

Klinsmann is hopeful that future generations of American soccer players will have a similar burning desire as Rooney and Ibrahimovic. "If young kids in Germany or Mexico are playing soccer four or five hours a week with their teams but then spending another fifteen or sixteen hours on their own banging the ball around in their neighborhoods, that's going to show later on. Their technical abilities, their passing abilities, and their instincts will be better. A kid in Buenos Aires is playing five hours a day, and so he's always going to be ahead of the curve. But it doesn't have to always stay like that. That's where the U.S. needs to improve."

The closest analogy to that kind of drive that he has seen in the United States is some youngsters building their lives around basketball—playing pickup games for hours upon hours every day, all year. "We all came from families with modest incomes and fought our way through," he says. "You need to keep that kind of hunger burning inside you. You see that with basketball—the way the guys play it all the time in the inner cities."

In an article in the *San Diego Union-Tribune* called "U.S. Soccer and the Perilous Road Ahead," sportswriter Mark Zeigler wrote that the U.S. Men's National Team showed in Brazil that it has gone a long way to narrow the gap to the world's top teams, but at the same time it also showed how far it still has to go. He concluded that America's failure to produce any kind of world-class outfield player was a worrying indictment of American youth soccer.

"Despite constant initiatives and residential academies and coaching handbooks, the massive youth soccer machine and its obsession with winning under-10 State Cups continues to churn out serviceable college players and B-level MLS guys but not elite talent, or at least not enough of it. The United States, with 318 million people, still has never produced a genuine world-class field player who could stick with Europe's biggest clubs. Belgium can, with 308 million fewer people and a worse World Cup record over the last 25 years than the United States. The Netherlands can. Uruguay can. Croatia can. Chile can."

Jürgen Klinsmann is convinced that the United States can too.

# LAY OF THE LAND

IT IS IRONIC that Jürgen Klinsmann is now trying to change what he once treasured about the United States—a national indifference to soccer. It had been about the only place on earth he could go to get away from the sport, a place where the game didn't matter to the general public. Now, some two decades later, he's trying to make soccer as popular and powerful in the United States as it is in Germany, Italy, France, England, and Brazil.

He is as curious as always, with a vociferous appetite to learn, and especially learn more about what makes Americans tick and how they play soccer at the grassroots levels. He didn't at first fathom the heavy influence that the U.S. school system has on sports because in Germany and many other countries the purview of sports like soccer is with private clubs without any affiliation to the schools.

"It took me years to understand how important the whole educational system is for Americans," says Klinsmann, who got to see it firsthand as his son and daughter both played youth soccer. "But I finally got it. Sports in this country are driven by the educational system. When people asked me, 'Where are your kids going to school?' I'd always say, 'To the next-closest school. Why? Is that a big deal?' I didn't really get that at first." Klinsmann wasn't in Stuttgart anymore. That might be the way parents pick schools for their children in Germany because the schools are, in general, pretty much all the same. But schools and sports systems in the United States are different, as Klinsmann discovered soon enough. "I looked at this as a huge learning opportunity," he says.

Still in top condition with a yearning to work out that was showing no signs of waning in his late thirties, Klinsmann grabbed his cleats two or three times a week and joined pickup soccer games—just for fun and fitness—near his home in Orange County with some of the locals, onetime high school players and former college players. It was not only a chance to stay in shape doing what he loves doing, but the low-key, low-level games and workouts also gave him some valuable insights into the game in the United States.

"At that level you got to see how totally fragmented soccer is in the United States," Klinsmann says. "I got to see that in this whole amazing country there are so many disconnected pieces."

He learned that soccer in the United States can be a prohibitively expensive sport. Also striking was that there was no clear soccer pyramid as in Germany, Italy, France, and England. Those countries have a single system with various levels in the hierarchy that feed players and teams up through the ranks from lower divisions to the first division, one step at a time.

By contrast, the main goal for young Americans seemed to be to use soccer as a springboard to get a college scholarship. The main goal for young Germans was to make it to the next level up on the pyramid and possibly one day play professionally or, ultimately, at a World Cup.

In soccer nations in Europe, the pyramid is a remarkably efficient system. In essence, if you're a good enough player or on a team that's good enough, you or your team will keep rising through the ranks. That meritocracy means, in theory, players can rise all the way to the top professional league or even the national team. But Klinsmann couldn't find anything resembling that straightforward soccer pyramid structure in the United States, even though basketball and football did have something of a hierarchy, with twenty-five thousand high schools feeding into three thousand colleges, which in turn feed their best into the few dozen teams of the NBA and NFL. The closest thing to a pyramid structure was in baseball, where the major league teams have minor league farm teams.

There are rival youth organizations in the U.S. pyramid, such as the American Youth Soccer Organization, U.S. Youth Soccer, U.S. Club Soccer, and the Soccer Association for Youth (SAY Soccer) at the entry level. For young adults and adults above that, the options include the USASA Elite Amateur League with twelve state and regional leagues, National Premier Soccer League with seventy-eight clubs, and the Premier Development League (PDL) with sixty-three clubs. And at the top are three professional leagues that are not linked in a clear hierarchy as in other countries. The United States League (USL) has twenty-four clubs, the North American Soccer League has fourteen clubs, and MLS has twenty teams. MLS, which played its first season in 1996 with ten teams, has a limited cooperative working agreement with USL. NASL, started in 2009, considers itself a rival of MLS, not subordinate or a feeder. For the most part, the leagues are not connected and there is no promotion or relegation of teams.

The pickup games that Klinsmann played in California were mostly informal, not unlike the sorts of games he played in his neighborhood as a youngster in Germany a quarter of a century earlier. At one point in 2003 there was a window of a few months when some local college players joined the pickup games whenever they could make it. Some were on the Orange County Blue Star, an amateur team in the PDL. They played their home games at a local high school with fewer than one hundred spectators. Klinsmann, thirty-nine at the time, was enjoying the low-key, just-for-fun games. Many of the players on opposing teams didn't even know who he was.

Unbeknownst to him, someone on the Blue Star had listed his name in the lineup as Jay Goppingen, based on the first initial of his first name and the town where he was born. Several games into the season, a sportswriter at a newspaper in San Diego spotted Klinsmann and wrote that he was playing under an alias, which wasn't quite the whole story but nevertheless got covered by newspapers in Europe.

"It was just a little team where we'd just kick a ball around two or three times a week," Klinsmann says. "It was just for fun. It was like, 'If you can make it, great. If not, that's okay too.' Then comes this three-month window between the spring and fall season for the college boys, and since we have better players coming in now with the college boys, we played in that little league, the PDL, for a few months. And that's all it was. The players were actually decent. I had a good time until they [some journalists] started to blow it up. After about eight games, I said, 'Hey, guys, this is really just to stay healthy and kick the ball around,' but if this is becoming something used to promote the team with . . ." So he stopped playing in the PDL games but kept working out quietly with many of the same players. "Whenever I got the chance, I played with those guys because it was a great workout—nothing special but it kept me going."

# CONNECTING THE DOTS

Jürgen Klinsmann had long been interested in one day coaching the U.S. soccer team, and U.S. Soccer president Sunil Gulati was long interested in hiring Klinsmann. It seemed like a natural fit. "To Gulati, Klinsmann was what U.S. Soccer needed: a coach European enough to command the players' respect, but American enough to embrace new advances in training and technology. He also saw Klinsmann as someone who would be able to relate to an ever-growing fan base that was looking for something—anything—fresh," wrote Sam Borden in *The New York Times Magazine*.

It took five years to reach an agreement. They first had talks in late 2006, again in 2007, and then again in 2010 before finally shaking hands in July 2011. At a joint press conference in New York on August 1, the persistent Gulati hailed the signing: "Today starts a new era for us. . . . We're heading in the right direction. We're excited to have Jürgen Klinsmann leading our team and technical program." Klinsmann told the journalists that he was really excited about the opportunity. "I've studied the U.S. the last 13 years, and it's going to be quite a challenge," he said.

It had been a long journey to get to that point, and both sides sounded thoroughly pleased and as if it had been worth the wait.

Klinsmann had been successful during his two years coaching Germany because he had the freedom to do everything he thought was necessary to turn the team around for the World Cup and the long term, and the DFB had essentially turned over the keys to him after they couldn't find any other takers for the job. As interested as he was in the challenges of the U.S. coaching job after spending more than a decade watching soccer grow in the United States, Klinsmann knew that his changes would cause pain and upset some people, leading to powerful headwinds blowing against him sooner or later. He wanted to be sure he would have the mandate and time he needed to push through the reforms.

"When we talked first after the 2006 World Cup and then again after the 2010 World Cup, it was all about the question: 'Are we on the same page going into a time of change?'" Klinsmann says. "It's not necessarily about the control. I said from the beginning that if you want progress, I believe that you need to change certain things. We had very positive conversations."

Klinsmann had long been fascinated by the challenges and great potential of soccer in the United States. But at the same time he was patient and wasn't looking to take any job at any price. He was perfectly content, and busy enough, with other assignments—analyzing his two years coaching in Germany, working on SoccerSolutions's consulting projects, learning Spanish, working toward his helicopter pilot's license, and working as a TV analyst at the 2010 World Cup in South Africa for ESPN, the BBC in Britain, and Germany's RTL.

"There are a lot of complexities with the way everything works here in the United States," Klinsmann says, referring in general terms to why the earlier talks had often ended without an agreement. Among the complexities was that Major League Soccer plays a calendar different from the rest of FIFA, a major disadvantage for U.S. soccer teams competing against countries with domestic leagues that play the FIFA calendar, running from early July to late May. Another difficulty is that the top pro league is not connected to the lower leagues the way the top leagues in other countries are. As noted earlier, there are different youth leagues, competing and overlapping systems everywhere he turned. "Because of all these things, it was really difficult to get a feeling that everybody's on the same page," Klinsmann says. "I said, 'If you want me to do that, I'll take on all these issues, but if I feel like something is wrong, I'm going to say it's wrong.' So we didn't come to an agreement. It's as simple as that. The same thing happened in 2010 as well. I said, 'Either you buy into it, or if you don't, that's okay too,'" he said, referring to his philosophy of reforms.

Klinsmann simply wanted to make sure that he and U.S. Soccer would be aligned about what was needed to develop youth soccer and make the foundation for the U.S. Men's National Team stronger. He also wanted assurance that U.S. Soccer would provide the backing a reform-minded coach would need to push the players and the federation to the next level.

"Oh, yes, I was absolutely interested in the job," Klinsmann says. "I've lived in the country for so long, I love it, and I watch soccer here every weekend. My boy is playing, and I know what's going on at the youth level and the education system. I had a good feel for where MLS was compared to other leagues around the world, and could feel the game was definitely on the rise in the United States, and that it'll only get bigger. And then at the end it was the same discussion, and we said, 'Okay, no problem.'"

Klinsmann expected it to take years—perhaps a decade or more—for his reforms to bear fruit. He knew the changes he wanted to implement couldn't produce results overnight or even within a single four-year World Cup cycle. He feared he might be wasting his time as well as that of U.S. Soccer to try to satisfy the yearnings for instant gratification with a long-term strategy that might not necessarily produce satisfactory short-term results. He wanted to set things in motion that would make a big difference down the road. The most successful soccer clubs and national teams thrived only after getting enough time for the reforms to take hold in order to make a difference.

One of the most famous examples of a club having enough faith in the vision of a new coach to have its patience rewarded is Manchester United, which Sir Alex Ferguson coached from 1986 to 2013. Ferguson had a most difficult start, finishing eleventh twice and second once in his first four seasons, from 1986/87 to 1989/90. Manchester United chairman, Martin Edwards, was criticized at the time for his reluctance to fire Ferguson—he nevertheless thought that in the long run, the Scottish coach would do the job well. He certainly got that right. Ferguson praised Edwards and Bobby Charlton, a key ally and member of the board of directors, in his autobiography *Alex Ferguson* for keeping the faith and taking a long-term view. "It reflects well on those two men that they had the courage to stick by me in those dark days," Ferguson wrote. Ferguson, like Klinsmann, was sometimes second-guessed for frequently changing his lineup in search of the best possible formation and to adjust for injuries. Ferguson once went nearly three years—more than 150 games—without fielding the same lineup twice in a row. And yet he ended up winning thirty-eight trophies for ManU in his twenty-six seasons, including thirteen Premier League titles and two Champions League titles.

Gulati bumped into Klinsmann on July 17, 2011, at the Women's World Cup final in Frankfurt, where Japan upset the U.S. Women's National Team in a penalty shoot-out. Gulati suggested they meet again. Just a month before, Klinsmann had been invited to a White

House state dinner on June 7 to honor German chancellor Angela Merkel with the Medal of Freedom. Merkel had been a steadfast supporter of Klinsmann and his reforms in Germany, and the two had remained in contact. She had even awarded him the country's prestigious *Bundesverdienstkreuz*, or federal cross of merit, in 2007 for his outstanding contributions to Germany in his leadership of the German national team. At the White House, Merkel introduced Klinsmann to President Barack Obama as the coach who had put the Germany team back on a winning track.

"I said, 'Sunil, we can always talk,'" Klinsmann recalls saying when they met in Frankfurt in 2011. "'We get along. But you know my approach: to really go for it, to shake things up, and try to connect these pieces that are floating around and driving everyone nuts in this country.' He said we should just sit down and meet. So it was the two of us in New York, and we got all our intentions down on a piece of paper in a letter of intent. It was a happy moment for both of us."

Once he was installed in the job, Klinsmann didn't lose any time introducing reforms and trying to "connect the dots" between the various soccer organizations and systems in the United States. One of his very first acts for his first game as coach of the U.S. Men's National Team, a friendly against Mexico in Philadelphia, was to take away the players' usual jersey numbers and assign the starting team the numbers 1 through 11. He said it was a signal that there was going to be open competition for all the starting positions.

He introduced a new attacking style of play designed to create more scoring opportunities, which he believed better reflected the country's ambitious attitude, scrapping the reactive style that U.S. teams had used before. He wanted his team to play with confidence, courage, and creativity. As he had done for Germany and Bayern Munich, he put a focus on conditioning and nutrition, introducing yoga as well. He increased the number of workouts from one to two or even three a day.

"Jürgen talked about a broader vision for American soccer," writes Tim Howard in his autobiography *The Keeper,* saying he understood where Klinsmann was coming from because of his experience at Manchester United and Everton in England's Premier League. "He wanted to install a more proactive philosophy throughout all levels of the sport—from youth clubs to the national team, Jürgen was an Americanized German but the man was still a German at heart."

The initial results were nothing to write home about. While adjusting to the changes, his team lost four of its first six games with one draw, scoring just two goals and getting shut out four times. But Klinsmann didn't sound at all discouraged about the first six months in an interview at one of his favorite Pacific Coast Highway diners in early January 2012. "This transition will take time," he said. "To tell the general American public that this is a longtime process is very difficult, because Americans, like Germans, are impatient and they want to see results. So while always working with the players in changing their mind-set, you've got to provide some results. It's a tricky one. You want to have the results while going through changes."

He knew that a time would come, after the initial euphoria wore off, when the daggers would come out. Famous player or not, the past would be worth precious little to fans craving results. He also knew that it would take time to build the United States into a global powerhouse. He was trying to show the players what it meant to live and think like a pro soccer player twenty-four hours a day, seven days a week.

He was in high spirits on that bright sunny January morning as he outlined his plans for U.S. soccer. "I'm having a blast," Klinsmann said. Above all, he wanted the teams to develop their own signature style, to put their own stamp on the game that would not only suit the American mentality but also enable the team to stand up as equals or near equals against Spain, Germany, and Brazil with their own distinctive brands of soccer.

"I thought it was important from the beginning that we transition from a reactive style of playing into a more proactive style. We will never play the same controlling type of soccer that Spain or Germany or Brazil play when you're playing against them. That's just reality. But you want to get to the point where you're closer to playing against them instead of just defending and hope for a counter-break score. You can win maybe one game out of ten with a counter-break philosophy. But that's not my philosophy, and actually that's not Americans' philosophy. Americans are not reactive types of people. It's not in their DNA. It's not in their culture. So I wondered: Why do you play with a style that's not in your culture?"

Switching from reacting to the opponents to trying to dictate the terms of play was a major change. "In the past, the U.S. teams were always used to just reacting to the big teams they were playing against," Klinsmann says. "If they were playing against some Central American countries, or the so-called small teams, they knew they could set the pace. But if it was against the bigger European countries or the bigger South American countries, the U.S. teams were often reactive. This transition will take time."

The results were only marginally better in the next six months to the middle of 2012. In Klinsmann's first full year, his team won only five games, lost seven, and had three ties. But there were signs that the reforms were having a positive impact. "The scoreboard hasn't always reflected it, but Klinsmann has instilled (or at least tried to) an attacking, flowing, possession style devoid of frantic long balls," wrote sportswriter Mark Zeigler in an analysis in 2012 in the *San Diego Union-Tribune* of Klinsmann's first year. "Has it worked? It's probably too early to say. In this current stretch of games, the Americans looked sensational against Scotland . . . and had their moments while being outclassed by Brazil. It should be noted, though, that Klinsmann's system didn't immediately take root in Germany, either, and it wasn't until the 2008 European Championships and 2010 World Cup under his former assistant Joachim Löw that it fully blossomed."

The results continued to improve in his second full year. From mid-2012 to mid-2013, his team won sixteen, lost three, and had three ties. He experimented with his lineup and bringing in younger players. Eager to open up the team for new leaders to emerge, he changed captains, taking the armband from thirty-three-year-old Carlos Bocanegra and trying it out with Tim Howard, Jermaine Jones, and Kyle Beckerman before finally settling on twenty-eight-year-old Clint Dempsey as the new captain. It rankled some fans of Bocanegra, but it was the same strategy of shaking things up that Klinsmann had used so effectively when he relieved Oliver Kahn of his captain duties at the age of thirty-five and gave the armband to Michael Ballack, age twenty-seven. That strong run that came in 2013 included a record-breaking twelve-game winning streak and a historic first-ever win against Mexico at Estadio Azteca as well as wins against Germany and Bosnia.

Klinsmann wasn't able to make the wholesale changes of players that he made with Germany because the U.S. talent pool wasn't as deep. But he and his staff did what they could to identify and invite Americans with dual citizenships living and playing abroad in soccer nations to consider playing for the U.S. team. The players with one American parent who grew up in nations where soccer is the number one sport had in some areas an enormous advantage—they had been exposed to the competitive pressures of the game their whole lives. Klinsmann also started trying to implement a universal set of standards to synthesize the great diversity of soccer programs and interests across the country into one great single orchestrated effort to make the United States a winner.

Klinsmann found and recruited four German American dual nationals with experience on top European clubs—sons of U.S. servicemen stationed in Germany—in that first year: Fabian Johnson, John Anthony Brooks, Timmy Chandler, and Julian Green—who became cornerstones of his 2014 World Cup team. Jermaine Jones had already joined the U.S. team in 2008. He also reached out to an Icelandic American, Aron Jóhannsson, who was born in the United States. Mix Diskerud, a Norwegian American with an American mother, decided to play for the U.S. senior team in 2010.

Turning to dual nationals to strengthen the national team is something that the United States, and other countries, have been doing for decades. Former U.S. captain Thomas Dooley, who had 81 caps for the United States between 1992 and 1999, is the son of a soldier in the U.S. Army and a German mother who grew up in West Germany, while another former American captain Earnie Stewart, the son of a U.S. serviceman and a Dutch mother, grew up in the Netherlands before earning 101 caps for the United States between 1990 and 2004 while playing for Dutch club teams for most of his career.

There were six British-born players on the U.S. team at the 1930 World Cup and even the U.S. team at the 1950 World Cup in Brazil that pulled off a miraculous upset win against England, a 1–0 victory in a group game at Belo Horizonte, had a lineup notable for its foreign-born players, including three added to the roster before the tournament who didn't even have U.S. citizenship. It was the first time the United States qualified for the World Cup since 1934. It would also be their final appearance until 1990. Joe Gaetjens scored the winning goal in the 38th minute; the son of a Haitian mother and Belgian father had only moved to New York from Haiti to study accounting at Columbia University and was allowed to play for the

United States without being a citizen because he expressed his intention to become a naturalized citizen, even though he never did. He later played for Haiti. The captain of the U.S. team, Eddie McIlvenny, was Scottish and also pledged to become an American citizen but never did. And defender Joe Maca was Belgian in 1950, although he did later take U.S. citizenship in 1957. The United States lost its other two group games to Spain, 3–1, and Chile, 5–2.

Despite the rich pool of its own talent to choose from, Germany had also enthusiastically started tapping into its own immigrant community after France won the 1998 World Cup with the help of many immigrants. Two of the starters on Klinsmann's Germany team were dual nationals with Polish roots, Miroslav Klose and Lukas Podolski. Oliver Neuville was born in Switzerland to an Italian mother and German father. It is interesting that Germany and other countries wholeheartedly welcome dual nationals if they make their teams stronger while in the United States, a nation of immigrants, there is still sometimes a leeriness and even opposition to using dual nationals, a sentiment expressed by former U.S. coach Bruce Arena. "Players on the national team should be—and this is my own feeling—they should be Americans," Arena said in a 2013 interview with ESPN's *The Magazine*. "If they're all born in other countries, I don't think we can say we are making progress." Klinsmann, who has faced criticism for including a number of dual national Americans who have spent most or all of their lives outside the United States, said everyone is entitled to their own opinion on the question. "That's just his opinion and that's totally cool with me," Klinsmann told a news conference in Denver in 2013. "The world is changing. It's a global game. I believe Americans are Americans, no matter if they grow up in Japan, South Africa or Buenos Aires. Our job is to identify the best talents with an American passport and see if they are good enough to come into that elite group. It's different times now. We have a lot of kids breaking through in different countries based on where Americans have spread out in the world. For me personally, America is a melting pot, not only here in the U.S. but it's a global melting pot."

The newspaper *USA Today* summarized the opposition to dual nationals in some quarters in the United States in these terms: "Should a player with little connection to the country take the spot of someone who came up through the American system and helped the team qualify for Brazil? Will a player raised elsewhere fight for the flag and care as much as someone raised in red, white and blue?" The newspaper also noted that two players born in the United States were on Mexico's World Cup team and one player born in the United States was on the Iran team. Dual nationals are a part of the game. Of Algeria's twenty-three players at the 2010 World Cup, seventeen were born in France.

"I brought in players who were not even on the radar playing in the MLS," Klinsmann says. "There were also [American] players in Mexico who were not on the radar. You also have a generation of kids coming through with dual citizenships. It's just a fascinating side aspect of globalization. I think America lost out on a lot of really good talent over the last fifteen to twenty years to the other side of the dual-citizenship question. We will dig into that. We don't want to lose another Giuseppe Rossi," he said of the Italy player with U.S. citizenship who was born in the United States and grew up in New Jersey but decided to play for the country of his ancestors. "We lost one big talent in that process with Rossi. We'll always lose some dual-national players to other teams. We'll lose some players to Mexico, we'll lose some players maybe to Germany and Argentina. But on that path we'll also win over some. The face of the U.S. National Team has changed over the last two or three years. It's fascinating for me to be in the middle of all that as coach. It's really fun."

The Giuseppe Rossi case is an illuminating example of a highly talented American-born player who got away from U.S. Soccer. The gifted forward grew up in Clifton, New Jersey, and played in youth leagues there. Just before turning thirteen, Rossi went to Italy to the youth academy of Parma, a club that plays in the Serie A. He later played for clubs in England, Spain, and Italy. Arena had extended an invitation to eighteen-year-old Rossi to join a U.S. training camp before the 2006 World Cup but he turned down the offer. A few months later at the 2006 World Cup in Germany, Arena spoke critically of Rossi's decision to reporters at the team's base in Hamburg, saying he thought the young Italian-American was being unrealistic to think he could play for Italy when he was only spending most of his time at Manchester United on the bench. Rossi's career soon took off after he was transferred to Spanish club Villareal in 2007 and he was picked to play on Italy's senior team in 2008, where he had thirty appearances through 2014.

To be fair, Rossi might never have played for the United States under any circumstances because he had made clear it was always his dream to play for Italy, as he explained in a 2014 interview with Jack Bell in *The New York Times*. But who knows if he would have still decided to play for Italy if the United States had been a top soccer power at the time and if he had been more heavily recruited. Rossi did note one factor behind his decision to play for Italy was the opaque system in the United States, a country without a clear-cut pyramid like in Italy or Germany. "The systems are totally different," Rossi said. "In America, it's a little confusing with so many different leagues, high school, college. It's hard to distinguish yourself. In Italy, it's there, you know the structure, you clearly know what you need to do to compete at a high level."

Rossi is hardly the only top international player to get away. There are a number of top players for other countries around the world who learned how to play soccer or sharpened their skills in the United States. Neven Subotić, for instance, plays for Serbia but grew up in Utah and Florida. His parents fled the wars in former Yugoslavia when he was a young child in the early 1990s, living for a while in Germany before settling in the United States. Subotić even played on the Under-21 team for the United States before switching to Serbia in 2008 when the Borussia Dortmund defender turned twenty-one. Forward Vedad Ibišević has earned more than seventy caps for Bosnia and Herzegovina even though he fled his native country with his family as a five-year-old, first to Switzerland and then a year later to St. Louis, where he grew up. As a freshman at St. Louis University, he was the NCAA rookie of the year and first played for the St. Louis Strikers and Chicago Fire in Major League Soccer in 2003 and 2004 before moving to Europe, where he has been a top goal-scoring forward for clubs such as Hoffenheim and Hertha Berlin. Andy Najar moved to Virginia from Honduras with his family as a three-year-old and played for D.C. United in MLS. At the age of nineteen he decided to play for Honduras while waiting to get his U.S. citizenship. Roger Espinoza, who moved from Honduras to Denver at the age of twelve and later played soccer at Ohio State, played in two World Cups and two Olympics for Honduras. Also, Premier League goalkeeper Glyn "Boaz" Myhill of Wales has an American father and Welsh mother who was born in Modesto, California.

Another player who, under different circumstances, might have opted to play for the United States was Brede Hangeland, the Norway captain who has had a long career as a central defender in England's Premier League. Hangeland was born in Houston while his parents were working in the United States. If the United States had been a soccer power in 2002 when he opted to join the Norway team and if he had been effectively recruited, it's not hard to imagine that Hangeland could perhaps have decided to play for the United States. So step back for a moment and imagine if the U.S. soccer team had those seven players available to strengthen their team at the 2014 World Cup: Rossi and Ibišević as forwards, Najar as a winger, Espinoza in midfield, with a defense anchored by Subotić and Hangeland, and perhaps a player like Myhill in goal.

Aside from doing all he can to identify and recruit players like that, Klinsmann also has been busy spreading U.S. Soccer's feelers out to the Hispanic leagues in the United States, some of which are unofficial and not even registered. "A lot of Hispanics who don't have the money to play in official organized leagues are playing in their own low-cost leagues that are based on the Central American or European model: Teams are coached by someone who once played the game himself working as a volunteer," Klinsmann says. "We didn't even know about thousands of highly talented American kids playing in these Hispanic leagues. They get scouted away by Mexican clubs and later on we'll hopefully find them again. That's how we found Ventura Alvarado. He's a super talent."

Klinsmann keeps track of his players—and potential new players—by watching a lot of soccer games each week. He can watch MLS games but also European, South American, and Central American leagues. "For a European person it's difficult to imagine," he says. "We have five channels here that show soccer nonstop. It's not that we're disconnected to soccer. On TV it's the opposite. We're overloaded." Klinsmann says that U.S. Soccer staff can quickly send him film material of young prospects that might not be on any of those networks. "We have the technology," he says. "They can get me any game I want to see, of whatever talented young player is coming through. If you want to see films of that one seventeen-year-old kid, it's no problem." Klinsmann tends not to watch the entire matches.

"I filter a lot of stuff. I don't watch ninety minutes and wait for the one moment. I'd rather summarize things and see what is really important."

The reforms were finally starting to have an impact by Klinsmann's second year—his team won nine games in 2012 with two losses and three ties, and then sixteen wins and four losses with three ties in 2013. The U.S. Men's National Team also won the CONCACAF Gold Cup for the fifth time and qualified for the World Cup for a seventh straight time atop the standings in CONCACAF. Klinsmann sounded pleased but hardly complacent during an interview at the end of 2013. "I think we're developing, and still in the middle of it, a very competitive environment," he said. "The players have learned to push themselves, they understand now that we empower them to take care of their own environment. We made it clear that it's all about competition, it's all about performance. It's not about how many caps you had in the past, what you did in the past. It's always about the moment, the present and future. In 2013 I think we achieved a lot in becoming more consistent. This is all a process we're going through, but it's coming along."

Klinsmann's reforms, in particular his nutritional ideas, are colorfully described by goalkeeper Tim Howard in *The Keeper*. He writes that Klinsmann discouraged sugary snacks and unhealthy food, and he lamented what had become of the peanut butter and jelly sandwiches he used to love. "I'd spent my whole life eating PB&Js. Somehow, under Jürgen, the sandwich morphed into a natural version of the staple that was practically unrecognizable—and to my taste buds, inedible."

# COMPETITIVE INTENSITY

ONE IMPORTANT AREA Klinsmann has identified that could help the USMNT toward its goal of winning a World Cup is improving the competitive intensity of the country's top professional league, Major League Soccer. Klinsmann has no control over the MLS, even though the league's players aspire to play for the USMNT and many of the league's brightest stars are on his squad. Other than his bully pulpit as U.S. coach and technical director, Klinsmann has no say in how the league is organized. But he nevertheless has some interesting ideas about changes that could make the MLS more competitive and exciting from top to bottom, more in sync with leagues in the rest of the world, and which might be able to nurture and produce more outstanding talent that the United States needs to win the World Cup.

Klinsmann believes that the MLS, its players, and the U.S. National Team would benefit considerably in the long run from increased competitive intensity that keeps everyone on every team on his toes right up to the end of the season. An example of such a format is the promotion-relegation system that is used in every other major soccer league around the world. But it runs counter to the MLS's business model. Klinsmann understands that but still hopes the MLS will find ways to increase season-long competitive intensity for all its teams from the best to the worst, from the start of the season until the final game.

It is normal for there to be some creative friction between the heads of the top professional clubs and the head of the national team, as their interests sometimes diverge. National team coaches want to win tournaments and as many international games as possible, while the leagues, who pay the players' salaries, are interested in winning their leagues and club competitions as well as safeguarding their best assets—their players. The clubs have concerns their players could get overused or injured through regular call-ups to their national team.

The model that the MLS uses comes from the professional football, basketball, baseball, and hockey leagues in North America. Even though most of Europe plays an August-to-June season, the MLS regular season runs from March to October, followed by play-offs running to December, which start with the top twelve of the league's twenty teams. At the end of the season, all twenty MLS teams stay in the top division—no matter how well or how poorly they performed during the season.

The excitement of the MLS tends to be concentrated around the top teams and the play-off races, with the public and media interest dwindling for teams at the bottom of the standings with no hopes of reaching the play-offs. The development of most players on those struggling teams out of play-off contention also suffers, as they often just "play out the season" and are competing only for pride. In America, the worst finishers even get *rewarded* for their poor results by getting the first draft choices from among the pool of players entering the next MLS SuperDraft.

That egalitarian system in the United States might work well in a closed national environment, but it is out of sync with the rest of the world when it comes to soccer. Even in countries with Socialist leanings, from Scandinavia to Germany, and former Communist nations such as Russia, soccer teams engage in Darwinian battles to survive each season. The two or three bottom teams in the major leagues in Europe and South America are relegated to the next-lowest league while the top teams from that league are "promoted" to the top league.

In the twenty-team English Premier League, as noted earlier, the bottom three teams are relegated to the second tier, the Football League Championship, for the next season. In the eighteen-team Bundesliga, the bottom two teams go straight down to the second division for the following season. Consequently, late-season relegation battles offer fans around the world some of the most exciting soccer there is: epic fights for survival with hundreds of jobs with the club resting on the shoulders of the players on the field. Entire cities can go berserk amid the frenzy of a good relegation fight and attendance at the stadiums often rises with players on the bottom five to eight teams going all out every weekend to keep their team out of the "drop zone."

Klinsmann says those existential battles benefit everyone by bringing out the competitive best from the players and coaches caught up in these fights to keep their teams from going down. Sometimes the relegated teams keep falling, stumbling dramatically over the course of several poor seasons from top flight all the way down to the third, fourth, fifth, or even sixth league. BFC Dynamo Berlin was once the dominant team in Communist East Germany, with ten league championships. It also reached the semifinals of Europe's 1971/72 Cup Winners' Cup before falling to the seventh division several years after reunification. BFC now plays in the fourth division.

But other teams have risen just as far, such as TSG 1899 Hoffen-heim, which climbed from the eighth division in the amateur leagues in the early 1990s to top flight in the Bundesliga in 2008.

"I think the intensity of competition as seen in promotion-relegation systems really helps the development of soccer and also helps national teams in the long run," Klinsmann says. "These are just unforgettable games that people will talk about for years to come," he adds, after all, as a nineteen-year-old player in 1983/84, he got swept up in a memorable relegation battle himself with his second-division team Stuttgarter Kickers.

"We need our players to live with and cope with season-long competitive intensity," he says. "Our players in Europe already know all about that. There's something at stake week in, week out. It doesn't matter if you're near the top or at the bottom—you always have to perform. I'm looking forward to MLS, NASL, and USL continuing to evolve their competitive formats so that our players, and soccer fans, can get to experience that high-level excitement from the first game of the season to the last."

The promotion-relegation battle is in a sense a microcosm of what the game is all about. Players who are constantly fighting to reach the next level will be infinitely better prepared for the pressure at the more competitive international level. It is all about the best rising through the ranks to the top. Just as their teams are striving to win a promotion, so too are the individual players doing everything they can to raise their game in order to make it to the next-higher level themselves.

That is how the game of global soccer comes to appeal to young players—fostering a mind-set of continuing to climb to the next level that infects the players everywhere from the youth leagues on up. From the moment he started playing soccer as a precocious eight-year-old, Klinsmann had a powerful inner drive to advance.

"Rising to the next level is something I've always wanted to do, and I think it's a driving force for kids everywhere," he says. "I wanted to play on a better club in my neighborhood. I wanted to play a year up in my age group. You always look upward. You can always learn more at the next-higher level. It's important to see that desire to rise up and advance is encouraged at the youth levels in soccer. It's important that youth clubs also build their own tier system and that clubs identify themselves based on how good they are, on performance. That's the way it is everywhere in the world.

"In a promotion-relegation system, the risk for those who invest in a club is high even though there are clear benefits from the sporting side of things," Klinsmann says. "The U.S. Men's National Team is trying to compete against global competition with players everywhere else facing the challenges of promotion-relegation their whole careers. My point is that our domestic leagues need to foster the same level of competitive intensity, using their business model, that other leagues around the world generate using their model if our players and National Team are going to successfully compete on the international stage."

MLS commissioner Don Garber made his case for the unique American league structure in a speech in Manchester, England, in 2015. "Promotion-relegation would create a level of instability in our league in an immature market that could crater the very existence of our league," he said. "Who is that good for?" He is concerned that fans of relegated MLS teams might be lost forever if they do not have a chance to build up ties to the teams over generations.

U.S. Soccer president Sunil Gulati has also spoken on promotion-relegation in the professional soccer structure, telling *Bloomberg* soccer writer Tariq Panja at a conference in New York in 2014, "People often reach out: 'Why doesn't the federation mandate this [promotion-relegation]?' Because we're not in the business of expropriating assets. . . . When the system came into play in Europe and the rest of the world, that was the agreement coming in. So if you're an owner and you buy into a system right now and you pay X amount of dollars to get in, and the rules of the game change the next day, essentially expropriating assets that were worth X— that's not something we're going to be doing."

Klinsmann welcomes the open exchange of controversial ideas. "At the end of the day, it's about player development and the ability of our players individually, and our ability as a nation, to compete internationally," he says. "It hurts player development and the National Team when the season is effectively over for a significant number of MLS teams two-thirds of the way in because they're not going to make the play-offs. That makes it very difficult for the players on those teams to reach the next level. So I think we need to find ways to improve the competitiveness of our professional leagues."

# BEST COLLEGE SOCCER
# IN THE WORLD

No OTHER COUNTRY in the world has better university soccer leagues than the United States. There are 1,667 colleges with varsity soccer teams, and 37,890 men and 37,760 women were playing on those teams in 2014. Many of America's best players have sharpened their skills at colleges over the years and Jürgen Klinsmann is convinced that the American college soccer system could be an even more important cornerstone for greater success in the future for soccer in the United States—and ultimately success for the Men's National Team at the World Cup. He thinks the sky is the limit if scholastic soccer can be better integrated into the U.S. soccer pyramid.

"The college system is a huge opportunity for U.S. soccer," he says. "If some changes could be made, the college system could be turned into a really big advantage for the United States." To prepare Americans to better compete at the highest levels of the global game, college soccer would have to extend training and playing opportunities from a single three- or four-month season to multiple seasons in the fall-to-spring academic year as some other sports already do, ramp up the training, and use FIFA rules, including for substitutions. If some four thousand American colleges and universities have long been the proving grounds for athletes who later make the leap to professional stardom in the NFL and NBA, why can't these same universities also feed the country's best soccer players into the professional and international game?

"It could be a great opportunity," Klinsmann says. "If college soccer could be treated as a year-round competitive system, it could be the ideal building block for the professional game. If American kids could play ten or eleven months a year throughout their college careers, that would be comparable to a third or a fourth division in Europe. The college kids are talented. They're obviously ambitious and they're eager to learn. What they're not getting is consistent training and enough games year-round compared to what other players at their age are getting in other countries. College soccer could be the ideal bridge to the pro game."

Women's soccer in the United States has already proved the value of a thriving college system behind it. The U.S. Women's National Team, which played its first match in 1985, has won the World Cup three times. There were more women varsity soccer players at Division I colleges (8,998) in 2014 than men (5,750). There were an average of fourteen athletic scholarships a year per women's team compared to an average of just under ten scholarships for each men's team.

Title IX, the game-changing 1972 law prohibiting sex-based discrimination in federally funded education programs, took effect in 1978. It had a major impact on women's sports, as colleges were suddenly required to offer equal scholarships for men and women. Because there are male-only sports such as football teams taking a large number of scholarships for men, colleges needed to award an equal number of scholarships to women, which is one of the key reasons that women's soccer boomed and put the U.S. Women's National Team so far ahead of its competition in the rest of the world. The number of women playing soccer in high school and college soared after 1978. There are 1.7 million women registered with U.S. Soccer compared to 2.5 million men. The United States invests more in women's soccer than any other country in the world.

"The U.S. women have developed their skills along the years through a system and via infrastructure that is world-class when compared to women in the rest of the world," wrote Robert Wilson in *The Huffington Post*. "No other country in the world has an NCAA."

Klinsmann agrees that the university system is an essential part of the mix. "Sports here in the United States are driven by education," he says. "The main goal of sports for a lot of people is: Maybe I can get a scholarship at a good, prestigious college? That's what is driving the women's side of the game. The women having won the World Cup again for a third time is really big for soccer in terms of how many people talk about soccer in public and on the streets now."

He believes that with a slightly revamped men's college system, the United States could make leaps forward in catching up with the rest of the world. Because college education is such a central pillar of American lives, it often plays a role for years to come—unlike in Europe or South America, where in general fewer people go on to higher education. Soccer players abroad rarely go to college, not necessarily for a lack of desire but simply because soccer is more than a full-time occupation for pro soccer players from the time they are about fifteen.

By contrast, some of the best American soccer players of the last generation played at college: Clint Dempsey (Furman), Geoff Cameron (Rhode Island), Brad Guzan (South Carolina), Tab Ramos (North Carolina State), Carlos Bocanegra (UCLA), Brad Friedel (UCLA), Claudio Reyna (Virginia), Eric Wynalda (San Diego State), Kasey Keller (Portland), and Brian McBride (Saint Louis). In other countries, it is hard to find any of the world's best international players who attended college; they left school in their teenage years to focus on the game. At the same time, Americans' desire to go to college makes them comparatively uninteresting from a financial point of view for the agents and talent scouts roaming Europe and South America searching for young talent. Because many young American soccer players want to keep their college eligibility, the agents run the risk of wasting a lot of time, money, and effort on connecting an American youngster with a top club in Europe. That is another important reason there are so few Americans playing in the top leagues.

"Having lived here for so long, I've come to understand that Americans have a really deep connection with their educational system and the college they went to," says Klinsmann, who finished school in Germany at fifteen and became an apprentice in his father's bakery where he got his training degree there three years later. "That's what they talk about their whole life. You meet someone on the airplane flying across the country, and it's not, 'Where do you work?' or 'What's your profession?' but 'Where did you go to school?' In Europe, no one would ask you where you went to school. It's a completely different approach here, which is difficult for people on both sides of the Atlantic to understand."

The U.S. college system was long seen as an obstacle rather than an asset because college soccer players do not get as much game experience or time training as their European and South American peers. By the time Americans have graduated, at about twenty-two or twenty-three, their counterparts abroad have been playing year-round for eight years or more and might have already played in a World Cup and the Champions League. How can American college soccer players, playing only four months a year, compete against that?

"I think the college system is both an advantage and a disadvantage," says Klinsmann. "I've been digging into this question for quite a while and really believe that if the college game could be stepped up, it could really help U.S. soccer in the future. If the college system could be changed to have more games and a whole-year season and the players could have the chance to continue training eleven months a year, it would be on the right path. I think that would provide a pathway to help the United States produce better players."

Yet college soccer is a uniquely American sport with its own set of rules. The NCAA rules are oddly out of sync with FIFA's Laws of the Game—a standard that is followed almost everywhere else in the world. Around the world, teams are allowed only three substitutions per game, there are no time-outs, and the clock is not stopped—although referees generally allow games to carry on for two to three or four minutes beyond ninety minutes to compensate for the cumulative total of those brief breaks in the action after goals, fouls, or injuries. But under the NCAA rules, there are hardly any limits on substitutions and time-outs, and the clock is stopped multiple times during a game for multiple reasons. The differences compared to FIFA's rules used elsewhere around the world impact the development of college players in game strategy and flow of the game.

The virtually unlimited substitutions rob the college game of some of its more fascinating subplots—conditioning, overcoming fatigue, and the opening up of late-match scoring opportunities against tiring defenders. Reflecting an American aversion to ties, college games go to sudden death overtime to determine a winner and end up in a tie only if neither team manages to score a "golden goal" in one of the two ten-minute overtime periods.

Elsewhere, many games end in a tie. It is simply a third possible outcome alongside victory or defeat. Savvy soccer fans around the world fully understand that although a tie might ostensibly seem like an unsatisfying result, it can nevertheless be an exciting or a disappointing outcome; in other words, a tie can and often does feel like a "victory" for an underdog or like a "defeat" for the favored team.

"College soccer needs to follow the same rules as the rest of the world," says Klinsmann. "The substitution rule, with unlimited substitutions and one reentry per player in the second half, is a disaster. The college kids never get a rhythm and never have to fight through tiredness. As soon as the coach sees that after twenty minutes someone is breathing hard, they get subbed out."

At a spirited UCLA game against the University of California–Riverside on a brilliant fall day in 2015, it was easy to see what Klinsmann is talking about—the substitution rule changed the character of the game. There were eight hundred spectators at UCLA's Drake Stadium, which has a capacity of seven thousand. UCLA, ranked in the nation's top ten, has won four NCAA national championships since 1937 and produced a number of National Team players, such as Bocanegra, Friedel, Frankie Hejduk, Cobi Jones, and Nick Rimando. In the first half, UCLA coach Jorge Salcedo sent in a wave of five substitutes, mixing and matching his multinational team made up of players from the United States, Spain, Germany, New Zealand, Ghana, and Mexico, and then again sending some of the same subs in the second half, while his Riverside counterpart Tim Cupello sent in four substitutes both before and after intermission. UCLA lost 2–1 on an own goal five minutes into the first ten-minute overtime period.

Soccer was introduced at colleges in the United States at pretty much the same time as football but was soon eclipsed by football, which was developed in the United States as a unique hybrid between rugby football and association football played in Britain in the 1800s. The first soccer match was played on November 6, 1869, between Princeton and Rutgers, according to David Wangerin in *Soccer in a Football World*. It was a game based on London FA rules, and Rutgers won 6–4. But football soon won the upper hand. "Well into the 1960s, . . . many colleges regarded the soccer team as little more than a training fillip for other, more important, sports such as football or even wrestling," Wangerin writes. "The formation of a team on campus often had more to do with the presence of a soccer-disposed member of the faculty than any groundswell of interest. In 1922, the University of Florida became one of the earliest colleges in the Deep South to form a team. But when its coach, Harry Metcalf, died in 1925, the team disbanded—and did not reform until the 1950s. As late as 1918 only twelve colleges played soccer against each other, all in the east and all to little public attention. Training began in December—after the end of the football season—and the fixtures often not until January, continuing as best they could through the brunt of the winter. Although this often resulted in wretched playing conditions, there was little hope of beginning any earlier and interfering with gridiron, in some cases because soccer teams depended on football players to make up their numbers."

There are some dynasties in modern college soccer, such as at the University of Indiana, the University of Virginia, the University of Connecticut, UCLA, the University of North Carolina, and Wake Forest. The women's college game has been dominated by the University of North Carolina, which has won twenty-one NCAA tournaments.

That the popularity of soccer at U.S. colleges is growing steadily can be seen in the top attendance in 1998 compared to 2012. The University of Connecticut had the largest total home attendance in both of those seasons. In 1998 there was a total of 33,830 spectators at the Huskies' fourteen home games, and by 2012 the total had climbed to 59,192, also for fourteen games. In 2013 more than thirty American colleges had an average home attendance above 1,000, and some of the most important matches were broadcast on national television.

American colleges are becoming an increasingly attractive

destination for European soccer players who have not quite made it into the professional ranks in the more competitive leagues as teenagers but are still trying to keep their careers alive—or possibly jump-start them. About six hundred British students are awarded soccer scholarships at American universities each year, according to a 2015 report by the BBC. One reason for the growing awareness abroad of American colleges as a pathway into MLS is that the MLS drafts some of the nation's top players each year in its SuperDraft.

At least six British soccer players whose careers appeared to be stalled at home have made it to the MLS after studying at American colleges. Dom Dwyer went to Sporting Kansas City after playing for the University of South Florida, Matt Watson went to Chicago Fire from the University of Maryland, Otis Earle went to FC Dallas from the University of California–Riverside, Luke Mulholland went to Real Salt Lake from the University of North Carolina, and Andy Rose went to the Seattle Sounders after playing for UCLA.

"It's pretty amazing—I'm a little kid from England and last year I was at the White House," Dwyer told the BBC after his team won the 2013 MLS Cup. "I just thought, 'What are they doing, letting me in here?'" Just a few years earlier, at the age of nineteen, Dwyer had been dropped by Norwich City, his club in England. Yet with the help of a specialized matchmaker company in England, which for a fee helps talented young players find college scholarship opportunities in the United States, Dwyer moved to America. He has scored more than thirty goals in the MLS and was on the 2014 All-Star team.

# THE PASSION OF COLLEGE SPORTS

JÜRGEN KLINSMANN SAYS the United States is fortunate to have such an extensive college system that gives so many athletes from around the country and the world a chance to get a degree while playing soccer or other sports. It might seem to some as a disadvantage for an ambitious young athlete to spend four such important years in college, but he doesn't see it that way.

"I think the educational opportunities through sports in the United States is unique in the world," he says. "You can get a scholarship for playing a sport or being good in art or music or whatever you are really good in. There's the opportunity for you, not only to go into college with that sport. You can actually prepare for your life after college or your professional career while getting a great education. I think it's unbelievable. It's fantastic."

Klinsmann is, however, concerned about how American soccer players can overcome the advantage that young players elsewhere get with their head starts. The best soccer players in Europe and South America tend to leave school at the age of fifteen to concentrate full-time on soccer with clubs or academies. That might improve their ability to score goals, make pinpoint passes, or chest down a long ball while running at full stride. But it can also be detrimental to their intellectual development, which he says can end up stagnating in their teenage years.

The emotional development of many of those young prodigies can be further stunted because they usually move away from their homes and families at such formative ages and into boarding-school-like soccer academies—often in different countries and sometimes even on different continents. David Beckham was sixteen when he left home to go to Manchester United's youth academy, Lionel Messi was just thirteen when he left Argentina for Barcelona's famous La Masia youth academy, while Cesc Fàbregas entered at ten, Xavi at eleven, and Andrés Iniesta at twelve. Cristiano Ronaldo left home on the Portuguese island of Madeira at twelve to move to Sporting Lisbon's youth team. One young American, Ben Lederman, moved with his entire family from California to Barcelona at the age of eleven after he was accepted at La Masia. The first U.S.-born player invited to La Masia, Lederman joined the academy in 2011 and stayed there until he was fifteen before moving to the IMG Academy in Florida. It is unknown if their emotional development suffered because they moved away from home at such young ages, but it is in any case a sacrifice and challenge for teenage boys to go off to polish their soccer talent at such a high-intensity level while most of their friends are staying home and going to school.

That is one reason that Odell Beckham Jr., a wide receiver for the New York Giants, decided not to pursue a soccer career even though he dreamed about playing internationally as a youngster. Instead, he turned to football. "I started when I was three years old and played until I was about 14," Beckham said of his early love for soccer in a TV interview in England in 2014. "My coach was pushing to try to get me on the national team and tryout. At that age, you're 13, 14 years old, you know that to make it big in soccer you are probably going to have to go overseas. Obviously that would be a goal and that would be the dream. At that age it would have been hard for me to leave my family and just go. I played every other sport, soccer, basketball, baseball, football. And I just said, 'I don't think I can leave my family.' So that's when I kind of put the soccer dreams aside and stuck close to home with the other sports." In another interview, while watching the 2014 World Cup, he was asked if he thinks back and wonders if he made the right decision at fourteen. "All the time, all the time," he said. "Soccer was my first love so whenever I think back on those moments, I think of what could have been." He's not the only one. Klinsmann hopes the day isn't far off when athletes like Odell Beckham opt for soccer instead of American football. "Just imagine Odell running down the wing on the soccer field. Awesome!" he says with a smile.

Klinsmann understands that the European and South American models have their flaws. Thousands of young boys leave their homes to be groomed for pro soccer, even though only a very small percentage will make it to the top of the sport. "What basically happens around the world is that the best kids at the age of fourteen, fifteen, sixteen, or seventeen get pulled into the academies of Barcelona or Madrid or Tottenham or Bayern Munich or Hertha Berlin or wherever," he says. "We take kids out of their environment, take them away from their families even before they might have become socially developed, and put them into an environment where you've got to become a professional soccer player and their life is nothing but soccer now. At the same time they're developing in that professional soccer environment, they might not be developing as a person anymore, and their brains become wired to soccer. You'll see this kid then at eighteen or twenty or twenty-two, and he's probably improved a lot as a soccer player, but did he improve the same way socially as a human being? It's a development you see everywhere in the rest of the world. But in the United States, it's like, 'I'll take the education first ahead of the career.' The education will last the rest of your lifetime. It's rare that someone makes it to the pros."

Klinsmann freely admits he would have liked to have continued on at school and gone to college, but it was not an option for a sixteen-year-old in West Germany wanting to pursue a pro soccer career. "I started playing professionally at sixteen. I got a baker's degree, but where's my education?" he says with a shrug of his shoulders. He nevertheless got an extraordinary education during his travels as an expatriate in four foreign countries around the world, yet he sees the great advantages of the college system in the United States.

That absence of a more traditional childhood as well as any kind of a formal higher education might be one of the reasons that sportswriters sometimes struggle to find enlightened observations from among the ranks of the world's best soccer players—possibly due to a lack of confidence, or a lack of interest in making comments on anything beyond their field of expertise—which is scoring goals or stopping them. Fortunately, the players' genius on the field is more than enough to write about. There are, of course, exceptions: players known for thought-provoking musings.

Klinsmann believes that the current college soccer system is a tremendous strong point of the United States. If some of those important adjustments can be made in college soccer to bring it in sync with the professional game in the United States and the way it is played around the world, it could become an incubator and conveyor belt of superbly trained talent similar to the way American colleges feed the NFL and NBA with some of the planet's best football and basketball players. The 75,650 American men playing college soccer at 1,667 schools in 2014 compares with 90,136 men playing varsity football at 891 colleges.

Klinsmann and his team are doing all they can to strengthen the ties between U.S. Soccer and the NCAA. He takes part in conference calls with college coaches, and U.S. Soccer holds "identification camps" for college players. "I think there's a lot of appreciation for what we're trying to do, to connect the dots," he says.

He keeps a close eye on college soccer and even made a daring invitation to a player from Stanford, Jordan Morris, to play on the senior team in 2014. He was the first college student to play for the senior team in two decades. The twenty-year-old sophomore scored in his second game, getting the first goal for the USMNT in the 49th minute to lead the United States to a 2–0 win against Mexico.

"He was already part of our Under-20 national team, but I brought him up because he is really good, not because he was playing college soccer for Stanford," says Klinsmann. "But maybe that will help with those efforts with the NCAA to make the college game more in line with the international game. We've still got a long way to go."

Klinsmann hopes to see the college game playing a greater role in the sport's development in the United States. Why hasn't that happened already? He says that behind the scenes, U.S. Soccer officials and NCAA officials are studying changes that could help the national team in the future. But he fears it will take some time before there are tangible results.

"If the NCAA would say, 'We get it now, we understand that soccer is a global sport and so kids need to prepare for an eleven-month season physically and mentally. So we'll stretch the college season to thirty or forty games a year with workouts once a day and then they go to their classes.' If those things could done, it would give the United States a big advantage."

Another aspect of college sports that fascinates Klinsmann is the passion Americans have for their favorite college football or basketball team. Those intense, emotional ties are the closest thing he has seen in the United States that are anywhere near comparable to the passion that Europeans have for their favorite soccer clubs.

"Many Americans have their emotional connection to the schools, not to professional sports," says Klinsmann, who has turned into a big supporter of the University of California at Berkeley since his son started playing soccer there. "It's one of the big differences between the United States and Europe or South America—people identify as closely and passionately with their college teams. In the United States, sports are driven by the educational system. If you grow up in Europe, you are either a Tottenham or Arsenal fan, you are either an Inter Milan or AC Milan fan. So you develop an emotional connection to a professional team at an early age."

Klinsmann's own first emotional connection was to Hertha Berlin in the Bundesliga. Why Hertha from the Northeast even though he lived in the Southwest near Stuttgart? It was because his father had grown up in a small town outside Berlin. "So the first game I ever went to was VfB Stuttgart against Hertha Berlin," Klinsmann recalls. "I was out there in the standing-room section of the Stuttgart stadium and waving a Hertha Berlin flag. I was the only kid in the stadium with a Hertha flag. So you choose pretty early on and have an emotional connection to your professional team."

Klinsmann says that he has become thoroughly Americanized after nearly two decades of living in the country and even proudly wears University of California–Berkeley colors when he watches his son's team play. "Because my son is going to Berkeley, I wear a T-shirt now with a bear on it when I go to a game because, hey, my boy is going to Berkeley."

It is an entirely different world in other countries. Universities in Germany don't have sports teams, let alone major college leagues watched on television. Universities tend to be sober institutions of learning, underfinanced academic centers with no or low tuition fees. There are neither booster clubs nor reunions and for most people little or no lasting connection to their schools.

"Americans have an emotional connection to college sports. The pro game in America is seen as entertainment, while the emotional connection, the place where Americans really let themselves go, is at the college game," Klinsmann says, although he notes there are some die-hard fans with a visceral attachment to their favorite pro sports teams. "So generally speaking, you don't see anybody getting up during a college basketball game to get a burger or a sausage and a beer," he says, referring to that uniquely American practice of going for food or drinks while the games are in full swing. "There could be ninety thousand people at the Rose Bowl watching UCLA against USC, and nobody cares about the concessions. If you go to see the Lakers play and they lose, you don't leave the Staples Center in a bad mood. You say, 'Oh, well, they had a bad day today.' But if people go and watch their college basketball team and they lose, it really upsets them because they are emotionally connected."

# LANDON DONOVAN

PEOPLE SOMETIMES JOKE that there are eighty-two million *Bundestrainers,* German National Team coaches. In other words, all eighty-two million Germans feel they are entitled to voice their opinion and second-guess every decision. Jürgen Klinsmann has had to make many difficult decisions in his years coaching Germany and the United States, and there was often plenty of second-guessing. It's the nature of the job. Such was the case with his decision not to include Landon Donovan on his 2014 World Cup team. Some called it a courageous move, leaving behind an aging forward who might not be content in a backup role on the bench. But others called it madness, leaving America's all-time leading scorer and a poster boy for U.S. soccer off the team.

Klinsmann said at the time that he saw other players slightly ahead of Donovan. "I have to do what I believe is the right thing as of today, and time will tell now over the next seven weeks if it was the right move," he said. "I am very strongly convinced this is the right way to go, this is the right decision."

The Los Angeles Galaxy forward, the all-time leading scorer in the MLS, had had a long goalless streak before the World Cup training camp started in May 2014 with a preliminary team of thirty players. At the age of thirty-two, he had not scored a goal in his previous nine MLS games for the Galaxy, a frustrating dry spell that stretched back to the end of the 2013 season. A prolific scorer earlier in his career with at least one goal every second game in five of his first MLS seasons through 2011, Donovan's scoring output had fallen off in 2012, 2013, and 2014 to just one goal per three games. In 2013, he had scored only ten goals in twenty-seven games. In early 2014, he hadn't scored in nine straight games.

In the midst of that scoring drought, Donovan had also raised doubts about his own ability to cope with the intensity of the month-plus World Cup grind with comments right before the training camp in May 2014. "I can't train twelve straight days in a row and have twelve great days in a row—physically, it's not possible," Donovan, who had taken a controversial four-month sabbatical until early 2013, said in an interview for an ESPN documentary. "My body breaks down, I'm getting older." Klinsmann was quoted in the same documentary warning that there would be no automatic passes to Brazil for anyone based on past performance.

In a general reflection on the importance of team chemistry at big tournaments based on his experiences as a three-time World Cup player in the 1990s and coach of Germany in 2006, Klinsmann noted, "A World Cup team will be together, live together, travel together, and practice together for nearly two months. You cannot have players in those backup roles at the World Cup who might actually take more attention than the guys on the field." This may or may not have been part of his thinking when he selected the U.S. Men's National Team for the 2014 World Cup. Klinsmann is loath to speak in any detail about Donovan because he has tremendous respect and admiration for all that Donovan has done to help soccer in the United States.

Yet it lingered as a topic of heated discussion after the World Cup even though there were those before the tournament who observed it was the coach's prerogative and that ultimately it was only what happens on the field that matters. As Grant Wahl wrote at the time in *Sports Illustrated,* "Dropping Donovan was undeniably bold, but now the coach will have to back it up. If the U.S. defies the odds and gets out of its group in Brazil, then Klinsmann will be a visionary." The U.S. Men's National Team did indeed get out of the Group of Death and, defying expectations, made it to the Round of 16.

"For all the uproar that followed Donovan's cut—and whether you agree or disagree with how Klinsmann handled it—this much is clear: The confidence Klinsmann had in making his decision is exactly what U.S. Soccer was looking for when it hired him as its coach," wrote Sam Borden in *The New York Times Magazine* just before the World Cup started.

A month after the World Cup, Donovan announced he would retire from the Los Angeles Galaxy at the end of the 2014 season. He played one final farewell game for Klinsmann and the U.S. Men's National Team, a 1–1 tie against Ecuador, on October 10, 2014. It was his 157th appearance for the United States. He didn't score but ended his career as the all-time leading scorer with fifty-seven goals and fifty-eight assists.

# EXPERIENCE IN EUROPE

THE WORLD'S BEST soccer leagues are in Europe. So the conventional wisdom has long been that the best players in the world ought to be playing in England, Germany, Spain, Italy, or France—or at least aspire to play against the best there. But, strangely enough, that doctrine doesn't always apply for the best American soccer players. The United States is on a different page on this issue than the rest of the world—which is an unsettling development for U.S. Men's National Team coach Jürgen Klinsmann.

Soccer players from across Europe and around the world are eager to match their skills against the world's best clubs in the sport's best leagues in Western Europe, and national coaches from around the world are eager to fill their rosters with as many players on the top European clubs as possible. It's just the way the international game of soccer works. But in recent years, some of the best Americans have left some of the top clubs in Europe, in the prime of their career, for MLS clubs—a less challenging league with less pressure. It's a marketing boon for the MLS to sign American stars from overseas, but it's arguably a setback from a sports point of view for the players' development and a worrying trend for the U.S. Men's National Team as well. Since 2013, three top USMNT outfield players returned to the MLS from Europe: Michael Bradley (from AS Roma to Toronto FC in 2014); Clint Dempsey (from Fulham to Seattle Sounders in 2013); and Jozy Altidore (Sunderland to Toronto in 2015). Their performances slipped upon their return to the MLS, and none of them was selected to the 2014 or 2015 MLS Best IX team of top performers, as voted on by MLS players themselves, club executives, and members of the media.

"The recent exodus of top U.S. players from Europe to Major League soccer . . . is great for MLS, raising the profile and quality of the league, but not so great for developing national-team players," wrote Mark Zeigler in the *San Diego Union-Tribune* in July 2014, mentioning Dempsey, Bradley, as well as Maurice Edu from the top league in Turkey, Clarence Goodson from Denmark, Carlos Bocanegra from Spain, and Michael Parkhurst from Germany. "The MLS is comfortable. It's an easy life. A less demanding game, less demanding coaches, less demanding media, less demanding fans, less demanding culture. But the cold reality is that for the U.S. national team to take the next step, it must reverse that trend and start sending more players to a place where they wake up every morning wondering if the gritty Romanian midfielder is going to take their spot. Not one or two or 10 [American] players, but 50 or 60 or 70 [need to go to Europe]. Not all will make it. Some will wash out, unable to handle the pressure and perceived prejudice against American players. But some won't."

In many sports, it's the other way around, and the best leagues are in the United States. The world's top professional basketball, football, baseball, and hockey leagues, for instance, are in North America. So the world's most talented players aspire to reach the NBA, NFL, MLB, and NHL—going in the opposite direction across the Atlantic Ocean as the world's best soccer players. When twenty-year-old Dirk Nowitzki was playing for the German basketball club

DJK Würzburg in the Basketball Bundesliga, his dream was to one day make it to the NBA to play against the world's best teams. Just about every basketball fan in Germany was duly proud that Nowitzki made his mark with the Dallas Mavericks and developed into a bona fide NBA all-star. Similarly, Germans cheered for Sebastian Vollmer when he made it onto the starting lineup of the New England Patriots, and no one holds it against the powerful offensive tackle that he opted not to spend the rest of his career with the Düsseldorf Panthers.

Jürgen Klinsmann, like every other national soccer coach, would like to see the best and brightest in his country putting their skills to the biggest possible challenge on clubs playing in the top European leagues—once they're ready for the jump. It's an article of faith accepted around the world that the best leagues are in Europe. He believes the constant competitive pressure of playing in a soccer nation, and trying to win a spot on the club's starting team against hungry and talented rivals, elevates the players' skills. He says it gives them precious experience coping with pressure that could one day prove crucial at crunch time in the latter rounds of a World Cup. The social pressures from the entire community, in most cases ardent fans of the club, can give the players even more drive, he says.

"If you want to measure yourself against the world's best, you've got to go to Europe, you've got to go where the world's best players are—it's as simple as that," says Klinsmann, who has at times faced criticism from some quarters in the United States for that view. "If you try to make that step, you throw yourself into the shark tank, and it's gonna get nasty. And you gotta fight your way through it. But ultimately it's gonna make you stronger."

As much as he would like to see some of the best Americans on top clubs in Europe, he realizes it might not be the right move for every player, and some are probably not ready for a move overseas; it's always a case-by-case decision. It's obviously more conducive for their development to be regularly playing games in the MLS or Mexico's Liga MX than not getting many minutes playing in games in Europe. But there is also an argument to be made that even spending a season mostly on the bench could benefit some players because of the intensity of practicing at the top level in Europe and competing for a spot on the team amid the surrounding social pressures—provided there are prospects of more playing time in the future.

Klinsmann's difficulties are compounded by the fact that he, like other national team coaches, gets to spend a cumulative total of only a few weeks each year with his players—when clubs are required to release the national team players by FIFA. The half dozen or so FIFA International Match Calendar windows each year are determined by the world's governing body.

It is thus hardly an understatement to say that the fate of the U.S. Men's National Team hinges to a considerable degree on the level at which Americans play their club soccer. Most of the top players on the Brazil and Argentina teams play for clubs in Europe, as do an increasing number of the players on the Mexico national team. Over the years, thousands of soccer players from Argentina and Brazil have spent their careers on clubs in Europe. At the start of the 2014/15 season in Europe, there were eight Americans in the Bundesliga, seven in the Premier League, one in France, and one in Portugal, but none in Spain or Italy. At the same time there were 21 Argentines playing in the Premier League, 4 in the Bundesliga, 35 in Italy, 34 in Spain, 8 in Portugal, and 9 in France. There were also 38 Brazilians playing in Italy, 23 in Spain, 106 in Portugal, 19 in France, 13 in England, and 16 in the Bundesliga. Those players spend far more time honing their skills with their clubs—about forty weeks a year—than with their national teams. And that's why Klinsmann feels it is so vital to play against the best players on the best clubs in the world.

"I just believe that the more you play in an environment where there is this peer pressure on you every day, the better you'll become and the more you'll be able to handle the big pressure moments of a World Cup, to stay calm and not lose your head and stay on course in order to get further in a World Cup than ever before," he says. "It takes that kind of mind-set that will make a difference in a big tournament. When players are in a highly competitive peer pressure environment for eleven months a year, they are far better prepared for that huge level of expectations when it comes down to a World Cup—which is the ultimate benchmark for everyone. So that's why I'm saying if you can play against Manchester United on the weekend, or against Inter Milan or Bayern Munich, you'll be better prepared for that moment when you face all these top players in a World Cup. If you've never had any experience playing against Ronaldo or Messi, and suddenly see players like that lining up against you in a World Cup game, you might be a little bit intimidated. It's only natural. I would be too."

Klinsmann's seventeen years playing in four top European leagues taught him that learning to handle the pressure and criticism in countries where soccer is treated as a 24/7 way of life is essential to succeeding on the biggest stage of all at the World Cup. "Our players who go to England, Germany, Spain, or France get used to the pressure and are used to getting criticized if they have a bad game," he says. "They hear about it from the local people in the supermarket or in the shops or on the streets. The pressure is everywhere. They're used to having to justify themselves for their performances all the time." He sounds hopeful that the day might not be far away where MLS fans will be more demanding. "If an MLS player has a bad game, we want them to be accountable for that. We want them to be pestered and bothered by the people in the supermarket or the baker or the butcher because that's the way people react to the game all over the world where soccer is the number one sport."

There have been discussions and, at times, disagreements between Klinsmann and MLS commissioner Don Garber. Because their interests sometimes collide, there are similar discussions and disagreements between national coaches and the leaders of domestic leagues in countries around the world. Klinsmann has faced criticism for urging the best American players to play or stay with European clubs and develop their game, while the MLS wants the top Americans playing in North America. It surprises Klinsmann to hear charges that his views are harmful to the MLS, because he has every interest in a thriving league, whose players he has regularly selected for the U.S. Men's National Team.

"My point is to explain that players need to always strive to the highest possible level," Klinsmann says. "I'd never criticize MLS or the clubs. I simply try to help players understand where they are right now and where they could be, and let them know if I see them taking a step backward a little bit. I just try to wake them up and say, 'You need to go in the other direction.' I'm not being negative. I'm just being realistic."

Some MLS officials back his point of view. Grant Wahl in *The Beckham Experiment* quotes Tim Leiweke, the chief executive of Anschutz Entertainment Group, which owned the Los Angeles Galaxy, saying that Klinsmann was absolutely right to encourage the best Americans to play on European clubs to improve in order to make the U.S. Men's National Team as strong as possible. "Whatever vision we have today, Jürgen Klinsmann had a lot to do with it," Leiweke said. "What we ought to be doing is taking the best young American kids and shipping them over to Europe to learn how to play against the best players. Until we learn to compete, we will not win a World Cup." He admitted it could take many years, however, before the MLS would be competitive enough.

Klinsmann notes the anomaly that a number of American goalkeepers have had strong careers in Europe while outfield players have yet to make a major mark and explains there are reasons for that. "Traditionally, over the last two or three decades, the best kind of players the United States produced were goalkeepers," he says. "That's a tremendous compliment. But it's because goalkeepers can react to the game. It's a very specific position, where you read the game and react to the game. What's needed for all the other positions, midfielders, strikers, and defenders, you have to be more proactive to establish yourself with the world's best. There's been some decent success, but not yet world class."

He says Brian McBride at Fulham, Claudio Reyna at Manchester City, and Clint Dempsey at Fulham all had success in Europe, but "we've never had a world-class outfield player overseas yet." It's a challenge trying to field a world-class team when so few Americans play in the world's best leagues. "Everyone wants to have the game growing as fast as possible. We have to improve every element of it. You always have to look up to improve. You're not going to improve your game dropping down a level or two. It's the same with life. Life is about, What can I learn next? By challenging yourself you can grow as a person."

The Champions League is the premier testing ground for soccer of the future, the cutting-edge environment where the tactics, strategies, and styles of play being tried out there will be used by the top national teams at the next World Cup. For that and other reasons, Klinsmann would like to see more Americans on teams in the Champions League one day. Most of the world's top national teams are stocked with players on clubs that play in the Champions League. Mexico has more players on the teams in European leagues playing in that elite tournament than ever before. In 2015, when Mexico faced the United States in a play-off game to represent the CONCA-CAF region at the 2017 Confederations Cup in Russia, there were seven Mexico players in their lineup who also played on a Champions League team in Europe, while the United States had only one player who also played for a club in the Champions League—Fabian Johnson of Borussia Mönchengladbach.

"It's just a great experience for every player. Of course, it's faster," Johnson said of the intensity in the League after becoming only the sixth American to score a goal in the Champions League, in Mönchengladbach's 1–1 tie against Juventus on November 3, 2015. He scored again, a spectacular goal three weeks later, in their 2–0 win over Sevilla. Speaking about the intensity and quality of the Champions League, Johnson was quoted by ESPN FC's Jeff Carlisle: "We had a very tough group with world-class players. And if you play in the Champions League, it's going to be more about the details: how good your first touch is, how you defend."

The Champions League is an international competition with midweek matches played from September to May—running parallel to the August-to-May season that the European clubs play. A total of seventy-eight clubs from fifty-three soccer federations in Europe were in the Champions League at the start of the 2015/16 season, with the top thirty-two emerging from the Qualifying round from June to August. The Group Stage runs from September to December with the knockout rounds running from February to May. The Spanish, English, and German leagues sent the top four clubs from the previous season into the Champions League, while Italy, Portugal, and France sent their top three clubs.

"With the world's best players and coaches packed together, the world's best soccer is constantly being refined there," write Kuper and Szymanski in *Soccernomics*. "The best soccer today is Champions League soccer, Western European soccer. It's a rapid passing game played by athletes. Rarely does anyone dribble, or keep the ball for a second. You pass instantly. It's not the beautiful game—dribbles are prettier—but it works best. All good teams everywhere in the world now play this way."

The 2015 Champions League final in Berlin, where Barcelona beat Juventus 3–1, was watched by a TV audience of 180 million people around the globe, according to the UEFA. By comparison, the 2015 Super Bowl in Phoenix, where the New England Patriots beat the Seattle Seahawks, was the most-watched TV program in U.S. history, with 114 million people in the United States tuned in, NBC reported. The Super Bowl was broadcast worldwide, but only about 38 million people outside the United States watched it a year earlier in 2014. By comparison, the 2014 World Cup final in Rio de Janeiro, where Germany beat Argentina 1–0, was watched by one billion people worldwide and 26.5 million in the United States.

Another challenge for the U.S. Men's National Team against its global competitors is the schedule of the professional league in North America. Unlike most of the countries in FIFA, MLS has a completely different calendar, with the season running from March to December. An MLS calendar in sync with the rest of the world would benefit the USMNT—first and foremost because the World Cup, normally held in June and July, comes at the end of the club season for other countries when the performances of many players are peaking. But the MLS is opposed to changes to its calendar. Garber said in September 2015 that he hopes FIFA, the world's governing body, would not pressure the North American league to change its calendar. "We are certainly hopeful that they [FIFA] will continue to allow us to do what we have done pretty effectively, which is grow the game in our country in ways which have probably exceeded most people's expectations," Garber said at a soccer conference in Manchester, England. "I would hope that those who are involved in governing the sport would say—we need to do things in ways that ensure it is all for the good of the game. I don't know who we are harming? Our calendar works for us because it would be really bad for our fans and players to play in February when it's 10 degrees and there is four feet of snow on the ground. Who is that good for?"

# WHY SO FEW AMERICANS
# IN EUROPE?

SOME INTERESTING THEORIES abound about why there have been so few American outfield players making any kind of a lasting mark with top European clubs. Longtime U.S. goalkeeper Kasey Keller suspects there have long been prejudices among clubs, with players from some nationalities overrated while Americans were underrated.

Another theory is that some Americans are put off by the cutthroat competition and the intense year-round pressure both with the club and in their private life. Another notion is that many European clubs have a condescending attitude toward American players, looking down on them as hardworking but less skilled players from a nation that doesn't take soccer seriously—a self-perpetuating fallacy. Yet another factor is that, as mentioned earlier, European agents have little incentive to track and sign young Americans. The agents have been active in the lucrative trade of discovering African or Eastern European teenagers for top clubs but have struggled to find American prospects between fifteen and seventeen years old willing to give up their college eligibility to turn pro.

That hubris against American players could vanish if, for instance, the United States one day produced a soccer superstar of the caliber of Gareth Bale (Wales), Wayne Rooney (England), Cristiano Ronaldo (Portugal), or Lionel Messi (Argentina).

Landon Donovan was once touted as a potential global superstar from the United States. But he gave up on Europe early in his career and played mostly in the MLS. The Californian will never forget working out in the wet and cold German winters while at Bayer Leverkusen. "Germany doesn't work well for me," Donovan said openly at the U.S. team headquarters in Hamburg just before the start of the 2006 World Cup. "I've learned my lesson. Our styles don't match. It's hard for me to be successful over here. Maybe it's too brutal, I don't know. It just doesn't go well with my style. Soccer-wise, I became a better pro. I remember seeing the captain, Jens Nowotny, making sliding tackles in the mud early on a Monday morning and thinking, 'Jesus, if he's doing that, I'd better start doing that too.'"

Three months later, Donovan was happy to elaborate in another interview, in California, on his reasons for staying away from the Bundesliga and Europe—after scoring a goal for the Los Angeles Galaxy in a 2–1 home loss to the Houston Dynamo. "I love my life here," he said, flashing a wide smile. He was twenty-four at the time and lived near the Pacific Ocean in upscale Manhattan Beach and was clearly tired of questions about playing in Europe. "It's the furthest thing from my mind, to be honest. I don't think about it unless I'm asked. I'd probably become a better soccer player just from the day-in, day-out grind of it there. But I wouldn't be a better person. I wouldn't be a happy person. I'd be pretty miserable. I'm not going anywhere for a while. I have no time for going over and trying out and doing things like that. That doesn't interest me." In Europe, Donovan had once famously complained about the food, calling it "crappy" and saying he missed American hamburgers, the beach, sun, and American women.

It is an impossible dilemma for Klinsmann and U.S. Soccer, as

Dirk Chatelain wrote in an insightful article in the *Omaha World-Herald* in July 2014 right after the team's strong run at the World Cup, called "What Will It Take to Win?" "The United States will win the World Cup when MLS becomes one of the world's best leagues. Here's the Catch-22 for American professionals. You can't hone your skills at a world-class level unless you opt to play in Europe. But American soccer can't truly flourish until its best players are performing for American audiences in MLS." He put his finger on the predicament that the U.S. soccer team faces. There is no easy way to resolve the mutually conflicting positions of having the best Americans play in the best leagues in Europe to get better while making the MLS one of the best leagues with the best American players. It's a quandary that won't be resolved anytime soon.

While some Americans have flourished in the pressure-packed environment in Europe's top leagues, others have struggled to cope with the expectations in nations where soccer is the only sport people care about and just about everything the players do on and off the field is under a magnifying glass. American Brek Shea spent two years in England with Stoke City and on loans to second-division clubs Barnsley and Birmingham City before returning to MLS to Orlando City at the end of 2014. "One of the reasons I didn't enjoy England so much is that it's so small and soccer is the biggest thing there," he said in an interview with the multimedia Fusion Media Network. "So everything you do is magnified times a thousand. So me posting a picture doing something like this [fishing] in England, everyone would be like, 'He's not concentrating on soccer. What's he doing? He's not focused.' Here, I can do this, because I can be me. It helps me, in the end, play the way I know how to play." He later told *Sports Illustrated,* "It's more like a 9–5 job over here. In America, you're having fun and you're with a group of friends. It's still very serious—you want to win—but you have that camaraderie. It's just different [in England]. It's a job. You go in and you go home and in MLS, you have a team barbecue once a week. You hang with people outside the facility."

Simon Evans, a veteran English soccer writer based in Florida, reflected on the difficulties some Americans have had in Europe, where soccer is anything but a nine-to-five job, in a thought-provoking column in *WorldSoccerTalk*. "I wonder if enough modern American players have the hunger and desire to take the risk and test themselves in Europe. Yes, soccer is the biggest thing in England and there is a lot of attention on it. The same goes for Germany, Italy or Spain. Being a professional footballer is a job and people approach it as work." Evans asked, "How many American players actually prefer the lack of intense pressure in MLS and the relative anonymity of being an MLS player? How many, like Landon Donovan, just prefer the comfort of living and playing in their own country to proving themselves in the best leagues in the world?" Evans added there are many Under-20 Americans playing in Europe and wonders if they will fare better in the years ahead: "These are players who have had no experience of MLS and who have been living in Europe, playing at top pro clubs throughout their formative years as players. Will they emerge in the coming years as a new kind of American player—to whom there is nothing strange at all about being under constant scrutiny and pressure? It will be fascinating to see and potentially crucial to the national team program."

There are other Americans with different attitudes about Europe. U.S. goalkeeper Tim Howard has spent most of his career in England at Manchester United and Everton. He writes in *The Keeper* that ever since his childhood he had a burning desire to make it onto a club in Europe and in 2003 fulfilled that dream by moving from the MLS team New York/New Jersey MetroStars to Manchester

United in the Premier League. "I [wanted] to go to Europe. Just as graduating to a travel team was the obvious next step from the Brunswick recreation league, a move from MLS to Europe became the way forward," says Howard, who has played for Everton since 2007 after three seasons at Manchester United. "European clubs are institutions, often more meaningful than the local governments or cultural landmarks. The best players on Earth wind up in Europe. If I was going to become the best, that's where I needed to go."

His predecessor as the U.S. Men's National Team keeper, Kasey Keller, played in four World Cups and for sixteen years in Europe: for clubs in England, Germany, and Spain. Near the end of his long career in Europe at the 2006 World Cup, Keller elaborated to a small group of reporters at the U.S. team base in Hamburg on his observations about how European clubs treat the nationalities differently. "If you are Dutch or Brazilian, it's just a lot easier—that's just the way it is," he said, adding that if a Brazilian prospect turned out to be a flop it wouldn't cause any managers problems because the thinking is "at least he's a Brazilian." He saw the anti-American prejudice firsthand. "If you look at your own teams, you see certain players from certain countries get the benefit of the doubt [because of their nationality]."

Even though there are not many American players in Europe, there are a surprising number of American owners of clubs in England. Six of the twenty teams in the Premier League— Manchester United, Liverpool, Arsenal, Aston Villa, Fulham, and Sunderland—in 2015 had American owners. "The Premier League obviously has a huge global audience," American Shahid Khan, the owner of Fulham who was born in Pakistan and also owns an NFL team, was quoted saying in an article called "U.S. Owners Buy in to New Era for Premier League Finances" by Keith Weir of Reuters.

"It's got a great media deal, it's got great leadership at the top and most importantly a very, very passionate fan base and it's an excellent business platform."

In *Soccernomics,* Kuper and Szymanski note that the American owners were looking to reach a global audience in ways that American sports can't. "These people come from a country where many sports franchises actually make money," they write. "Most of these people didn't buy into soccer because they love the game, but as a business proposition. They think soccer has the power to capture foreign markets in a way that American sports don't." Kuper and Szymanski add that soccer fans in the United States prefer to watch the world's best players on television from the Premier League in England, even though it means getting up early on Saturdays because of the time difference. "The market for sports fans is becoming global. If you live in the United States and like soccer, you are more likely to support Manchester United than your local MLS team. Even in Argentina, with its great historic soccer clubs, people increasingly watch United on TV. That's all the more true in the US, China, or Japan, countries whose soccer fans mostly came of age during the second wave of sporting globalization." The authors of the seminal book on global soccer developments conclude, "These people want to see the real thing. Global fans want global leagues. For most of them, that means the NBA, the NFL, or the Premier League."

# HOW U.S. SKIERS WON BY GOING TO EUROPE

Just as the world's best soccer players are in Europe, so too are the world's best skiers. American Lindsey Vonn was an unknown teenager when she decided to move to Europe to pursue her dream of becoming a world-class skier. After more than a decade of disappointing results in international competitions, several U.S. skiers began resettling in Europe for at least part of the year around the turn of the millennium to try to get faster by living with, training with, and being more like the world's best—traditionally from Alpine nations like Austria and Switzerland.

As most of the International Ski Federation's Alpine World Cup races take place in Europe, and especially the Alps, it made eminent sense for American skiers to put down roots in Europe, and Vonn was at the forefront of that movement. The idea was to become better acquainted with the mentality, habits, training, diet, and way of life. It was also important to feel at home in Europe, have home-cooked meals, and not have to live out of a suitcase in hotels all winter long. Vonn learned to speak German fluently—and she learned how to ski faster than the Austrians.

"It definitely helped me to live in Europe," says Vonn, whose hazel eyes light up when she talks about her experiences handling the intense competition in Alpine skiing's elite world by living right there in the heart of the competition. "It's not just a different culture but it's also a different way of living. It's a different mentality. It's good to live in a culture where everyone goes skiing all the time. They have so much more respect for skiing than other nations because they all ski. Everyone in the country pretty much skis, so they really understand. That helped me. I learned a great deal. It helped me understand my competitors better as well as improve my skiing."

Alpine skiing is not a major sport in the United States, but it is the most popular winter sport in most European countries. And because Alpine skiing is so hugely important in Austria and Switzerland, the social and public pressure to succeed is enormous—not unlike the pressure that soccer players in many European nations face. As Alpine skiing grew in the 1960s and '70s, it offered a path out of poverty in some parts of Europe, and in recent decades it's become connected with wealth and glamour. Each weekend's race throughout the winter season is broadcast on national television, and significant parts of alpine nations come to a standstill for important races. Vonn and other top Americans, such as men's skier Bode Miller, who also moved to Europe at a formative age to learn both the sport and German, probably would not have been recognized walking down most streets in the United States, but they became celebrities in Alpine countries. Vonn totally immersed herself in Austria, learning how to speak the Austrian dialect, and even joined the vaunted Athletes Special Projects personalized support program operated by Red Bull and run by former Austria downhill coach Robert Trenkwalder. Patrick Riml, an Austrian native coaching the U.S. women's team at the time, also played a key role in Vonn's development in Europe in the winter ski season running from October to March.

By the time she was twenty-one in 2006, Vonn had become one

of the world's top skiers and her heroics in the downhill, super-G, giant slalom, and slalom disciplines helped rejuvenate enthusiasm for international skiing in the United States. She went on to win a record sixty-seven World Cup races in the next nine years, four overall titles, two world championships, and the gold medal in downhill at the 2010 Olympics.

"I started traveling abroad when I was nine years old," Vonn says. "It gives you another whole perspective on everything—not just sports but on culture and the whole language barrier and everything. That's why I started learning German, because I didn't like not being able to communicate with people and to be able to embrace the culture the way I wanted to. Learning German was important to me because it was an important language for my sport. I couldn't really be part of the ski culture if I couldn't speak with my competitors."

Vonn smiles when asked if she thinks more American soccer players should make their way to Europe in the years ahead. She says she would love to see the United States win the World Cup. "I'd definitely recommend it. It's a great learning experience. We have the talent to win the World Cup. It's just a matter of putting all the pieces together."

The U.S. Ski Team also benefited by resettling in Europe. Phil McNichol was head coach of the U.S. Ski Team's men's alpine team from 1997 to 2008, and its head coach from 2002, and was part of the same movement to help his skiers restore some glory to U.S. skiing after more than a decade of slow decline. He was determined to help his skiers become more comfortable, and above all more confident, skiing against the fastest in the world as they plunged down the sides of mountains at speeds of up to ninety miles per hour.

"Staying in Europe for the season clearly was having a positive influence on our performances," McNichol says. "I think it was because success is born out of confidence. You need to be comfortable, relaxed, and you need to be supremely confident. If you're living there with them and realizing your competition is nothing special, this is a big confidence boost. You become much more able to enter an optimal performance state if you can relax about where you live, if you enjoy where you live, if you like the food and understand the language. You're not on edge. Your mind is not in a different place. It was really important for us to see there was no difference."

McNichol adds that it was understandable that just about every other nationality felt daunted racing against the Austrians back then. For years they had been the world's dominant team, and their skiers were national heroes. He thought it was important for the American skiers to become more familiar with the Austrians in their own back-yard and realize they were hardly superhuman. "I think spending time there and being comfortable in that culture showed the boys themselves that this was actually no different than skiing in Colorado," McNichol says. "We discovered that the snow is still the same color in Europe and gravity still works the same way over there." The U.S. men's team started having more success than ever. Led by Bode Miller, Ted Ligety, Steve Nyman, Daron Rahlves, Marco Sullivan, and Erik Schlopy, the team scored forty-two World Cup victories during his six-year tenure and got the first Olympic gold medal in a dozen years when Ligety won the combined title in 2006. In 2005 and 2006, the U.S. men's team was second overall behind only the mighty Austrians in the World Cup standings, and American skiers won four medals at the 2003 and 2005 World Championships.

# FRIENDLY FIRE

FROM THE MOMENT he took the job, Jürgen Klinsmann has gone out of his way to schedule the most difficult opponents he can for friendlies, the exhibition matches national soccer teams around the world play against each other in between tournaments and qualifying games for tournaments. In the short term, it can be a perilous exercise because the results may disappoint impatient fans, and there is always a risk of getting trounced by top teams like Brazil.

But Klinsmann is confident about what he is doing and has a long-term strategy in mind: He is adamant that there is no better way to get his players confident for the excruciating pressures of the World Cup games in 2018 than by playing friendlies against the best teams that the U.S. Men's National Team might face in the tournament. He believes that playing the toughest teams possible in games in which the results *do not* really matter will make his players more confident, aggressive, proactive, and resilient under pressure in the games that really *do* matter.

"The ultimate goal over the years is to become a more proactive team," Klinsmann says. "Traditionally, the way the U.S. teams saw themselves on the global stage was reactive because they never build up the confidence to move further up the field and to put the other teams under pressure—and maybe dictate games here and there. It's a process that will only happen over a longer stretch of time. That's why you have to risk playing a lot of friendlies against the best nations in the world. You might lose here and there, but you'll get some positive results—and you'll get the feeling that you can actually play with these teams and give them a game."

The United States only rarely made trips across the Atlantic to Europe for friendlies before 2011, in part because European teams were reluctant to play against the United States for commercial reasons, and when they did venture into the heartlands of the sport, they sometimes seemed overwhelmed. In *The Beckham Experiment,* Grant Wahl captures a sense of how daunted some American players were at a friendly in England in May 2008. Not only had England thoroughly outplayed the U.S. team, the U.S. team played like they were afraid. "In the end, the game was a disaster for the United States, which played like a collection of amateurs in a 2–0 loss that didn't fully capture the embarrassing disparity in performance. Afterward, one England player would tell associates that the American players' hands were trembling during the pregame handshakes . . . England fans saw an outclassed U.S. team and presumably confirmed their suspicions that David Beckham was wasting his time in a third-rate American league." A year later, however, the United States managed to pull off a spectacular win against Spain in the Confederations Cup to end its 35-game unbeaten run at the time.

Klinsmann was determined to build the confidence of his players from the outset by scheduling as many such exhibition games as he could. He believes that once the Americans are as fit, as skilled, and as experienced as players on top teams, the difference between winning and losing in a big tournament is confidence and frame of mind. "The only thing that matters is who's stronger mentally," he says.

His first string of European friendlies came just three months into the job, in France in November 2011, which the U.S. lost 1–0, and on the same trip against Slovenia, which they won 3–2. In 2012, the U.S. Men's National Team got their first-ever win against four-time World Cup winner Italy, 1–0, in Genoa, beat Scotland 5–1, and played a 2–2 tie in Russia. They also lost to Brazil 4–1 and got their first-ever win against Mexico in Mexico City, a historic triumph in a hostile environment for Americans. In 2013, the U.S. beat Bosnia and Herzegovina 4–3 and Germany 4–3, but lost to Belgium 4–2 and Austria 1–0, and had a 0–0 tie against Scotland. In 2014, the U.S. beat South Korea 2–0, Turkey 2–1, the Czech Republic 1–0, and Nigeria 2–1 in friendlies, lost to Ukraine 2–0, Ireland 4–0, and Colombia 2–1, with ties against Mexico 2–2, and Ecuador 1–1. In 2015, the U.S. lost to Chile 3–2 and Denmark 3–2, tied Switzerland 1–1, before beating Mexico 2–0, the Netherlands 4–3, and Germany 2–1. Klinsmann was pleased with the wins in exhibition games against two of the world's top teams but pointed out they were only friendlies, and the results— just as close exhibition game losses to Denmark and Chile earlier that year—were not as important as the experience gained.

One of the first things Klinsmann did when his friends and former coaching allies in Germany, Joachim Löw and Oliver Bierhoff, called to congratulate him upon being hired in 2011 was to ask for friendlies. "Right away I said to Jogi and Oliver that, 'Whenever there's a chance, we'd love to host you, wherever you want,'" he says. "If we get a friendly, that would be awesome." In its first friendly against Germany in the Klinsmann era, in Washington in June 2013, the United States won 4–3.

The confidence against the big teams was certainly on display in the second friendly against Germany on a lovely summer evening in Cologne on June 10, 2015, when the U.S. team came from a goal down to win—the eighteenth friendly against a top European team in his first four years. Even though it was a friendly, Klinsmann was in high spirits, especially with the way his team had fought to win it. He said the United States had deserved to come away with the win. After struggling in the first half against the World Cup holders, Klinsmann's team dominated the world's top-ranked team throughout the second half—to the delight of a large crowd of fans from the American Outlaws, who surprised Germany with their intensity— and could have scored more goals with better finishing. "I don't know what happened to us in the second half," Germany's exhausted captain Bastian Schweinsteiger told reporters after the match, looking stunned that the Americans had beaten Germany twice in the last three years. "Obviously we wanted to win this. Something like this [losing to the United States] shouldn't happen."

Klinsmann is convinced the friendlies against the world's best will help the U.S. team at the next World Cup. "Going up against the big teams on a regular basis is really valuable in helping the players understand what it takes to go eye to eye against the best," he says. Klinsmann has also taken the U.S. Men's National Team to play friendlies in Mexico City against one of the best teams in the Western Hemisphere—Mexico.

Even though the victories over the Netherlands and Germany in 2014 were friendlies, they were important after the U.S. Men's National Team had suffered two tough friendly losses after giving up late goals earlier in the year against Denmark 3–2, and Chile 3–2, which triggered a round of second-guessing about the strategy. "There were some matches this year we should have won but gave up late goals—against Denmark and Switzerland," Klinsmann said in Cologne. "Now, we're turning those around with late goals."

Klinsmann has come under pressure before from impatient fans about friendly defeats, even while coaching Germany. But by the time he stepped down after the stirring run to third place at the 2006 World Cup, they were clamoring for him to stay. The merits of friendly results are relative, of course. To some they matter a lot. To others they are meaningless. To Klinsmann, the experience is priceless.

"The information you get out of these games against top teams is so valuable that it's definitely worth taking the risks of [losing]," he says. "The only way to get a positive psychological learning curve is by playing against teams ranked higher. The players can get positive results and experiences, and grow a mind-set that they can believe they can beat those top teams one day when it counts. Now you suddenly face Germany or Holland or Switzerland in the World Cup, and there's no fear anymore. There's still respect. You always have to have respect. But there's not too much respect. When I look back at the World Cup, I think we had too much respect for Germany and maybe even too much for Belgium."

At the World Cup, Germany gave the United States their only defeat in the Group Stage, winning 1–0. Klinsmann believes his team played Germany as equals that day and had a chance to come away with at least a tie. After finishing the Group in second place behind Germany, the United States was beaten in overtime by Belgium 2–1 in the Round of 16—another defeat that Klinsmann believes could have been prevented. "It took a while to get to the point that we can at least dominate in our region and we can also beat Mexico. We had some historic wins [in friendlies] in Mexico and against Italy and Bosnia," he says, but he warns that sometimes the lessons are forgotten: "This process made a big step forward, but then there are steps backward. All of a sudden you're going up against Belgium at the World Cup, all their famous players from the famous clubs, and your head starts turning, and you're maybe feeling small out there. But overall I think things are going in the right direction. I think it's growing, that mind-set of, 'Okay, we go to Europe to play a game and we're not going to Europe to just defend. We're there to take a game to them and see how it ends up.'"

At first it was easy for Klinsmann to schedule friendlies against European teams. But after the United States had upset Germany, Italy, Turkey, the Czech Republic, and Bosnia and Herzegovina, and thrashed Scotland, it was becoming more difficult for a while to find sparring partners—at least in the run-up to the World Cup where teams headed to Brazil were looking for easy opponents to tune up their game against. Under Klinsmann, the United States won four of its nine matches against top-ten teams through the end of 2015, lost three, and played two ties.

Despite playing such an ambitious schedule of friendlies, Klinsmann still has one of the highest winning percentages of any U.S. soccer coach. "It takes a bit of bravery to schedule games that could, and maybe should, end badly," wrote Brian Straus in *Sports Illustrated* after the victory against Germany in Cologne. "But credit to Klinsmann. He's willing to risk defeat, and the criticism that often follows, in an effort to get his growing team the experience and exposure to top-class competition it needs. Wins make people happy, but they don't always make people better."

# AMERICAN ANOMALIES

PERHAPS THE MOST attractive aspect of soccer, for some, is that it is so different from other sports. It's an incredibly fluid game of nonstop action where the players on the field make the countless split-second decisions, the creative passes, the quick touches, the clever shots on goal, or the well-timed tackles. It's all about instincts.

"One of the joys of soccer is seeing how different cultures view, interpret and celebrate the game in their own distinct ways," wrote Jonathan Clegg, a native of England, in "The Problem with American Soccer Fans" in the *Wall Street Journal*. "I find it fascinating, for example, that while we see soccer as a broad narrative that unfolds over 90 minutes, your fans tend to think about the sport as a series of discrete events."

There are some unique aspects of soccer in the United States that are evolving. One thing Americans sometimes struggle to understand, for instance, is that the role of the coach during the games is minimal—or at least it should be. At some levels in the United States, soccer coaches can be seen barking a steady stream of instructions and plays onto the field from the sidelines as if they were coaching a football or basketball team. Soccer is a game where, unlike any other sport, the players have the main say in the outcome, and the impact from the coach is limited. That's just one of the mis-understandings and misconceptions about soccer that Jürgen Klins-mann hopes will be sorted out as the game matures in the United States. At the same time, he hopes that the quality of soccer coaching in the United States will keep improving each year and that standards continue to rise. He also hopes that more and more young players will develop the skills and confidence to take control of the game themselves.

"Soccer is a players-driven game," Klinsmann says. "I think one of the biggest riddles for American soccer [is] that some people still think it's a coaches-driven game, like American football or baseball. It's not like basketball, where you have time-outs and set up plays that you study and repeat. It's very difficult for a lot of people, espe-cially at the grassroots level, to understand that we need to inspire the kids to play the game and we need to leave the game up to them. We need to stand back and let them develop their game."

Ruud Gullit, the former World Player of the Year from the Neth-erlands, also struggled with the very different American mentality on the same issue while he was the coach of the Los Angeles Gal-axy. As Grant Wahl notes in *The Beckham Experiment,* Gullit said, "When I see the American sports, it's stop-and-go, it's more like people following an assignment. The only one who has some diver-sion is the quarterback. The rest just play the scheme, almost like soldiers. So I was afraid of having people who would only follow orders. I don't want that. I want to be creative on the pitch. Because of the mentality of sports in America, this is going to be the most difficult issue, to get players to be creative."

Whenever he can, Klinsmann stresses that soccer is different. In an interview in 2014 with Steven Goff of the *Washington Post,* Klins-mann said, "The biggest educational problem is people think it's a coaches' game in the United States. It's not. It's a players' game.

There's too much emphasis on telling people what to do. If the teaching part is too big, you will only have players who react to what the teacher or coach tells them. I am looking for personalities. I am looking for players that drive the game. I am looking for them to step it up and say they can do this. I hope to see more. No matter whether they are playing in Europe or Mexico or MLS, we hope to see more of them take the game in their hands. We need people to understand the players have to drive it, take initiative, make decisions and get it to another level, and then you [as a coach] are a guide on the outside and you can help. You need them to understand, 'I can give you all the information I can, but I'm not going to score the goals for you. You have to go in there and beat the [heck] out of defenders and put the ball in the net and figure it out yourself.' "

By contrast, coaches in football, basketball, and baseball can and often do have a major influence—calling time-outs, calling for set plays, or making strategic decisions for the players on the field as well as through the unlimited substitutions. But there are no time-outs in soccer, set plays happen only occasionally, and decisions are mostly made by players on the field. At the 2014 World Cup, German players attempted on average more than 650 passes per game, a dizzying number for ninety minutes that shows there is no time or need for consultation from coaches on the sidelines.

"This is something that hopefully over time people will understand, 'Okay, if we get into soccer, we need to understand that the player is the main driver of everything,' " Klinsmann says. "Over time there needs to be more education that soccer is very different from American football, baseball, basketball, and hockey. And the parents need to understand that it's not the coach who will create the next Messi—but it's the kid himself."

On the one hand, Klinsmann admires the uncomplicated American can-do spirit when it comes to coaching, in sharp contrast to

Germany, where licenses and rigorous training are required for every level of coaching. But on the other hand, he notes that those coaches with the formal training have the right qualifications to coach young players, whereas many Americans are confident to coach soccer even if they have never played the game themselves.

"I think baseball, basketball, football, and hockey are part of the DNA in America, the emotional DNA," Klinsmann says. "They grow up with those sports, love those sports because it's what they know from a young age and it's been like that for many years. This process is only just starting now with soccer. Because you've grown up with several sports over the years, your brain thinks, 'I know American football, I know some plays, so I can coach it. And now I want to become a soccer coach because my kid wants to play soccer,' which is great. But they tell themselves they know the game, which isn't the case."

He is optimistic that as Americans become more knowledgeable about the nuances of soccer, they will be able to distinguish between coaches with qualifications and those without. "As the knowledge grows, parents can judge their kids' coaches better, and they'll realize that soccer is a players-driven game and a good coach won't be trying to control every move their kids make from the sidelines."

Another uniquely American aspect is that many young athletes play different sports, while in other countries around the world they are playing only soccer. In the long run, Klinsmann believes that Americans who want to excel in soccer at the international level will have to start focusing on the sport. "The traditional American grows up with the seasonal sports of their school system," he says. "There's three months of basketball, three months of soccer, and three months of football or baseball. That's all great. But I think at some point people will have to look at that model and realize that if their kid wants to become really good in soccer, he'll have to focus all year round on soccer. That's just the reality of the way it is in other soccer nations."

He is also surprised and concerned by the expense of soccer for youngsters in the United States and worried about what that means for the growth of the game for children from working-class families. That soccer is so expensive in the United States seemed strange to him because traditionally it has been such an inexpensive sport for the masses pretty much everywhere else.

"This is the only country in the world that has the pyramid upside down," Klinsmann says, with a look of bewilderment written all over his face. "You pay so that your kid can play soccer, because your goal is that your kid can get a scholarship to college—which is completely opposite from the rest of the world. It should be the cheapest at the bottom of the pyramid; you shouldn't have to pay more than a small membership fee for your club. Soccer is a lower-class environment sport around the world."

Tim Howard, in *The Keeper,* also expresses concerns about the rising costs of soccer in the United States and the implications that it's a game for the well-off. It wasn't always easy for his mother, a single mom, to pay for his youth soccer. "I worry for the kids who can't afford that," he writes. "It's become even harder for working families today than it was for my mom. They have less recreational time, less wiggle room in their budgets. In much of the rest of the world, kids begin playing soccer in pickup games—a loose, often barefoot scramble in scrubby patches of dirt or smack dab in the middle of the street . . . We could use a little more of that in America—a little more scrap, a little more pickup, a little less structure . . . The truth is, until we get that right, I'm not sure we'll ever become the nation of soccer champions that we all want to be."

In Germany, the *annual* membership fees for a soccer club are about €40 ($45) for children and €80 ($90) for adults. But in the

United States fees might be $1,000 to $4,000 or even $6,000 if travel expenses are included.

"Soccer in America turned into an upper- and upper-middle-class sport somewhere along the line and disconnected itself from its Hispanic environment," he says. "Because soccer is seen by many as a sport that might get you access to a better school or a college education, that drives people to pay for anything connected to the sport. So people pay for private lessons for technical things such as private lessons for goalkeepers or private lessons for strikers. It's crazy. Soccer in America turned into a pay-for-play system over the decades, and that's completely the wrong direction."

Klinsmann fears that the pay-for-play model is harmful for the United States in the long run. "It hurts American soccer because that's not driven by the kids but instead it's all planned through for them. It's the opposite way everywhere else around the world, where soccer is affordable for everyone. There, it's driven by the kid because he's hungry to succeed, he's hungry to rise up socially through soccer. They want it badly and they're highly driven on their own. Here it sometimes seems like the attitude is, 'Oh, I'm talented,' and the parents say, 'Okay, he's talented, let's get him extra sessions here and extra sessions there.' That all means extra money. The goal is often a college scholarship, but the goal isn't, 'My kid needs to play on the Galaxy one day.'"

Klinsmann says that as a result there is a dual system in the United States. Many Hispanic children with a passion for the game but without the wherewithal for youth soccer leagues and the pay-for-play model organize themselves in their own leagues based on the international model: low membership fees, volunteer coaches who once played the game themselves, and lots of practice, practice, practice on their own.

"There were thousands of highly talented American kids playing in Hispanic leagues that we didn't know about," says Klinsmann. One of the first areas that his coaching staff worked on improving was its ties to the Hispanic communities. As late as the 2006 World Cup, U.S. soccer players were discouraged from answering questions in Spanish at U.S. Soccer press conferences at the team's base in Hamburg—even if they could speak Spanish—and only given the chance in so-called "mixed zones" afterwards to pose questions in Spanish. "It's a process that still needs time," says Klinsmann, who takes and understands Spanish-language questions but usually answers in English. "There are fifty-five million Hispanics living in the United States who are driving that process a bit faster because they live and die for soccer. It's their sport, it is their only sport because it's coming from their Central American countries or [from] South Americans that are now part of our community here. It's a wonderful development. That's one of the big reasons that soccer is on the rise here—because of the huge Hispanic influence coming through."

# TEN-POINT PLAN

JÜRGEN KLINSMANN HAS one major goal for the U.S. Men's National Team—to one day win the World Cup. It's a long-term target, and here is the essence of his plan to get there.

1. *Change the mentality.* Instead of looking with trepidation at teams like Germany, Spain, Italy, Netherlands, Croatia, the Czech Republic, Brazil, and Argentina as invincible, Klinsmann wants Americans to take it to the top teams with their own unique American "never-say-die" style. Toward the goal of playing without fear, he has gone out of his way to schedule as many exhibition matches as possible against the world's top-ranked teams. That has helped the Americans discover that the other teams may not be much better, if at all, than they are, and that in soccer any team is beatable.

2. *Change the youth programs and start early.* Klinsmann is investing enormous energy in helping U.S. Soccer develop youth soccer academies across the country—and making them open for talent regardless of a family's ability to pay. He wants to see American universities make some changes as well, to prolong their seasons to be in sync with the rest of the

world in the hope that the educational system can become a launching pad for the best soccer players in the United States.

3. *Open up to more players.* Klinsmann has thrown open the door to the Hispanic community in search of top players. He has also gone out of his way to find Americans abroad, the children of American parents who have grown up in countries around the world where soccer is the number one sport. It is those dual-national players, some of whom are the children of American soldiers or business executives, who formed the core of the team that impressed at the 2014 World Cup. There were five German Americans on the team, one raised in Norway, and another from Iceland.

4. *Change the programs, connect the dots.* There are thirteen million Americans playing soccer already, but there has been frustratingly little to connect the youth leagues, academies, university leagues, and professional teams. Klinsmann wants the various leagues and programs to be better coordinated and, ideally, to feed into each other and ultimately the Men's National Team with the best and brightest players of the generation. His goal is to have a pyramid system—the way the game is structured in other soccer nations.

5. *Get experience abroad.* Klinsmann makes no secret of the fact that he wants as many of the best American players as possible to compete in the world's best leagues. Those are in Europe—in England, Spain, Germany, Italy, France, and the Netherlands. Soccer is 24/7 in those countries. Players and the fans live, eat, and breathe soccer. Have an off game in Europe? You'll hear about it at the café, the grocery store, or the gas station the next day. It is that pressure to perform 24/7 and "social accountability" that will make American players

better, sharper, and able to win the World Cup one day. The idea is controversial in a country that likes to see itself as number one in everything, and perturbs some who have different ideas about the relative strength of the MLS, whose goals diverge from Klinsmann's.

6. *Help the MLS reach its goal to be one of the top leagues in the world.* This means increasing the competitive intensity of games from the first day of the season until the last day. Most of the rest of the world uses promotion-relegation to ensure competitive intensity. If the MLS sticks to its current business model, it needs to develop its own method for increasing competition. Also, it would help player development and the U.S. Men's National Team for the MLS to follow the FIFA calendar like other leagues do.

7. *Tap the fan culture.* In many countries, soccer fans have a visceral attachment to their favorite club and their national team. Klinsmann hopes that fan culture for the national team will continue growing in the United States. There is hardly anything more exhilarating than entire nations celebrating as one or coming to a standstill to watch a World Cup match.

8. *Think long term and have a multicycle plan.* Americans want quick results. Long-term goals might seem anathema and boring to many U.S. sports fans, but winning the World Cup won't happen overnight. There are too many good teams. Yet the United States is finally waking up to the glory of the beautiful game. It will take (at least) a few more four-year cycles to win the World Cup, but Klinsmann is putting the country on the right track. The U.S. team's strong showing at the 2014 World Cup in Brazil turned a lot of heads inside the United States and around the world. "We're a lot more

respected in Europe and South America now—thanks to
what we did at the World Cup," Klinsmann says.

9. *Think global.* Soccer is above all a global game. Winning national championships, domestic cups, or even the Champions League title are all fine, but that pales in comparison to
winning the World Cup. It is the tournament that every soccer player, coach, and fan looks to. Americans might think
there's nothing bigger than the Super Bowl, the NBA finals,
the World Series, or the Stanley Cup—but these epic annual
North American title fights don't come close to capturing as
much of the globe's imagination as a World Cup. "In soccer,
your competitors are global and your way of thinking has to
be global," Klinsmann says.

10. *Change the playing style.* Before Klinsmann arrived, U.S.
teams pulled off the occasional spectacular win or tie against
top teams with a defensive style of playing combined with
counterattack goals against the run of play. But the United
States never got close to winning the World Cup with that
tactic, and it probably never will. It might work in a single
game or two but not in the six or seven in a row needed to
win the Cup. Klinsmann also believes it's not the American
way—lying back and reacting. He switched his teams to a
proactive style as one of his first acts. "Americans are not
reactive types of people, it's not in their DNA. So why do
you play a style of soccer that is not in your culture?" he asks.

# AFTERWORD

## BRIGHT FUTURE

Soccer has come a long way in the United States in the last twenty-five years—the game is growing, people are talking about it more than ever before, and there are a lot of positive things happening across the country. The U.S. Men's National Team qualified for the last seven World Cup, defied expectations in 2014, and made it through the Group Stage to the Round of 16 in Brazil, and many people who closely follow soccer around the world took notice of the United States' strong performance at the World Cup.

"We all want a brighter future for the U.S. Men's National Team, and we want the United States to become established as one of the world's top ten teams," says Klinsmann. "But it's not going to be easy considering how many strong soccer nations there are around the world. We set an ambitious goal for the 2018 World Cup—to reach the semifinals. And, if we start with the end goal in mind, we obviously want to win the World Cup one day. There are huge challenges, and it will take a lot of hard work. But things are definitely moving in the right direction. Our goals are challenging but achievable."

Klinsmann says the growth of Major League Soccer has been

"absolutely fascinating" over the last twenty years—with twenty teams, packed stadiums, a growing fan base, and more followers on TV. He's also pleased that soccer is continuing to grow at the youth levels, at the high school and college levels, and adult amateur levels. There are millions of children playing soccer now. They will be pushing the game forward and shaping its future in the United States.

"Soccer has clearly made it in the United States. It's mainstream. It's established. It's recognized as a major sport. People like it. And it's growing," Klinsmann says. "The next step is to become one of the best soccer nations in the world." One of the key differences between soccer and other major U.S. sports is that soccer is an international competition. That makes the big tournaments like the World Cup and Copa América Centenario all the more exciting—and all the more challenging. It's the arena where the world's best teams are competing in the game they care so passionately about. By contrast, the NFL, NBA, MLB, and NHL are domestic competitions.

"The U.S. Men's National Team has become an important engine for growth in the United States," Klinsmann says. "We're trying to do everything we can to make the national team as successful as possible in the World Cup, which is the benchmark for everyone around the world. The attention that soccer in the United States gets at the World Cup is what pushes the game forward for the next four years. And because we made it out of the Group of Death in Brazil, the game got another big boost emotionally—from millions of American soccer fans and from the media."

He hopes the United States can keep that momentum going to 2018—and beyond. "A lot of things have gone well these past years, but a lot of things need to get better. It's a long-term process and there's no room for complacency. We're working on becoming a more proactive team; we're working on developing a style in which Americans recognize themselves. Over time, we want to develop a belief that, 'If I'm really prepared, if I'm physically and mentally at the top of my abilities, then I'm actually able to compete with the best in the world.' We want to develop that mind-set that, yes, we can do it."

Klinsmann believes that in the long run the senior national team can be successful only if the foundation of the game in the United States—the youth system—keeps improving and developing. It's an evolution, not a short-term process. He realizes that Americans are impatient and want quick results, but he keeps warning that it is going to take time and there will be setbacks along the way.

"The foundation in the United States is still fragile and disconnected compared to other countries," he says. "The youth leagues do their own thing, the professional system is not really connected to the amateur system, and that's not really connected to the college system. So there are holes in the system, like in a Swiss cheese, and there's a loss of quality. We're working on connecting those pieces, on connecting player development, and on continuing to build a pyramid in this amazing country."

Klinsmann is convinced that the foundation of the game is the youth sector. Just as in every other country, it's how much effort children put into the game and how well they're being coached that will be decisive in the long run. "That's our future," he says. "In essence, it's the more you play, the better you'll get. If you kick a ball against a house wall or against the garage for hours on end, you'll get better. It's as simple as that. At the end of the day, the big question is: What is it that gets kids outside to play soccer for so many hours every day? What gives them that drive to do what's needed to make themselves better, every day, all year round?"

Klinsmann says that is one of the biggest challenges facing the United States—getting children out and playing more soccer. In Mexico and Argentina and Italy, youngsters are playing soccer sixteen or twenty hours a week or more plus going to practice and playing maybe another four to ten hours a week with an organized team. "All those hours of practice in the streets are going to show up in their game later on when they're adults with better technical skills, with better passing skills, and better instincts," he says.

There's another aspect of soccer that makes it unique: Soccer is different from American football, baseball, and basketball in that it's a players-driven game. There are no time-outs and you can't sub in and out as much as you want. In soccer it's the players on the field who drive everything during the games, not the coaches on the sidelines. "There's sometimes a perception in America that the parents drop their kids off, and the coach is there to make him a better player and drive him," Klinsmann says.

Another long-term challenge facing the U.S. Men's National Team coach is that, traditionally, Americans grow up playing two or three seasonal sports at school—baseball, basketball, and soccer or football. "That's terrific," he says. "But kids in other countries are playing only soccer ten or eleven months a year. American kids never really develop that rhythm, stamina, and soccer focus." He believes Americans will keep wrestling with this issue, and eventually they'll realize that to become really good in soccer they have to focus exclusively on the game.

When will the United States have its first international soccer superstar the caliber of Argentina's Lionel Messi, Portugal's Cristiano Ronaldo, Germany's Bastian Schweinsteiger, England's Wayne Rooney, or Wales's Gareth Bale?

"That's a great question that I get asked a lot," Klinsmann says, adding he hopes the answer will be sooner rather than later. "The one common denominator you see with all the top players is a mind-set of total determination they had as youth players and kept that right up to their national team careers. They were absolutely driven to become the best players at every level along the way, and were never satisfied. I'm not sure if the United States has developed that mind-set yet. I'm not sure why it seems that some Americans with talent sometimes reach a certain level in soccer and then settle with that instead of pushing themselves to the next level."

He adds that it takes more than just talent to become one of the world's top twenty soccer players. "You need talent but also to be extremely hungry and driven, driven by the people around you who keep pushing you, and it doesn't help to be surrounded by people who compliment you every day and give you pats on the back."

Klinsmann notes that one of the important reasons that soccer is on the rise in the United States is the Hispanic influence. According to the Census Bureau, there were fifty-five million Hispanics living in the United States in 2014. "They're pushing that process forward a bit faster because they live and die for soccer," Klinsmann says. "It's their primary sport, and they're part of our community now, which is wonderful. Before we were losing a lot of talent to Mexico. They were playing youth soccer here and went to Mexico—and we didn't even know about them. That's changing now."

The same is true for the dual-national Americans who grew up overseas in soccer nations and have helped strengthen the U.S. Men's National Team in recent years. "It's a fascinating aspect of globalization," he says. "It happened in Holland in the 1980s with Ruud Gullit and Frank Rijkaard, in France in the 1990s with Zinedine Zidane and Youri Djorkaeff, and in Germany from the early 2000s with Miroslav Klose, Lukas Podolski, Mesut Özil, and Sami Khedira. Now it's happening in the United States. Where did they come from? The United States has people all around the world with businesses and the military, so there are a lot of dual-national Americans who grew up in countries such as Germany, Iceland, Norway, Peru, or in other places. It's the first time in American history when you have a generation of these dual nationals coming through."

The Netherlands won the 1988 European Championship thanks to two goals in a 2–0 final win against the Soviet Union from captain Ruud Gullit, whose mother was Dutch and his father was from Holland's former South American colony of Suriname. The integration of children of immigrants from Suriname in the 1980s strengthened teams from the Netherlands, whose all-white teams had so disappointingly lost the finals of the World Cup in 1974 to West Germany, 2–1, and in 1978 to Argentina, 3–1. After that, the soccer team and then the country embraced multiculturalism. Frank Rijkaard, Edgar Davids, Patrick Kluivert, and Clarence Seedorf also trace their roots to Suriname.

In a similar vein, France, a team known as *les Bleus* (the Blues), won its first World Cup in 1998 thanks to its opening up to a multicultural team of French-born and dual-national players with African and Caribbean heritage, which also furthered integration and assimilation in the country as a whole. Celebrated as a unifying force in France, the team got the nickname *"Black, Blanc, Beur"* (Black, White, Arab) and was led by Zinedine Zidane, born in France to Algerian parents; Lilian Thuram, born in the French West Indies; and Youri Djorkaeff, whose mother was Armenian and his father Kalmyk-Polish.

Klinsmann believes that those Americans growing up playing soccer in highly competitive peer-pressure environments overseas are better prepared for the rigors of a World Cup. He insists, however, that more important than *where* Americans play is *how* they play. "At the end of the day, what matters is your performance," he says.

He is pleased that soccer is growing in America so rapidly and that as the game becomes part of the sports mainstream, it's being discussed with all its passions and controversies more on TV and in social media forums. Klinsmann hopes that American soccer players will push themselves more in the future. "You want your players looking up to the next level," he says. "If you're a ten-year-old and a fantastic player, you want to play with the eleven-year-olds because the ten-year-olds might bore you. The same is true if you have a player on the verge of being a Champions League player. You want him to prove himself in the Champions League. You always want them to challenge themselves at the next-highest level."

Klinsmann can somewhat understand when top American players return to the United States from some of the world's best clubs in Europe to play for teams in Major League Soccer for lucrative contracts, but he regrets it in terms of the players' development. "When players at that level come back to the MLS, it's understandable, but it's not challenging for them. I can't blame someone coming back to make four times as much money. But for the talent they have, it's just not challenging enough. They're not playing at the highest possible level," he says. He wonders if it would be good for LeBron James's basketball skills to play in the French league. Or Kobe Bryant to play in Italy. Or Dirk Nowitzki in Germany's basketball Bundesliga? "No, they wanted to play against the best of the world in the NBA," he says. The same goes for Tom Brady. Would it have been good to send him to the American football league in Europe?

He believes that social pressure is definitely a good thing that keeps players on their toes. "Players at the professional level in MLS are not getting bothered at the supermarket the next day because they lost a game, which is what happens to you in South America or Europe," he says.

Klinsmann is thoroughly enjoying his job. "I'm having a blast. It's a fascinating challenge to help connect the pieces in this amazing country. It's a bigger puzzle in the United States than in other countries, and it's not perfect yet. That's what makes it so exciting; we're building something great here. We don't have a system in place like France or Germany or even South American countries. If you look at the FA in England, it's more than one hundred years old and they already have their infrastructure, they already have their scouting, their coaches' education, they have their national training center, and the pyramid is connected. There's relatively little infrastructure work to do in England because it's all there. Here in the United States, building that infrastructure is still important. That's what's so fascinating and rewarding about this."

He is pleased with the progress he's made in his first five years as the U.S. Men's National Team head coach and is confident of the longer-term outlook if Americans continue to embrace soccer so wholeheartedly as they have in recent years. "The transition is happening step-by-step," he says. "We're playing against the bigger nations, we're attacking those bigger nations and holding our own against them. But there's no gain without pain. There's no growth without taking risks. And there's no growth without failure along the way. We're getting out of our comfort zone, and we're making some big strides forward," he added, referring to historic wins in exhibition games in Mexico, Italy, Bosnia and Herzegovina, the Czech Republic, the Netherlands, and Germany.

"I think our mind-set is growing: 'Okay, we go to Europe and play a game, we're there to take a game to them and we're not going to Europe just to defend,'" Klinsmann says with a smile at the team hotel after the U.S. had just upset world champion Germany, 2–1, in a friendly played in Cologne in 2015. "Soccer is about what we do today and tomorrow. We're making progress. People interested in soccer both inside and outside the United States can all feel that there is so much potential for soccer here. There's a lot of work ahead of us, but we're moving in the right direction, and that's exciting."

# INDEX

Jakob Stielow

**ERIK KIRSCHBAUM** is a foreign correspondent based in Germany. Kirschbaum has worked for Reuters, the *Los Angeles Times,* and other newspapers from Europe since 1989. A native of New York City, he grew up in Connecticut and studied history and German at the University of Wisconsin. He has covered World Cups and Olympics, and is the author of *Burning Beethoven: The Eradication of German Culture in the United States during World War I, Rocking the Wall: Bruce Springsteen: The Berlin Concert That Changed the World,* and *Swim and Bike and Run: Triathlon — The Sporting Trinity.*